HOWARD GARRETT'S

T · E · X · A · S

ORGANIC GARDENING

B · O · O · K

HOWARD GARRETT'S
T·E·X·A·S
ORGANIC GARDENING
B·O·O·K

Gulf Publishing Company
Houston, Texas

Gulf Publishing Company
Book Division
P.O. Box 2608 □ Houston, Texas 77252-2608

10   9   8   7   6   5   4   3

Library of Congress Cataloging-in-Publication Data
Garrett, Howard, 1947–
    Howard Garrett's Texas organic gardening book.
        p.   cm.
    Includes index.
    ISBN 0-88415-505-6 (pbk.)
    1. Organic gardening—Texas. I. Title. II. Title: Texas organic gardening book.
[SB 453.5.G37   1995]
635'.0484'09764—dc20   94-24055
                                                                    CIP

Printed in Hong Kong.

to

MALCOLM BECK

The man who taught me how to see, enjoy, and learn from nature.

Contents

Acknowledgments

Many thanks go to the people involved in the production of the book. Donna Wilkins typed, retyped, and amended the text and as always put up with my changes, revisions, and additions. She also worked with my editor at Gulf Publishing, Joyce Alff. Editors have always bothered me because I haven't wanted anyone messing with my stuff. I have learned to take criticism better, but more importantly, I liked all of Joyce's suggestions and changes and the book is truly better because of her involvement.

Some of the artwork in the book is mine but I would also like to thank Neal Roper and his staff at Gulf Publishing for the overall artwork and cover design.

There are many organic growers, gardeners, manufacturers, and landscape people who have helped by trying my techniques, offering advice, and supporting the organic movement.

I would also like to thank those critics who have opposed me and the organic movement. You know who you are. Without your serendipitous help, I would not have studied and worked as hard as I have to understand nature and communicate her secrets to others.

Finally a very special thank you to Judy, Logan, and my folks for always being there.

Preface

Synthetic fertilizers and toxic pesticides were tools of my trade for years. I understand homeowners and landscape people who mistakenly think they are doing the right thing by using them. What changed my course was the birth of my daughter, Logan. It was at that point I seriously started investigating the organic alternatives. I now wonder why I was so foolish and how anyone can spray toxic pesticides where children play and taste everything they see. The challenges facing our environment are now my concern. Every continent is polluted, some worse than others. America is polluted and Texas has the dubious honor of being the most polluted state in the union, according to the *Dallas Morning News.*

My research uncovered that organics is much more than a human safety issue. Our entire planet earth is in serious trouble and the most significant discovery is that the organic approach—*the natural way*—works better than the traditional chemical approach. Organics is not just a switch of products, but a completely new way of life. It's about understanding and enjoying nature.

Organic gardening and landscape maintenance procedures are financially sound, environmentally sensitive, and safe to wildlife, pets, children, adults, and the earth.

Poor land management and the overuse of artificial products have created millions of acres of sick soils in Texas. These soils have been over-fertilized, over-grazed, over-cultivated, over-sprayed, and left to parch in the Texas sun. Our soils have been eroded, and little to no recycled organic matter has been added to rejuvenate them. That must stop. Sick soils lead to sick plants, which leads to sick animals and sick people.

Organic programs have been used off and on throughout history. There are civilizations that no longer exist because they departed from organic farming methods. The fall of the Roman Empire was largely due to the removal of the small, family-owned farms that were merged into large estates. Organic tools such as biodiversity, multiple cropping, wind breaks, crop rotation, and organic matter replenishment were eliminated. The state-owned farms grew monocultures of crops, destroyed the land, and ignored the real needs of the people. Sound familiar?

Organics as a modern philosophy and practice began in the early 1900s with the ideas and experiments of British agronomist, Sir Albert Howard. While working in India, Howard found fewer animal diseases on the native Indians' farms

than on the government farms where synthetic fertilizers were used. He set up scientific farm management based on the native method of using natural manure fertilizers. Sir Alfred taught the natives how to mix weeds, crop waste, and manure to make nature's most valuable soil conditioner—compost. He taught them how to manage the soil.

What Sir Alfred Howard had started with this work was the unteaching of the work of a German chemist, Justus von Liebig, who had declared that N-P-K (nitrogen-phosphorus-potassium) were the only elements in soil important for growth of plants. Liebig created the chemical fertilizer industry by ignoring the importance of organic matter, microorganisms, and trace minerals.

As Sir Albert Howard said in 1940, the earth's capital—its only real wealth—is the soil. His book *An Agricultural Testament* was one of the first attempts to point out the importance of death, decay, and life and the equal share each of these plays in the balance of nature. He also explained the importance of the soil's microscopic plants and animals. He warned about the harmful effects of artificial "manures." Howard learned the specific pieces of life's puzzle from other laboratory scientists, but he was responsible for putting the information together in order to understand "the whole" of nature.

Natural or organic—the term is not important. The process is fun and works so well that you'll have gardens that are more beautiful, more productive, and more manageable than you ever imagined. The facts about organics have been available for a long time. I hope this book presents those facts in a way that encourages you to use, enjoy, profit by, and tell others about—*the natural way*.

J. Howard Garrett

Differences in Chemical and Organic Approach

Chemical Approach

- Mow low and often.
- Catch grass clippings.
- High analysis fertilizers 4–5 times per year.
- High nitrogen fertilizers.
- Synthetic fertilizer—no organic matter, fillers.
- Fertilizer based on plant needs.
- Fertilizers have few or no trace minerals.
- Attempt to control nature.
- Treat symptoms (insects, diseases).
- Use chemical pesticides at first sign of pests.
- Poisons used on a calendar basis as preventatives.
- Discourage the use of beneficial insects.
- Use only university-tested products.

Organic Approach

- Mow higher and less often.
- Leave clippings on the ground.
- Low analysis fertilizer 2–3 times per year.
- Low nitrogen fertilizers.
- 100% organic fertilizer—no fillers.
- Fertilizer based on soil needs.
- Fertilizers loaded with trace minerals.
- Attempt to work within nature's systems.
- Treat soil and cultural problems.
- Use natural pesticides, but only as last resort.
- Prevention through soil improvement and foliar fertilizers.
- Use beneficial insects as a major tool.
- Use food products, teas, and homemade mixtures where appropriate.

CHAPTER 1

What is Organic
Gardening?

Environmentally Safe

In the 70s, there were only a few gardening books in Texas. Since then Texas garden authors responded to a need for more books devoted to the harsh and varied growing conditions in Texas. Many excellent books resulted.

Gardeners have now become aware of the dangers of pesticides and the damage toxic materials cause to the environment. This is the first gardening book to address organics just for Texas.

Organic gardening is a new idea that's catching on in Texas—a "new" idea that's several thousand years old. Organic gardening is gardening that uses nature's laws and systems. Unfortunately for us, Texas is the most polluted state in America. Local industries can be blamed for some of the pollution, but farmers and home gardeners are also responsible. The good news is that pollution and waste are on the decline and the public is demanding clean food and freedom from toxic sprays. Local, state, and federal governments are finally tightening the screws on air and water pollution, waste disposal, and destruction of the environment. Everyone is awakening to the fact that spraying or broadcasting synthetic poisons is not right. Forest clear cutting and worldwide loss of biodiversity have been identified as global criminal acts. The return of health to the planet, to wildlife, and to our children is now a clear and achievable goal.

Chemicals vs. Organics

It's not a chemical vs. organics question. Everything in the world is chemical; even air and water are composed of chemicals such as hydrogen, oxygen, nitrogen, and carbon.

The words, *chemical* and *organic,* are equally misused and misunderstood. For example, there are products acceptable for use in an organic program that have low toxicity but are not truly organic, and some organic products are extremely dangerous and not acceptable in a wise organic program. Likewise, not all chemical products are severely toxic. Confused?

The point is that the two words, *chemical* and *organic,* have become the buzz words of the two philosophies. Chemical represents the traditional approach of force-feeding plants using synthetic fertilizers and trying to control nature using synthetic pesticides. Organic represents the approach of working within nature's laws to improve soil health and of using the least toxic and most environmentally sensitive products available.

It's a serious misconception that organic methods are simply safer ways to kill pests. The basis of organics is an overall philosophy of life more than a simple decision about which kinds of garden products to use. The organic philosophy relates to the ability to see and understand nature's systems and work within those systems. The chemical philosophy teaches that man and his products can control nature. Nature can't be controlled—it's futile to even try. Many farmers are now realizing that we must stop taking the life out of the soil and the land out of production. The landscaping industry is also moving very quickly toward the organic philosophy, primarily because of the tremendous public demand for safer and more environmentally sensitive techniques and products.

Chemicals are not all bad. For example, some of the best tools in the organic gardener's arsenal include man-made, synthetic products like *Logic* fire ant control and *Precor* Flea Control, and other pest-control products. They work by regulating the growth of insects rather than by killing the pests. These products have very low toxicity to beneficial insects, pets, man, and the environment. On the other hand, some of the best organic tools are extremely toxic materials. For example, *Bt* and *Bti* are very toxic natural biological products. Fortunately, they are specific to the targeted pests, caterpillars and mosquitoes, and they don't hurt beneficial insects, pets, man, or the environment.

Another difference in philosophy relates to fertilization. Proponents of traditional chemical programs say that plants must be fertilized with high nitrogen, salt-based, synthetic fertilizers. Organic gardeners believe that the soil should be fed with 100 percent organic fertilizers and balanced. Plants do not need to be force-fed. Balancing the soil is not discussed very often, if ever, in traditional chemical programs.

It may seem like a strange thing for me to say, but the chemistry of the soil is a primary consideration. Remember that everything is chemical. If the chemistry of the soil is balanced, the physical properties will be correct, the pH will be between 6.2 and 6.5, and the living matter will also be in the proper proportions. In balanced soil, calcium should represent approximately 60 to 70 percent of the available chemical nutrients, magnesium 10 to 20 percent, potassium 2 to 5 percent, sodium .5 to 3 percent, and all the trace elements should be in their proper relative proportions.

Another advantage of balanced soil chemistry is that the frequency of fertilizing can be greatly reduced. In fact, once the soil is balanced, plants can be maintained primarily with mulches, organic matter, foliar feeding, and an occasional fine tuning of the balance of the minerals of the soil.

Therefore, if the chemicals in the soil are balanced (those chemicals that *should* be there, that is) everything else will fall in line. A balance of the soil will automatically create proper tilth, positive drainage, and the correct populations of beneficial microorganisms—*if you stop killing them with the quick-fix garden-care poisons.* The end result is healthy, nutritious plants, animals, and people.

So you see—chemicals aren't so bad and organics is just the rally cry.

Harmony with the Environment

No matter what term is used—*natural, ecological, organic, least toxic, sustainable, biological, IPM, low input*—the principles are the same—just plain good agriculture and horticulture. I prefer the term *organic* because it seems to be the most easily understood. Organics is about the soil, about

Healthy soil is the key to successful gardening.

the primacy of organic matter, about plants, and most importantly, about natural systems that have existed long before man. It's about balance.

Why aren't organic methods more universally understood and used? For one thing, nature and science have for some time been out of sync. The sciences of botany and zoology teach only about the growing half of life, nothing about the other half—death and decay. In the past we have failed to understand nature's powerful and resilient systems that respect birth, death, decay, and birth again—in other words—recycling.

Understanding how nature's systems work in detail is difficult because those systems are intricate and complicated. However, it's easy to understand how to put conditions in place that allow nature's systems to work effectively on their own. It's easy to convert from chemical-based programs to organic-based programs, and the transition can be made not only in small gardens but also on large projects, including golf courses, parks, college campuses, commercial developments, farms, and ranches—even Texas oil fields.

Traditional chemical landscape programs ignore the soil and treat plants with direct and artificial methods, similar to the way sick people are kept alive by drugs and machines. Soil health programs feed plants indirectly through a natural and balanced process, similar to the way people are nourished on healthy, balanced diets.

It has been said that there's only one cause of disease—malnutrition. I believe that! Diseases are most effectively controlled through balanced, nutritious diets. Nutritious food comes from nutritious soil.

Soil is the key to health.

Biodiversity

Nature works best when there is a variety of plant and animal life present.

Nature abhors straight lines and monocultures. Monocultures are masses of one plant type. They don't work. For nature to function properly there must be a mix of plant materials and animals. Home landscapes, vegetable gardens, farms, and ranches must have a mixture of soil organisms, insects, plants, small animals, and large animal elements. Large mass plantings of food crops or forests where only one variety has been used are examples of monocultures.

A field of corn, for example, can become much more successful if divided into smaller areas by other cash crops or by native plantings to provide food and shelter for birds and beneficial insects. It's quite simple—organisms living side by side will help each other. The natural checks and balances provide the long-term pest and disease control that we have futilely attempted to control with poisons.

Man has taken from the land for so long without giving anything back that much of the world has died and become desert-like where it was once alive, thriving, and productive. Biological diversity has been eliminated from landscaping and agriculture. That's a problem that must be reversed. Monocultures don't exist in nature and they should not be allowed to exist in horticulture and agriculture. Healthy mixes of plants and animals allow nature's checks and balances to properly function. Microbes, insects, snakes, lizards, toads, birds, mammals, perennials, annuals, grasses, shrubs, and trees are all important to the whole of nature.

Lack of biodiversity causes desertification. Deserts are not just sand dunes and barren land. Dead streams, rivers, and lakes that have lost their biodiversity are also deserts. Forests that have been clear-cut and replanted with monocultures are deserts and monoculture lawns using chemical maintenance programs are deserts. Chemically abused farms are deserts.

The reversal is easy. Stop using high-nitrogen, synthetic fertilizers; stop using synthetic pesticides. Plant a mixture of plant types, encourage beneficial insects, and start working within nature's systems.

Ready to Start?

If you are ready to start right this second and don't want to read the rest of the book, the guidelines that follow will help.

Please remember that you are dealing with living soil, living plants, and other living creatures. Nature is dynamic and always changing. No program is the best for everyone so start out with my program and then fine tune it into your own. No one organic program is perfect—except for nature's own.

Nature is dynamic and always changing.

The Basics of Organic Gardening

Test the soil. Send soil samples to a lab that uses the Cation Exchange Capacity (CEC) testing method. Test the different types of soil on your property separately. See Appendix for soil test procedures. The soil test will tell you how far you have to go to balance the soil.

Aerate the soil. Oxygen is the most essential fertilizer element and it is lacking in many soils. Punching holes in the ground and rototilling are the most common aerating techniques. Oxygen feeds microorganisms that feed on and break down organic matter.

Increase the humus in the soil. Organic matter breaks down into humus. Sources include grass clippings, compost, and living soil organisms. Covering all bare soil with rough-textured mulch is essential.

Start a compost pile. All vegetative matter should go into the pile. Never send any vegetative waste to the dump. Everything that's alive, dies, and everything that dies, rots; therefore, anything once alive can be composted. The best percentage for compost is 80 percent vegetative matter and 20 percent animal waste, although any mix-

By using simple organic gardening techniques, you can have a beautiful, healthy garden that will be the envy of your friends and neighbors.

ture will work. Grind limbs and other large matter into smaller pieces first. Keep the pile moist and turn it at least monthly. Finished compost can be tilled into the soil, and partially finished compost (raw material can still be identified) is an excellent top-dressing mulch. Do not put synthetic fertilizer, synthetic cloth, oils, or greasy foods in the compost pile. Containers are only for convenience, and tarp coverings are not needed. Compost piles work in sun or shade, and if they are kept aerated, they don't stink.

Stop catching the lawn clippings. Clippings are a source of organic matter and nutrients. Excess clippings after heavy rains or missed mowings can be put in the compost pile. **Never** send grass clippings or any vegetative waste to the dump in plastic bags. Do not scalp the lawn in spring, and mow regularly at a higher setting.

Start fertilizing with organic fertilizer. Stop using synthetic, high-nitrogen fertilizers and start using 100 percent organic fertilizers. The starting rate is about 20 lbs per 1,000 sq ft two or three times per year. After some soil improvement, the rate can be reduced to 10 lbs/1,000 sq ft. The best time to fertilize is immediately after aerating in early spring, early summer, and fall. For an added boost, spray foliage monthly with liquid organic fertilizers.

Start using beneficial insects and stop using toxic chemical pesticides. Good bugs should be released every two weeks starting in early spring until healthy naturalized populations exist. The best choices for general control of pests are ladybugs, green lacewings, praying mantids, and trichogramma wasps. Not only will herbicides, insecticides, and fungicides kill beneficial living organisms, but they are simply unnecessary.

Encourage biodiversity. Stimulate life of all kinds and avoid monocultures. Healthy gardens and farms need a mix of microorganisms, insects, plant types, and animals. Plant a variety of native and well adapted plants. Using exotic plants that are hard to maintain violates organic principles. Don't forget to feed the birds, and encourage other friends such as bats, lizards, toads, and insects.

CHAPTER 2

Organics Work Great in Texas

Consider the Soil

The soils in Texas are as varied as the people. Texas has a huge range of terrain, soil, and climate. It has seashore, wetlands, swamps, forests, deserts, grasslands, hills, and mountains. Although Texas can be divided into various geological and climatic areas, the basis for organic gardening is the same. You simply have to know where you're starting from and what is the targeted goal. The sandy soils of East Texas have certain advantages and deficiencies, and the black clay soils of North Texas do as well. Both can be converted into balanced healthy soil.

Consider the Climate

Climate is the one element we can't alter, so it is important to choose plant types that are suited to our climate. The plants I've listed in the book are those that are the easiest and most adaptable across the entire state. I don't mean that you should use just these, but these plants make a good starting point. Because they are so tough and easy to grow, they are also a good financial investment.

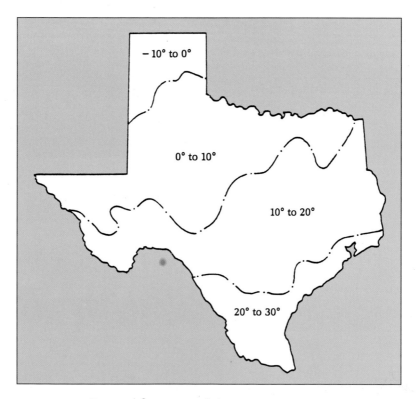

- 10° to 0°

0° to 10°

10° to 20°

20° to 30°

Ranges of average minimum temperatures.

Choose Native Plants

In order for nature's systems to work, native or adapted plants must be used. Good soil will never make palm trees grow well in Dallas. On the other hand, if good plant choices are made, and if they are planted in healthy soil, the organic system will work beautifully.

Recently, homeowners, institutions, and commercial developers have begun to rediscover native Texas trees, shrubs, annuals, perennials, grasses, and wildflowers. Landscape nurseries around the state are reporting a healthy increase in consumer demand for native plants and for information about how to grow them in residential gardens and urban settings.

There are more than 5,000 species of plants native to Texas. That's not counting the plants that have been introduced from other parts of the country that have grown to like it here and have decided to stay. Native plants have economic and aesthetic advantages over many fragile imports. Natives in most cases are hardy and well-adapted to Texas conditions and in general have low water and fertilizer requirements.

One reason native plants need less attention is that they naturally resist pests. Grown in healthy soil, they don't need pesticides to protect them from insects and diseases. While no plant is entirely pest-free, centuries of natural selection have built tolerances into native plants. Even with native plants, it is best to use a mix of different varieties.

Whenever plant, insect, or microbial variety is absent, nature's system of checks and balances has a harder time controlling pests. Balance and soil health are the key words in organic landscaping. Using a balance of plant types is also important. A landscape or garden consisting of only one plant species is an easier target for insect pests and diseases than a setting made up of various plant species. One-crop (or monoculture) conditions dramatically increase the potential for pest damage. This point is painfully illustrated in Central Texas with the destruction of acres of live oaks or the similar demise of elms in the Northeast and Midwest. In both cases, huge monocultures had been created. Devastation followed in the form of oak wilt and Dutch elm disease.

A variety of native plants attracts more wildlife. Landscapes that appeal to a variety of animal life can help to create a healthy, interconnected environment. Instead of constantly trying to reduce nature's influences, it's better to encourage nature's butterflies, dragonflies, fireflies, wasps, lizards, frogs, toads, turtles, earthworms, and other beneficial animals.

All wildlife needs some form of protection. Birds are attracted to tall trees and dense or thorny plants. They prefer a mix of evergreen and deciduous plants that provide year-round protection. Variation in the height and type of vegetation is also important in supplying hiding places and food for wildlife; whereas, overpruned and sparsely landscaped areas provide little cover.

Advantages of Native Plants

Lower maintenance
Hardy and well-adapted
Wildlife food and shelter
Reduced water requirements
Disease and pest resistance
Lower fertilization requirements

Scarlet buckeye (Aesculus pavia) *is a beautiful small-scale understory tree with red flower spikes in late spring.*

Best Texas Trees

Japanese Maple
Acer palmatum

This wonderful small tree is not native but adapts here very well. There are over 400 varieties of Japanese maple, but my favorite is the common green variety (*Acer palmatum*). It's the toughest, grows larger than other varieties, and has dramatic red fall color.

Pecan
Carya illinoinensis

The native varieties make better shade trees than do the improved hybrids, but all the pecans can be messy. In fact, these trees are usually dropping something year round. They

are also susceptible to the unsightliness of web worms, but they are fast-growing, magnificent specimens and well worth using in the landscape.

Texas redbud
Cersis canadensis

This native is easy to grow in any soil and quite drought-tolerant. The white variety seems more healthy than the purple native. The crinkled-leaf Mexican variety is the most drought-tolerant. 'Oklahoma' has dark green glossy foliage, and 'Forest Pansy' has red-purple foliage in summer.

'Forest pansy redbud'

Texas ash
Fraxinus texensis

One of our hardiest and most dependable native trees, Texas ash has been overlooked as a landscape plant. It is one of the few large-growing shade trees that allows sufficient light to reach the ground for healthy lawn growth. The foliage is a deep green that turns a luminescent yellow/orange/purple in the fall.

Deciduous yaupon holly
Ilex decidua

Possum haw is easy to grow in sun or partial shade and is striking in winter with red berries on bare branches. Only female plants have the winter berries.

Ginkgo
Ginkgo biloba

This wonderful tree has bright yellow leaves in fall and fan-shaped summer foliage. The female has bad-smelling fruit, so be sure to buy the male plants. Ginkgo has no problems other than its slow growth, but when planted in soil that is healthy and alive, the growth rate is dramatically increased. Split leaf cultivars seem to be the fastest growing.

Yaupon holly
Ilex vomitoria

Regular yaupon is evergreen, usually multi-trunked, easy to grow in any soil type, although it does best in a moist, well-drained area. Nursery-grown plants are a better investment than field-collected trees because the field trees are often dug from large clumps and have few roots, which can result in a high loss rate.

Eastern red cedar
Juniperus virginiana

Excellent evergreen native choice for screening or for use as a specimen. Its dense shade makes it difficult for understory plants to grow, but some thinning can reduce that drawback.

Chinese pistachio
Pistachio chinensis

The Chinese pistachio makes some of our native trees look sickly. This tree is outstanding. It has lovely fall color, no insect or disease problems, and is fast-growing. Chinese pistachio is also one of the best self-pruning trees which means that it naturally thins out its branching, so little pruning is ever needed.

Eldarica pine
Pinus eldarica

This is the best pine tree choice for the alkaline soils of Texas. It is quick-growing, upright and drought-tolerant. Loblolly, slash, and many other pines can grow in the sandy, acid soils of East Texas.

Mexican plum
Prunus mexicana

A native plum with small edible fruit that ripens in late summer. It has small thorns, white flowers in the spring, and lovely orange fall color. The summer foliage is dark green, and the bark has an interesting flaky texture.

Bur oak
Quercus macrocarpa

One of the most spectacular trees in the country. Beautiful branching structure and overall grandeur. Few trees grow larger or live longer than bur oak. Fast-growing tree and drought-tolerant.

Chinkapin oak
Quercus muhlenbergia

This rarely used native oak has large, chestnut-looking leaves and graceful branching structure. The fall color is so-so, but it is a fast-growing, desirable oak choice and should be

used more often. Doesn't transplant from the wild very well; best to buy container grown trees.

Red oak
Quercus shumardi

Fast-growing quality shade tree, with colorful foliage late in the fall when many other varieties have gone bare. It is the most graceful tree of all in the summer. Red oaks will cross breed with other oaks and unless the tree you choose is shumard red oak (*Quercus shumardi*) or Texas red oak (*Quercus texana*), it will not do well in alkaline soils. Almost any oak will grow in sandy, acidic soil, but that's not the case in the black clays and white rock areas.

Live oak
Quercus virginiana

Live oak has been over-planted in some areas, but if used with faster growing deciduous trees, can be an excellent landscape tree. It is evergreen but slow-growing and requires more pruning than most other trees. It can suffer freeze damage in severe winters and can be susceptible to oak wilt. Use it, but sparingly. Many tree experts say that *Quercus fusiformis,* the escarpment live oak, is better adapted for use in North Texas.

Eve's necklace
Sophora affinis

Texas sophora is an excellent small tree for residential gardens or commercial projects. It's native, so it likes our soil, has pink wisteria-like flowers in the spring and black, bead-like seed pods in the fall. The foliage is delicate and similar to honeylocust, but unlike honeylocust, it loves it here and is very easy to grow.

Bald cypress
Taxodium distichum

The stately bald cypress trees can survive and grow in wet areas, but they prefer healthy, well-drained soil.

The cypress has lacy foliage and is pleasant in all seasons, even in the winter when the tree displays its splendid branching structure. Pond cypress (*Taxodium ascendens*) is more slender but a harder-to-find variety.

Lacebark elm
Ulmus parvifolia

The real Chinese elm is a tough, fast-growing shade tree whose foliage in late summer is just as green and undamaged by insects and disease as it is in the early summer. Its fall color is less than spectacular, but the branching structure and color of the bark in winter are quite pleasant. Few deaths result from transplant shock, and lacebark elm has substantial resistance to drought and harsh weather.

Other good trees include goldenrain, cedar elm, raywood ash, white ash, Mexican buckeye, catalpa, chitalpa, magnolia, mesquite, wax myrtle, sweetgum, persimmon, western soapberry, durrand oak, and desert willow.

There is a group of trees that hate the alkaline clay soils of Texas but love the sandy, acidic soils of East Texas. They include pin oak, water oak, willow oak, dogwood, black gum, hickory, and several pines such as slash, long needle, and loblolly.

Worst Texas Trees

In addition to the good tree choices for Texas, it's important to identify the bad choices. Here they are.

Arizona ash is short-lived, a high water user, has destructive roots, is subject to several insect and disease problems, and will suffer freeze damage.

Chinese tallow freezes back every hard winter in the northern part of the state and has lots of insect and disease problems.

Cottonwood trees are stately and beautiful when healthy but are a bad investment. They are short-lived, have brittle wood, are subject to wind damage, insects, especially borers, and the female plants produce messy cotton that clogs air conditioners.

Siberian elm is the worst choice of all. It is incorrectly called Chinese elm. It has severe elm leaf beetle infestation every year and is susceptible to Dutch elm disease. Wind damage due to weak wood is also a problem.

Honeylocust continues to be used by some people but borers love it, and it just never seems to be healthy here.

Hackberry is just a big weed.

Mimosa is another real dog. Although beautiful when healthy, it never is. The root system is ravenous and destructive, and the tree is highly vulnerable to insects and diseases.

Fruitless mulberry is the most overused junk tree. It shades the ground too heavily, uses too much water, and is the target for several insects and diseases. Its root system is highly destructive to lawns, walks, driveways, and pipes. It is also short-lived.

Pin oak grows well in acidic, sandy soil but is a disaster in alkaline, clay soils. Red oaks accidentally crossed with pin oak will always be yellow and sick in alkaline soils.

Poplars in general are fast-growing, unhealthy trees and should be avoided.

Silver maple is a lousy tree. It is usually chlorotic (yellow from iron deficiency), subject to insects and diseases, and has weak, brittle wood.

Sycamore trees are gorgeous when healthy, but disease problems are wiping them out. Bacterial leaf scorch is the culprit.

Italian cypress trees are prone to freeze damage, insect problems, and diseases.

Working with nature is what organics is all about. Trying to use problem trees is fighting nature because these plants just don't like it here in Texas. Some of them don't like it anywhere. Stick with recommended varieties and enjoy your trees and the birds in them.

Best Texas Shrubs

Regular nandina is beautiful year round and pest free. It can be planted in sun or shade.

Abelia
Abelia grandiflora

Summer-flowering semi-evergreen shrub, 6 to 8 feet height. Dwarf forms include 'Sherwood,' 'Prostrata,' and 'Edward Goucher.' Sun or semi-shade.

Agarita
Berberis trifoliolata

Drought-tolerant evergreen shrub with yellow flowers in spring, red berries in winter. Sun or shade.

American beautyberry
Callicarpa americana

Sprawling native shrub, insignificant pink flowers in spring, showy purple or white berries fall into winter. 4 to 8 feet in partial shade.

Flameleaf euonymus
Euonymus alata

Also called Burning Bush. Deciduous, thick winged stems, brilliant red fall color. To 12 feet in sun or partial shade. Compact form grows to 4 to 5 feet.

Smoke tree
Cotinus sp.

Upright shrub with bright yellow-orange fall color. Purple leaf cultivars are 'Royal Purple' and 'Velvet Cloak'. *C. obovatus* is the Texas smoke tree. To 15 feet in full sun or partial shade.

Forsythia
Forsythia intermedia

Fountain-like growth, bare branches covered with bright yellow bell-shaped flowers in early spring that last about two weeks. Use as specimen plant. Grows 6 to 7 feet in sun to partial shade.

Red yucca
Hesperaloe parviflora

Slender, fountain-like blue green foliage that is fairly slow growing. Reddish pink flowers bloom almost all summer.

Oakleaf hydrangea
Hydrangea quercifolia

Good looking, coarse textured foliage with red fall color. Showy white flowers in late spring. To 6 feet in shade.

Althaea
Hibiscus syriacus

Summer-flowering shrub, bare branches in winter. To 12 feet in sun or partial shade.

Hypericum
Hypericum sp.

Low evergreen with yellow summer flowers. To 3 feet in sun or partial shade.

Dwarf Chinese holly
Ilex cornuta 'Rotunda'

Low-growing mass, very dense and spiny, no berries. To 3 feet in sun or shade.

Burford holly
Ilex cornuta 'Burfordi'

Large evergreen, leaves with single spine, large red berries in winter. To 15 feet in sun or shade.

Willow leaf holly
Ilex cornuta 'Willow-leaf' or 'Needlepoint'

Similar to burford holly but leaves are thinner. To 12 feet in sun or shade.

Dwarf Burford holly
Ilex cornuta 'Burfordi Nana'

Same as regular burford holly but smaller. To 5 feet in sun or shade.

Nellie R. Stevens holly
Ilex x 'Nellie R. Stevens'

Large dark green leaves, large red berries in winter, extremely durable. To 20 feet in sun or shade.

Dwarf yaupon holly
Ilex vomitoria 'Nana'

Rounded, compact, dense soft foliage, no berries. To 4 feet in sun or shade.

Texas sage
Leucophyllum frutescens

Silver-gray foliage and purple or white flowers in summer. A drought-tolerant shrub that grows to 6 feet in full sun. 'Compacta' is smaller growing. Also called cenizo.

Leatherleaf mahonia
Mahonia bealei

Distinctive upright plant with thick spiny leaves, yellow early spring flowers followed by blue berries. To 7 feet in shade.

Compact nandina
Nandina domestica 'Compacta'

Almost foolproof colorful evergreen shrub. Red berries in fall through winter and orange-red foliage in winter. Sun or shade to 4 feet.

Chinese photinia
Photinia serrulata

Tall evergreen shrub with large white flower clusters in spring and red berries in winter. Fraser photinia is the more popular hybrid but is actually less healthy. Chinese photinia grows to 15 feet in sun or partial shade.

Fountain grass
Pennisetum sp.

Showy perennial ornamental grass. White flower plumes from July to October. To 3 feet in sun.

Carolina buckthorn
Rhamnus caroliniana

Bushy shrub or small tree, large glossy leaves, yellow-orange fall color, red berries late summer turning black in fall. To 20 feet. Sun or shade.

Spirea
Spiraea sp.

Stemmy shrub with rounded overall form. Most varieties have white spring flowers, but 'Anthony Waterer' has long-lasting coral flowers. To 6 feet in sun or partial shade.

Flameleaf sumac
Rhus lanceolata

A large growing shrub or small tree growing to 10 feet in full sun. Other good sumacs include evergreen sumac (*R. virens*), Skunkbush (*R. aromatica*), Smooth sumac (*R. glabra*), Little leaf sumac (*R. microphylla*).

Coralberry
Symphoricarpos orbiculatus

Low-growing, deciduous, red-purple berries form in summer and last into winter. To 3 feet in shade to partial shade.

Viburnum
Viburnum sp.

Upright growth on thick stems. V. macrocephalum is the Chinese snowball bush and has large white flowers in spring. V. burkwoodi is an excellent semi-evergreen variety.

Best Texas Vines

The tropical vine bougainvillea used in pots or as an annual is spectacular by itself or with fall clematis.

Vines are one of the best values in landscaping. From an inexpensive 1-gallon container, a vine can create screening, provide shade, and flower in just one growing season. Here are the varieties I find work best in an organic program.

Cross vine
Bignonia capreolata

An evergreen vine for sun or partial shade that climbs by tendrils and has unusual yellow and red flowers in spring.

all summer. Bare in winter and will spread underground. Best in full sun. 'Madame Galen' doesn't spread as much as the native mother plant.

Fall clematis
Clematis maximowieziana

Incorrectly sold as *C. paniculata,* sweet autumn clematis is a vigorous perennial climber with a profusion of fragrant 1-inch white flowers in late summer. Usually bare in winter.

Trumpet vine
Campsis radicans

Large, sprawling vine with showy orange and red trumpet-like flowers

Hyacinth bean
Dolichos lablab

Annual climbing ornamental bean with purple flowers in late summer followed by purple bean pods in fall. Easy to grow from seed and very colorful. Best in full sun.

Carolina jessamine
Gelsemium sempervirens

Evergreen climbing vine that needs support. Has poisonous yellow flowers in early spring.

Coral honeysuckle
Lonicera sempervirens

A native climbing vine for full sun, has coral-red flowers all summer. Excellent for attracting hummingbirds.

Boston ivy
Parthenocissus tricuspidata

Non-flowering, fast-growing, clinging vine. Fall color ranges from reddish brown to bright red. Sun or shade.

Passionflower
Passiflora incarnata

Summer-blooming climbing vine with deeply cut leaves and spectacular purple and white flowers. Other flower colors are available. Bare in winter. Best in full sun.

Wisteria
Wisteria sinensis

Fast-growing twining vine that reaches great heights. Purple flowers in spring. 'Alba' has white flowers. Japanese wisteria (*W. floribunda*) has longer flowers that don't open until after the foliage has sprouted.

Best Texas Groundcovers

Gill ivy, Glechoma hederacea, *sometimes called ground ivy or wonder weed, is an aggressive, easy-to-grow groundcover for shady areas.*

Groundcover plants are low-growing plants used for a change of texture on the ground plane or for areas too shady for grass to grow.

Horseherb
Calyptocarpus vialis

Rough leaves and tiny yellow flowers in summer. Forms a dense mat in shade with little to no water.

Wood fern
Dryopteris sp.

Delicate perennial groundcover for softening effect. To 24 inches in shade or partial shade. Dies to the ground in winter.

Purple winter creeper
Euonymus fortunei 'Colorata'

Evergreen groundcover with thick leaves and stems, reddish-purple color in winter. Grows well in sun or shade. Good for large areas.

Liriope
Liriope muscari 'Big Blue'

Grass-like groundcover that spreads by underground stems. Blue flowers on stalks in summer. Best in shade or partial shade.

Houttuynia
Houttuynia cordata 'Variegata'

Colorful perennial groundcover herb that spreads aggressively and has yellow, rose, and red foliage in full sun. Used in Thai cooking.

Ophiopogon
Ophiopogon japonicum

Low-growing grass-like groundcover that spreads by underground stems. Best in shade to partial shade but will grow in full sun. Excellent choice.

Asian jasmine
Trachelospermum asiaticum

Dense, low-growing, evergreen groundcover that grows in sun or shade. Spreads by runners. Browns badly in severe winters.

Creeping thyme
Thymus sp.

Low-growing, spreading herb with flowers in white, pink, and lavender. Excellent in full sun as a border or between stepping stones.

White clover
Trifolium repens

Perennial legume with creeping stems. The common white clover (white Dutch) is the lowest growing clover and makes a good naturalistic groundcover in sun or partial shade.

Melampodium is an annual with long-lasting yellow summer flowers. Here it is planted with pink verbena for a stunning effect.

Even though annual flower color in the landscape can be expensive and fairly short-lived, the impact of large colorful annual beds has the greatest visual impact of all planting types. The following list describes the best choices for annual color in Texas.

Copperleaf
Acalypha wilkesiana

Fast-growing colorful foliage plant that reaches 3 feet tall. Best in full sun in prepared beds with good drainage. Use as a background planting.

Snapdragon
Antirrhinum sp.

Upright flower spikes available in many colors. Blooms in cool weather in sun or partial shade. Reaches height of 12 to 24 inches.

Begonia
Begonia sp.

Great for summer color, hanging baskets, and pots. Varieties with red or bronze leaves can take more sun than the varieties with green leaves. Blooms red, white, or coral throughout the summer and reaches a height of 6 to 15 inches.

Flowering kale
Brassica oleracea

Colorful cool-weather plant. Excellent for beds or pots. Mix with pansies and dianthus in a container for attractive winter color.

Cosmos
Cosmos parviflorus

Hardy summer blooming plant with lacy foliage and multi-colored flowers on long stems. Grows 12 to 18 inches in full sun.

Dianthus
Dianthus sp.

Delicate-looking cool-weather flowers that come in a variety of colors, ranging from reds and purples to pinks and whites. Common names include carnations, pinks, and sweet William. Plant in sun. Grows 8 to 12 inches.

Impatiens
Impatiens balsamina

Colorful, succulent annual with summer blooms of orange, white, pink, red, and purple. This is one of the best plants for shady areas. Use in beds, pots, or hanging baskets. Height of 10 to 24 inches.

Geranium
Pelargonium hortorum

Grows upright or trailing with clusters of red, orange, pink, or white flowers. Plant in sun or partial shade in well-drained beds or containers. Height of 18 to 24 inches.

Lantana
Lantana sp.

Native plant with bushy growth all summer and flowers of yellow, white, orange, pink, blue, purple, or mixed. Some tough varieties will return each year. Plant in sun. Grows 1 to 3 feet.

Poppy
Papaver sp.

Lovely flowers on long slender stems with lacy, hairy foliage. Blooms late April to early May (many colors) in sunny areas. Some varieties will come back each year. Height of 12 to 24 inches.

Penta
Pentas lanceolata

Blooms all summer. Colors include red, lavender, pink, and candy stripe. Easy to grow in well-drained soil in sun to partial shade. Grows to a height of 24 inches.

Portulaca
Portulaca grandiflora

Low-growing annual with succulent stems and rose-like flowers in summer. New flowers every day. Use in mass plantings or hanging baskets in full sun. Height of 6 inches.

Petunia
Petunia x hybrida

Good annual for cool months. Available in many colors. Most varieties do not take summer heat well. 'Madness' and 'Cherry Blossom' are more heat-tolerant. Plant in sun. Grows to a height of 12 to 24 inches.

Purslane
Portulaca oleracea

Low-growing annual that is related to portulaca and looks very similar. Showy summer flowers of white, pink, yellow, red, and purple. Good for rock gardens or hanging baskets.

Marigold
Tagetes sp.

Fast-growing plant with lacy foliage and yellow or orange flowers in the summer. Red spider mites usually attacks them when used for summer color. Problem not as bad when planted mid-summer for fall color. Plant in sun. Height of 1 to 2 feet.

Verbena
Verbena sp.

Low-growing annuals and perennials with blooms of red, white, salmon, or purple in spring and summer. Height of 9 to 12 inches.

Pansy
Viola hybrids

Low-growing winter-and spring-flowering plant with a multitude of color choices. Excellent for mass plantings or well-drained containers located in sunny areas. Reaches a height of 6 to 8 inches.

Zinnia
Zinnia sp.

Open, upright growing plant with flowers of all colors and sizes on long stems in summer. Easy to grow from seed in full sun. Mature height ranges from 8 to 36 inches.

Butterfly weed (Asclepias tuberosa) *is an excellent native Texas perennial.*

Perennials are semi-permanent to permanent. They usually freeze down to the ground in the winter but return each spring with lush foliage and inspiring displays of flower color.

Perennials can be used in large masses for dramatic impact or throughout the garden to add splashes of color. Because perennials can be divided and moved easily, experiment with different locations in your garden.

There are many wonderful perennials to choose from. Try some of the plants out of the following list for the best chance of success, but try others as well.

Yarrow
Achillea sp.

Upright, lacy foliage with flat-topped clusters of flowers. Colors include white, rose, pink, yellow, and red. Plant in sun. Height of 2 feet.

Aster
Aster sp.

Daisy-like perennial that has light blue blooms summer through fall. Divide established plants in spring every 3 to 4 years. Plant in sun or partial shade. Height of 1 to 3 feet.

Columbine
Aquilegia sp.

Delicate, woodsy-type flowers that bloom on long stems from lacy foliage. Dies to the ground at frost, but returns the following spring. Provides excellent color in shady areas. Height of 12 to 18 inches.

Chrysanthemum
Chrysanthemum sp.

Mums are fall-blooming with a wide assortment of colors and attractive foliage that looks healthy most of the year. Plant in sun. Height of 12 to 36 inches.

Will reseed and spread. Most common color is yellow. Plant in sun. Height of 12 to 24 inches.

Oxeye daisy
Chrysanthemum leucanthemum

Large showy flowers from early to midsummer. It has low water and fertilizer requirements. Established plants should be divided every few years. More freeze-tolerant than shasta daisy. Plant in sun. Height of 12 to 36 inches.

Purple coneflower
Echinacea angustifolia

Brightly colored flowers of dark pink with yellow centers in early to midsummer in sunny areas. Carefree and drought-tolerant. Reaches height of 2 to 3 feet. *E. purpurea* is a lower growing variety with larger, brighter flowers.

Coreopsis
Coreopsis sp.

Looks good most of the year and great while in bloom May to August.

Daylilly
Hemerocallis spp.

Foliage like large leafed grass. Many colors, shapes of blooms and heights of plants available. Blooms from late May until September.

Iris
Iris sp.

Lovely unique blooms available in many colors. Spreads by underground stems. Bearded and spuria iris like dried, well drained soil. Siberian and Louisiana iris like moist conditions. Plant in sun. Height varies from 6 inches to 6 feet.

Liatris
Liatris sp.

Also known as gayfeather. It has tufts of narrow stems topped by fluffy purple flower spikes. It is tough and drought-tolerant. Liatris makes a wonderful cut flower. Plant in sun.

Turk's cap
Malvavisars drummondii

Red-flowering perennial that grows to a height of 3 to 5 feet and blooms all summer. Good for attracting hummingbirds. Flowers resemble a fez— thus the name.

Narcissus
Narcissus sp.

Lovely bell-shaped flowers in early spring. Colors are white, yellow, orange, and combinations. Foliage forms vertical blades from the ground.

Foliage must be left to turn brown on the plant before removing to form bulbs for the next year. Larger flower varieties are called daffodils. Plant in sun. Height of 9 to 18 inches.

Nierembergia
Nierembergia sp.

Low bunch growth with blue or white flowers in summer. Perfect for borders, rock gardens, perennial gardens, or stone walls. Plant in sun to partial sun. Height of 6 to 12 inches.

Oxalis
Oxalis sp.

Tough, low-growing perennial available in several colors. Foliage looks like clover. It is easy to grow in light to

fairly heavy shade, and it retains a neat compact appearance. Grows to a height of 6 to 12 inches with a spread of 12 to 15 inches.

Phlox
Phlox sp.

Several varieties and colors. Hot pink is the most durable. Provides spring and summer color. Plant in full sun or partial shade. *Phlox paniculata,* 'Mr. Fuji,' is a lovely white selection. Louisiana phlox is a purple-flowered spring bloomer.

Thrift
Phlox subulata

Low-growing and spreading plant that acts like an evergreen in mild winters. Blooms in spring in pink, blue, and white. Hot pink is the most common color. Excellent for dwarf border, spring color, and stone walls. Plant in sun. Grows to a height of 6 to 8 inches with a spread of 10 to 12 inches.

Obedient plant
Physostegia sp.

A carefree plant that blooms in the fall and spring. It comes in several colors and is sometimes referred to as lionheart. Grows 2 to 4 feet in full sun

Old roses
Rosa sp.

Antique or heritage roses, especially the native varieties are very durable and pest-resistant. These roses are growing on their own rootstock, are more fragrant, and in general, are prettier bushes than the hybrids.

Wild petunia
Ruellia nudiflora

Wild petunia is a very tough long-blooming Texas native. Grows to 2 feet in full sun or shade.

Salvia
Salvia sp.

Hardy shrubby plants with attractive summer blooms. *S. greggi* (autumn sage) has red, pink, salmon, or white blooms. *S. guaranitica* has intense blue flowers and reaches 3 to 4 feet. *S. leucantha* is a large-growing perennial with beautiful foliage and purple flowers in late summer. *S. farinacea* (mealy blue salvia) has gray-green foliage and early summer blue flowers on long stems.

For other good perennials, see wildflower and herb sections.

Salvia
Salvia leucantha

Best Texas Herbs

Lamb's ear and Mexican mint marigold are excellent herbs for landscape use.

Herbs can be planted for culinary and medicinal uses, but they should also be used as landscape plants. They are drought-tolerant, grow in almost any well drained soil, provide color, texture, and wonderful fragrances.

There are bush-type herbs such as salvia and rosemary. There are excellent groundcovers like lamb's ear, creeping thyme, and Greek oregano, and many beautiful flowering varieties such as yarrow and Mexican mint marigold. Herbs also have effective insecticidal qualities. Some of my favorites that can be planted among the vegetable and ornamental plants to help ward off pests include comfrey, basil, lemon balm, garlic, and tansy.

Herbs are undergoing a revival in Texas. They fit perfectly into an organic program because they should only be fertilized with natural fertilizers and they should never be sprayed with chemical pesticides. In fact, herbs rarely are infested by insects or diseases.

Yarrow
Achillea millefolium

A very lacy, fern-like evergreen perennial with colorful flowers on tall stalks. Flowers bloom in the early summer in white, pinks, and reds. Plant in full sun to partial sun.

Garlic
Allium sativum

Of course, we have to have garlic for cooking and to ward off vampires and to make garlic tea, but it is also a good-looking landscape plant. The foliage of garlic is dark green and the flowers are very interesting as they curve around and finally burst open in the early summer. Best in full sun but can take some shade.

Chives
Allium schoenoprasum

Grows in clumps and looks a little bit like monkey grass. Onion chives have lavender flowers; garlic chives (*A. tuberosum*) have white flowers. Likes sun or partial shade. A member of the onion family, it is used to flavor everything from baked potatoes to vichyssoise. Chives are often rubbed on steaks prior to grilling. They make attractive ornamental plants and repel many insect pests.

Lemon verbena
Aloysia triphylla

A wonderfully fragrant addition to the landscape garden as well as the herb garden. It is sensitive to cold in the northern part of the state so it's best treated as an annual, although it can be used in a pot and brought indoors during the cold months. Best in full sun.

Southernwood
Artemisia abrotanum

Delicate looking, dusty gray foliage emits a lemony scent even when uncrushed but definitely a stronger fragrance when crushed. Full sun is best.

Tarragon
Artemisia dracunculus

An increasingly popular herb, valued for its versatility in the kitchen. Russian tarragon is often confused with French tarragon because it looks the same, but is absent of flavor. Plant in full sun.

Borage
Borago officinalis

A beautiful herb that grows to about 3 feet tall. The leaves are gray-green and have whitish bristles. Flowers are star shaped and peacock blue and bloom throughout the summer. Plant in sun or partial shade.

Saffron
Crocus sativus

The true saffron is an autumn-blooming, lavender-flowered crocus. The saffron food flavor is made from the red-orange stigmas of the plant. Plant bulbs in full sun during the late fall or early spring. They are easier to grow than rumored.

Epazote
Chenopodium ambrosioides

Grows like a weed and can become a pest, but it's worth it for its ability to de-gas beans. Just toss a few leaves in the bean pot when you start cooking. It's also used to flavor Mexican food. Plant in full sun.

Coriander
Coriandrum sativum

Known as cilantro, Chinese or Mexican parsley, this herb is often the distinctive mystery flavor behind many Mexican dishes. It is used a lot in salsas, and may be found in hot Thai peanut sauce. It has also enjoyed popularity in southwest cuisine.

Lemongrass
Cymbopogon citratus

A herb that looks like pampas grass. It grows to a height of about 3 feet, and has a wonderful lemony scent that's excellent for making tea. Although it rarely flowers, it has a lovely texture for a specimen landscape plant. If it freezes, just plant a new one each year. Best in full sun but can take some shade.

Bay
Laurus nobilis

Cold tender in the northern part of the state, bay should be grown in a pot and moved inside during winter. Leaves are very spicy and pungent, are usually used when cooking meat, and can be found in most types of cuisine. Only one or two leaves are needed at a time. Needs full sun.

Lavender
Lavandula officinalis

This herb has white velvety leaves and long spikes of lavender flowers. It grows best in well-drained, sunny areas. Excellent for planting in containers with other herbs.

Marjoram
Majorana hortensis

A mild, fragrant herb and close kin to oregano. It is used in sauces, vinaigrettes, and marinades. Although not used in volume, its availability is greatly appreciated by high caliber chefs.

Lemon balm
Melissa officinalis

An easy-to-grow, fragrant herb with leaves that are light green and oval with scalloped edges. It has a lemony fragrance and is excellent to interplant among vegetable and landscape plants to look good, help repel pests, and attract bees. Sun or part shade.

Mint
Mentha sp.

Makes a good landscape groundcover, but be careful, it spreads aggressively. *Mentha pulegium* is pennyroyal and is an excellent landscape groundcover reported to repel fleas. It will freeze in the colder parts of the state. Plant in sun or partial shade. Varieties include pepper, English, apple, orange, lemon, lime, chocolate, anise, and licorice. My favorite is chocolate peppermint.

Catnip
Nepeta cataria

A shrubby groundcover perennial with gray-green oval leaves. It will reach about 3 feet in height and has small white or lavender flowers. It is excellent for attracting bees and butterflies—and cats, unfortunately. Sun or partial shade.

Basil
Ocimum sp.

There are many types of purple and green basil. All make excellent annual plants to use as borders or low masses. Plant from seed or transplants in sun or partial shade. They will usually return from seed each year. Basil is often used in large volume as an ingredient for pesto sauce. It has also found a spot as a garnish herb. There are many types of basils such as lemon, cinnamon, anise, opal, or holy.

Oregano
Origanum sp.

Used extensively in Greek and Italian food, and sometimes in Mexican dishes. The strongest in flavor is Greek oregano, which is also an excellent cold hardy groundcover plant. Excellent in sauces, soups, and salads. Plant in sun or partial shade.

Dittany of Crete
Origanum dictamnus

This herb is excellent for hanging baskets or patio containers. It has small, soft, round, gray leaves and tiny purple flowers summer through fall. Best in full sun.

Scented geraniums
Pelargonium sp.

Excellent landscape plants because of the lovely texture and the nice delicate flowers, but more importantly, they give off a marvelous fragrance when rubbed or crushed. They come in all sizes and all leaf shapes including deeply cut leaves and those that are soft and velvety. Scents include rose, lemon, strawberry, peppermint,

and many others. Use as house plants in bright light or as tender perennials outside.

Perilla
Perilla frutescens

An easy-to-grow annual with dark burgundy leaves. Growth habits are similar to that of coleus or basil, in fact, it looks like opal basil. Planted from seed or transplants, it will reseed easily each year. It is beautiful in contrast with gray plants such as dusty miller, wormwood, or southernwood. Plant in sun or partial shade.

Parsley
Petroselinum crispum

Curly parsley is a favorite as a garnish due to its pretty leaf, but Italian or flat leaf parsley is a more flavorable herb. All parsley is high in Vitamin C.

Salad burnet
Poterium sanguisorba

A compact evergreen herb that will reach 2 feet tall with a rosette shape. It provides a pleasant cucumber fragrance and has flowers on long stems growing out of the center of the plant. Its lacy, symmetrical shape and nice texture make it a good accent plant. Use in sun or partial shade.

Rosemary
Rosmarinus officinalis

A beautiful gray-green shrub that can grow to a height of 4 feet. Freezes in hard winters, but it is worth replanting every year if necessary. Rosemary has a marvelous pine-like fragrance and beautiful light blue flowers. The low-growing groundcover type is *Rosemary prostratus*. Most chefs seem to prefer the flavor of *prostratus*, yet many chefs are still deciding.

Sorrel
Rumex acetosa

Looks somewhat like spinach but has a very sour flavor. French chefs puree it into a cooked green sauce that is poured over trout fillets. Fresh, young, and tender sorrel leaves are great for salads.

Pineapple sage
Salvia elegans

Has beautiful red flowers in the late summer or fall. It perennializes throughout all but the hardest winters, and grows in sun or shade.

Sage
Salvia officinalis

A very tough evergreen perennial with grayish-green leaves. It will develop woody growth after a while

and need to be replaced. It's easy to kill by overwatering. There are several different selections including some that have variegated foliage. Use in sun or partial shade. A little bit goes a long way, as just a pinch can pierce through any combination of foods. It is an important flavor for turkey dressing and sausage. Its thick gray-green velvety leaves and purple flower spikes make a stunning garnish as well as a beautiful landscape plant.

Elderberry
Sambucus canadensis

A large-growing, beautiful perennial often grown for its edible purple-black berries that ripen in August through September. It grows to a height of 10 to 12 feet in most soils and has lovely white flower clusters in the summer. It's known for its ability to produce very fine humus soil in the root zone and is a wonderful plant for attracting birds. Full to partial shade.

Savory
Satureja montana

Winter savory and summer savory (*satureja hortensis*), are identical in flavor and interchangeable in use. The most skilled chefs use savory to take the gamy flavor out of venison. It is also used in bean dishes.

Lamb's ear
Stachys byzantina

A tough, fuzzy-leafed, gray herb, that makes an excellent groundcover to contrast with darker green plants. It takes full sun up to some fairly heavy shade. Lamb's ear's velvet-like foliage and lavender blossoms are delightful to see and to touch. The leaves were the original Band-Aids and have antiseptic qualities.

Stevia
Stevia rebaudiana

This plant is many times sweeter than sugar. It is a coarse-looking herb with hairy stems, opposite toothed leaves, and small tubular flowers in spring. The dried and finely ground leaves can be used in anything that calls for sugar. One teaspoon of stevia replaces one cup of sugar. It tastes like the nectar of wild honeysuckle. *Lippia dulcis* is another sweet herb. It is more decorative and easier to grow.

Comfrey

Comfrey
Symphytum officinale

"The healing herb" has large, hairy, 10-to 12-inch long leaves. It will spread to 3 feet high by 3 feet wide and has lovely pink and purple bell-shaped flowers that hang gracefully from the stems most of the summer. Can grow in sun or shade and should be used as an accent plant or in a large massing. Comfrey will stay evergreen during mild winters but always comes back and establishes into a hardy perennial. Use the juice from the leaves and stems to take the sting out of insect bites and rashes. Comfrey contains lots of Vitamin B-12 and is good for cuts, bruises, and abrasions.

Mexican mint marigold
Tagetes lucida

A substitute for French tarragon and much easier to grow. It has a strong fragrance in the garden and produces a terrific display of yellow-orange blossoms in the late summer and early fall. It is used to flavor sauces and soups. Perennial in sun to partial shade

Tansy
Tanacetum vulgare

An easy-to-grow, fern-leafed herb that blooms with yellow button-like flowers in the late summer to early fall. Crushed or chopped tansy leaves emit a very bitter taste and are an excellent repellant for ants inside and out. Use in sun or shade.

Thyme
Thymus vulgaris

Pronounced "time," this is an excellent landscape plant. The creeping thymes make fragrant groundcover that is particularly effective between stepping stones and on borders. Creeping thyme also works well flowing over retaining walls. Full sun is best. There are many varieties such as English that has a round leaf, as opposed to French thyme that has a small pointed leaf. There are the flavored thymes such as lemon thyme and coconut thyme. Usually they are chopped finely and added to sauces, soups, or dips. Lemon thyme

when chopped and put on broiled fish is delicious.

Mullein
Verbascum thapsus

A Texas wildflower that looks like a large version of lamb's ear but is more upright and has larger foliage. It also has yellow, white, or purple flowers. Also called flannel leaf or old man's flannel, mullein is a distinctive specimen plant. Use in full sun to partial shade.

Ginger
Zingiber sp.

An easy-to-grow herb that needs warm air and soil around 70°. It can be grown in the spring from pieces cut from the roots (called hands). Plant 1 inch under the soil in pots or beds in sun or partial shade. Produces lots of canes and yellow and purple flowers. Harvest all roots in fall before freeze.

Other good Texas herbs include angelica, anise, arugula, chervil, dill, fennel, rue, and watercress.

Most herbs will do best in well-drained beds made of a mix of compost and native soil. The best location, in general, is full sun in morning and at least some shade from the hot afternoon sun.

Some herbs help with pest control. See Chapter 6, *How to Control Pests the Natural Way.*

Best Texas Wildflowers

Black-eyed Susan is an excellent, long-lasting Texas wildflower.

Wildflowers have always been popular in the wild, at least for those people taking the time to stop for a moment and look at them. On the other hand, many people have been frustrated trying to establish wildflowers on their own properties. Growing wildflowers can be easy, but it isn't as simple as throwing seed on the ground and waiting for the spring show. Once again we need to watch what works in nature and try to use those techniques and even improve on them where possible. (See Chapter 5 for planting tips.)

Yarrow
Achillea millifolium

Upright, lacy foliage, flat topped clusters of white or yellow flowers. Also clusters of white and pink.

Coreopsis
Coreopsis lanceolata

Yellow and red late spring blooming wildflower. Plants reseed and spread easily in any soil, sun to light shade, low water and food needs.

Indian paintbrush
Castelleja indivisa

An annual herb with a single erect stem. The terminal red-to-orange flower color is a misconception. Actually the flower is tiny, creamy white to pale yellow, encircled by the red and orange leaf-like bracts. The seeds are very small and should be planted directly on the soil surface. Adapted to low-lying moist areas in full sun. Perennial lavender and yellow forms are available.

Indian blanket
Gaillardia pulchella

A hardy, drought-tolerant annual found throughout the United States. Easily established from seed, it forms dense colonies of brilliant red flowers with yellow rims. Thrives in heat and full sun in well drained soils.

Gayfeather
Liatris pycnostachya

Tough, drought tolerant wildflowers that respond fairly well to maintained gardens. Make wonderful cut flowers because the purple color lasts indefinitely in a dry arrangement.

Bluebonnet
Lupinus texensis

The bluebonnet is an upright to sprawling spring wildflower that germinates from seed in the fall, leaves and stems are hairy, and flowers have a wonderful fragrance. Bluebonnets are sometimes hard to get going, but once established, are reliable each year. Nurseries are now selling 2¼-inch pots for planting in small garden areas in the spring.

Horsemint
Monarda citriodora

Beautiful, tall late spring blooming wildflower. Flowers when crushed or rubbed on clothes repel fleas and chiggers. Also called lemonmint.

Evening primrose
Oenothera sp.

This sprawling perennial has long-lasting showy white or pink flower display in the spring. It isn't a plant for well groomed gardens but is beautiful in grassy areas and carefree perennial gardens. The evening primrose, also called Texas buttercup, is a native from Missouri to Texas.

Mexican hat
Ratibida columnaris

A drought-tolerant annual to perennial native to the mid-West and has naturalized throughout North America. The characteristic black, cone-shaped heads are surrounded by dropping flowers. At maturity the upright branching stems may become woody. Prefers full sun in well drained soil.

Black-eyed Susan
Rudbeckia hirta

An upright annual or short-lived perennial that grows easily in any soil in full sun. It blooms midsummer, and under irrigation, it lasts several months.

Texas Wildflowers

Common Name	Botanical Name	Flower Color	Rate
Black-eyed Susan	*Rudbeckia hirta*	yellow	3 lbs/acre
Bluebonnet	*Lupinus texensis*	blue	30 lbs/acre
Butterfly Weed	*Asclepias tuberosa*	orange	10 lbs/acre
Coreopsis	*Coreopsis lanceolata*	yellow	10 lbs/acre
Coreopsis	*Coreopsis tinctoria*	red and yellow	2 lbs/acre
Cosmos	*Coreopsis* sp.	multicolors	15 lbs/acre
Crimson Clover	*Trifolium incarnatum*	crimson	15-25 lbs/acre
White Dutch Clover	*Trifolium repens*	white	5-10 lbs/acre
Engelmann Daisy	*Engelmannia pinnatifida*	yellow	5 lbs/acre
Evening Primrose	*Oenothera sp.*	multicolors	1/2 lb/acre
Gayfeather	*Liatris pycnostachya*	purple	10 lbs/acre
Horsemint	*Monarda citriodora*	lavender	3 lbs/acre
Indian Blanket	*Gaillardia pulchella*	red/yellow	10 lbs/acre
Indian Paintbrush	*Castelleja indivisa*	orange	1/4 lb/acre
Indian Paintbrush	*Castilleja purpurea*	purple	1/4 lb/acre
Maximilian Sunflower	*Helianthus maximiliani*	yellow	2 lbs/acre
Mexican Hat	*Ratibida columnaris*	red and yellow	2 lbs/acre
Oxeye Daisy	*Chrysanthemum leucanthemum*	white	5 lbs/acre
Purple Coneflower	*Echinacea purpurea*	purple	12 lbs/acre
Snow on the Mountain	*Euphorbia bicolor*	white	3 lbs/acre
Tahoka Daisy	*Machaeranthera tanacetifolia*	purple	5 lbs/acre
Verbena	*Verbena* sp.	purple	6 lbs/acre
White Yarrow	*Achillea millifolium*	white	1 1/2 lbs/acre
Gold Yarrow	*Achillea filipendulina*	yellow	1/2 lbs/acre

Many varieties of peppers grow well in Texas.

ASPARAGUS

Jersey Gem
Jersey Giant
UC 157

BUSH BEANS

Blue Lake
Contender
Derby
Jumbo
Pinto
Roma
Tendercrop
Topcrop

YELLOW BUSH BEANS

Goldcrop
Improved Golden Wax

POLE BEANS

Blue Lake
Kentucky Blue
Kentucky Wonder

PINTO BEANS

Improved Pinto

LIMA BEANS

Fordhook 242
Jackson Wonder

BEETS

Detroit Dark Red
Pacemaker
Ruby Queen
Lutz

BROCCOLI

Galaxy
Green Comet
Premium Crop
Emperor

BRUSSELS SPROUTS

Jade Cross
Prince Valiant
Royal Marvel

CABBAGE

Early Jersey Wakefield
Ruby Ball
Sanibel
Stonehead

CANTALOUPE

Ambrosia
Laguna
Magnum 45
Mission

CARROTS

Red Cored Chantenay
Danvers 126
Gold Pak
Imperator 58
Little Finger
Spartan Winner

CAULIFLOWER

Snow Crown
Snow King

CHINESE CABBAGE

Michihli
Jade
Pagoda
China Pride

CHARD

Lucullus
Rhubarb
Ruby
Fordhook

COLLARDS

Blue Max
Georgia
Champion
Vates

CORN

Calumet
Sweet G90
Kandy Korn
Merit
Silver Queen
Guadalupe Gold
Golden Queen

CUCUMBERS (Pickling)

Lucky Strike
SMR 58
Liberty
Carolina
Saladin
County Fair 87
Miss Pickler

CUCUMBERS (Slicing)

Dasher II
Salad Bush
Sweet Slice
Slice Master
Sweet Success
Burpless

EGGPLANT

Florida Market
Tycoon
(Small Fruited)
    Ichiban
    Imperial
    Karume
(White)
    Casper

GARLIC

Texas White

HORSERADISH

VNS (Variety not stated)

KALE

Dwarf Scotch
Dwarf Siberian
Blue Knight
Dwarf Blue Curled

LETTUCE

Black-Seeded Simpson
Buttercrunch
Oakleaf
Red Sails
Salad Bowl
Summer Bibb

MUSTARD

Florida Broadleaf
Green Wave
Southern Giant Curled
Tendergreen

OKRA

Burgundy
Clemson Spineless
Lee
Louisiana Green Velvet
Annie Oakley

ONION

(White)
    Crystal Wax

(continued on next page)

(Red)
  Red Granex
  Burgandy
(Yellow)
  Grano
Texas Supersweet 1015Y

PEAS (English)

Green Arrow
Laxton
Thomas
Little Marvel
Wando

PEAS (Snap)

Sugar Ann
Sugar Bon
Sugar Pop

PEAS (Southern)

Big Boys
Blackeye #5
Colossus
Cream 40
Mississippi Silver
Purple Hull
Zipper White Crowder
Red Ripper

PEPPERS (Hot)

Habañero
Jalapeño
Jalapeño Mild
New Mexico Big Jim
Cayenne
Serrano
Purple Peruvian
Hungarian Yellow Wax
Hildalgo

PEPPERS (Sweet)

Big Bertha
Biscayne
Cubanelle
Jupiter
Sharrock
Top Banana
Golden Summer (yellow)
Purple Belle (purple)

POTATOES

(Red)
  Norland
  Red LaSoda

(White)
  Kennebec
(Russett)
  Norgold

PUMPKINS

Autumn Gold
Big Max
Funny Face
Jack O'Lantern
Jackpot
Spirit
Connecticut Field

RADISHES

(Red)
  Champion
  Cherry Belle
  Crimson Giant
  Easter Egg
  Plum Purple
  Red Prince
(White)
  White Round
  White Icicle
  Snow Belle

RUTABAGAS

American Purple Top

SPINACH

Bloomsdale Longstanding
Coho
Fall Green
Hybrid 7
Melody
Ozarka
Iron Duke
(Summer)
  New Zealand
  Malibar

SQUASH (Summer)

Butterbar
Chefini
Dixie
Early Prolific Yellow
Straightneck
Goldbar
Multipik
Senator
Hyrikie
Sun Drops

SQUASH (Winter)

Early Butternut
Table Ace
Acorn Hybrid
Tahitian
Sweet Mama

SQUASH (Zucchini)

(Green)
  Senator
  President
(Yellow)
  Goldrush

TOMATOES (Paste)

(Indeterminate, Vining Type)
  Roma
  San Marzano

TOMATOES (Small fruited)

(Determinate, Bush Type)
  Small Fry
(Indeterminate, Vining Type)
  Porter
  Cherry Grande

TOMATOES (Large fruited)

(Determinate, Bush Type)
  Bingo
  Celebrity
  Cardinal
  Whooper
  Spring Giant
  Whirlaway
(Indeterminate, Vining Type)
  Better Boy
  Simba
  Superfantastic

TURNIPS

Just Right (fall)
Royal Globe II
Tokyo Cross
White Lady

WATERMELONS

Allsweet
Crimson Sweet
Dixie Queen
Jack of Hearts
Jubilee
Mirage
Royal Charleston
Royal Peacock

Note: *There are other varieties that will grow in Texas. This is just a good starting list. It's best to experiment (seeds are cheap) with lots of different kinds to see which varieties and cultivars do best in your specific soil and climate. A mix of varieties will usually bring the best results.*

Fruit and Nut Varieties for Texas

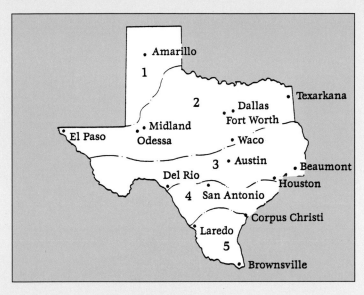

Some fruit varieties do better in certain zones. Compare the list with this map to see which fruits do best in your area.

ZONE 1

Apple—Granny Smith, Holland, Jerseymac, Prime Gold, Red Chief, Smoothee, Starkrimson Red Delicious, Starkspur Golden Delicious, Top Red, Gala

Apricot—Bryan, Hungarian. Moorpark, Wilson

Blackberry—Brazos, Rosborough, Womack

Sour Cherry—Montmorency

Figs—Celeste, Texas Everbearing

Peach—Bicentennial, Denman, Jefferson, Milam, Ranger, Redglobe, Sentinel, Springgold, Surecrop

Pear—Ayers, Kieffer, LeConte, Magness, Maxine, Moonglow, Orient, Surecrop

Plum—Allred, Bruce, Methley, Morris, Ozark Premier

Strawberry—Cardinal, Sunrise

ZONE 2

Apple—Holland, Jerseymac, Mollie's Delicious, Prime Gold, Red Chief, Smoothee, Starkrimson Red Delicious, Starkspur Golden Delicious, Top Red

Apricot—Bryan, Hungarian, Moorpark, Wilson

Blackberry—Brazos, Rosborough

Figs—Celeste, Texas Everbearing

Peach—Bicentennial, Denman, Dixiland, Frank, Harvester, Jefferson, Loring, Milam, Ranger, Redglobe, Redskin, Sentinel, Springgold

Pear—Ayers, Garber, Kieffer, LeConte, Maxine, Moonglow, Orient, Zyers, Asian

Persimmon—Eureka, Hachiya

Plum—Allred, Bruce, Methley, Morris, Ozark Premier

Strawberry—Cardinal, Sunrise

ZONE 3

Apple—Holland, Jerseymac, Mollie's Delicious, Ozark Gold, Starkrimson Red Delicious, Starkspur Golden Delicious

Apricot—Bryan, Hungarian, Moorpark, Wilson

Blackberry—Brazos, Rosborough

Figs—Celeste, Texas Everbearing

Peach—Bicentennial, Dixiland, Frank, Harvester, Jefferson, June Gold, Loring, Milam, Redglobe, Redskin, Sentinel, Springgold, Summergold

Pear—Ayers, Garber, Kieffer, LeConte, Maxine, Moonglow, Orient, Monterrey, Asian

Persimmon—Fuyu

Plum—Allred, Bruce, Methley, Morris, Ozark Premier

Strawberry—Cardinal, Sequoia, Sunrise, Tangi

ZONE 4

Apple—Anna, Dorsett Golden, Ein Shemer, Mollie's Delicious

Apricot—Blenheim, Royal

Blackberry—Brazos, Rosborough

Cold Hardy Citrus—Changsha Tangarinc, Eustis Limequat, Kumquat, Meyer Lemon, Satsuma

(continued on next page)

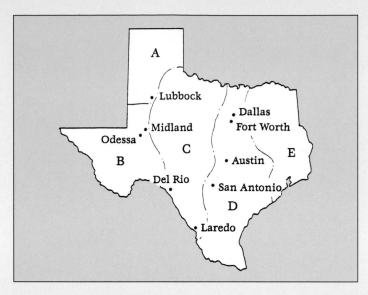

Compare this map with the list of pecan and grape varieties to see which plants do well in your area.

Figs—Alma, Celeste, Texas Everbearing

Peach—Bicentennial, Dixiland, Harvester, June Gold, La Feliciana, Loring, Redskin, Rio Grande, Sam Houston, Sentinel, Springold

Pear—Fan-stil, Kieffer, LeConte, Orient, Pineapple, Monterrey

Persimmon—Fuyu

Plum—Allred, Bruce, Methley, Santa Rosa

Strawberry—Douglas, Sequoia, Tangi, Tioga

ZONE 5

Apple—Anna, Dorsett Golden, Ein Shemer

Apricot—Blenheim, Royal

Blackberry—Brazos, Brison, Rosborough

Cold Tolerant Citrus—(Acid Citrus)—Calamondin, Eustis Limequat, Kumquat, Meyer Lemon; (Mandarin Types)-Changsha Tangerine, Clementine, Orlando, Satsuma; (Oranges)-Hamlin, Marrs, Navel

Figs—Alma, Celeste

Peach—EarliGrande, Early Amber, Flordabelle, McRed, Rio Grande, Sam Houston, Sun Red

Pear—Fan-stil, Kieffer, LeConte, Orient, Pineapple

Persimmon—Tanerashi, Tamopan

Plum—Bruce, Methley, Santa Rosa

Strawberry—Douglas, Sequoia, Tangi, Tioga

REGION A

Grape: Black Spanish, Carman, Champanel, Favorite, Golden Muscat, Herbemont

Pecan: Cheyenne, Mohawk, Shawnee, Shoshoni, Pawnee

REGION B

Grape: Black Spanish, Carman, Champanel, Favorite, Golden Muscat, Herbemont; *Vinifera* —Barbera, Chenin Blanc, Emerald Riesling, Ruby Cabernet, Thompson Seedless

Pecan: Cheyenne, Mohawk, Tejas, Western, Wichita

REGION C

Grape: Black Spanish, Carman, Champanel, Favorite, Golden Muscat, Herbemont

Pecan: Caddo, Cheyenne, Choctaw, Kiowa, Mohawk, Shawnee, Sioux, Western, Wichita

REGION D

Grape: Black Spanish, Carman, Champanel, Favorite, Golden Muscat, Herbemont, Reliance, Flame

Pecan: Caddo, Cape Fear, Cheyenne, Choctaw, Desirable, Kiowa, Shawnee

REGION E

Blueberry: Briteblue, Delite, Garden blue, Tifblue, Woodard

Grape: Black Spanish, Carman, Champanel, Favorite, Golden Muscat, Herbemont; Muscadine—Carlos, Cowart, Fry, Higgins, Jumbo, Magnolia, Regal

Pecan: Caddo, Cape Fear, Cheyenne, Choctaw, Desirable, Kiowa, Shawnee

Pecan Trees

Pecans have traditionally been a favorite tree with Texans.

For success with pecans, choose a mix of the varieties recommended for your part of Texas. Eastern varieties are resistant to leaf diseases and thus are more able to grow in humid areas. The eastern varieties can be grown satisfactorily in the west, but western varieties should not be used in the east because of leaf disease problems. For a rough boundary line for eastern and western varieties, draw a line from San Antonio through Fort Worth.

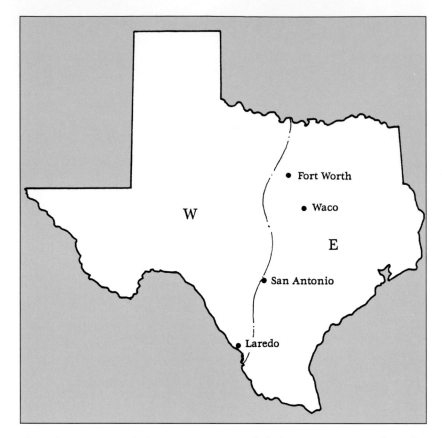

Certain pecan varieties are recommended for East Texas, others for West Texas. Check the accompanying descriptions for the varieties that do best in your area.

Caddo
East

A small, football shaped nut of excellent quality. Very disease-resistant. A vigorous grower and regular producer. Excellent choice for clay soils.

Cape Fear
East

A North Carolina variety with good disease resistance. Susceptible to foliage scorch but a vigorous and good producer. Nice shade tree. Good choice for central and north Texas.

Cheyenne
East and West

Small growing tree that is a cross of Clark and Odom varieties. Cheyenne bears heavily and early. The kernels are relatively loose, making them easy to shell. Good disease resistance and good pollenizer.

Choctaw
East and West

Good landscape tree with high quality nuts. Cross between the Mahan and Success. Choctaw does well in most pecan growing areas. The kernel is very smooth, high in oil content, bright in color, and rich in flavor.

Desirable
East

A heavy producer with large nuts that crack easily. It bears early and is disease-resistant. Very popular eastern variety.

Kiowa
East

A cross of Mahan and Odom. The nut is medium to large in size resembling the Desirable variety in shape and size. Tree shape is good. The Kiowa will make a good yard tree or choice for a commercial orchard. Produces early.

Pawnee
East

An early maturing cross of Mohawk and Starking Hardy Giant. Early ripening and aphid resistant.

Oconee
East

The newest release from the U.S.D.A. Pecan Breeders. The Oconee is a Barton-Schley cross. This variety has good nut size and good disease resistance.

Shawnee
East

Good quality medium-sized pecans. Productive and resistant to disease.

Shoshoni
West

Early ripening, cold tolerant tree with roundish nuts. Due to dramatic alternate cropping, sometimes over produces badly in central Texas.

Sioux
East and West

A Schley-Carmichael cross with excellent eye appeal, shape, taste, and ease of shelling. It has produced well in central Texas and westward.

Tejas
West

A medium-size, elongated nut. Shells into halves easily with a mechanical cracker.

Western
West

Excellent pecan tree choice for far western part of the state but scabs badly east of Abilene.

Wichita
West

Cross between the Halbert and the Mahan varieties. This pecan has an abundance of dark green foliage and is a consistent bearer of heavy, high quality nuts. Must be grown in the west due to its susceptibility to pecan scab.

The pecan varieties I do not recommend in Texas are: Burkett, Success, Barton, Mahan, Mohawk, and Stuart.

Best Texas Grasses

Native grasses help prevent soil erosion and add beauty to a landscape.

Grasses

The most common lawn grasses in Texas are Bermuda and St. Augustine, although tif bermuda hybrids, fescues, centipede, buffalo, and zoysia are used as well. Even ryegrasses are used in Texas for winter overseeding.

Bermudagrass

Still the most popular grass of all because it's relatively easy to maintain as a green turf and it's cheap to install. It only grows in full sun and can be a problem because of its aggressiveness in growing into planting beds while spreading by stolons and rhizomes. It looks fine growing mixed with St. Augustine. Tex Turf 10 is the first step down in the selective hybridization of dwarf bermudas. The next step down to finer textured bermudas is 419, then 328, and dwarf tiffs that are used on golf courses. Common bermudagrass is less susceptible to diseases and insects than the dwarf hybrids or St

Augustine, and freeze is rarely a problem. I still use bermuda some but prefer buffalograss in the sun.

Buffalograss

The best choice for Texas lawns in full sun. It's Texas' only native lawn grass, has a soft, beautiful appearance and requires little water and even less fertilization. Some people have tried hard to convince us that the flowers of the male plants are unattractive. The wispy white flags which are often misidentified as seeds are actually quite attractive. If you are hung up on their appearance, sterile female hybrid choices such as 'Prairie' are available. They are excellent but expensive. Whether you buy native or hybrid buffalograss, you'll be pleased with the results.

Fescue

Bunch-type grass that is planted as a winter overseeding or used in shady lawn areas. Fescue needs fertile, well-drained soil and should be planted in the fall (Sept.-Nov.) for best results.

St. Augustine

A wider bladed grass than bermuda, it can stand more shade—although it won't grow in heavy shade. It can freeze, as you know if you owned any in the winters of '83 or '89. St. Augustine decline is a problem disease in the common St. Augustine but not a problem with the hybrid cultivar 'Raleigh.' St. Augustine requires more water and care than bermuda and falls down somewhat on my recommended list for that reason. It's a good choice for semi-shady areas.

Texas bluegrass

A southerly adapted, rhizomatous, dioecious rangegrass that produces an abundance of quality forage.

Zoysia

An exotic looking grass with dark green, thick, and succulent foliage. The only problem with zoysia, other than it won't grow in shade, is that it is so slow growing. I would never use it in an area that gets much foot traffic from people or pets. A dog or the mail man walking the same path regularly will kill it out. For a beautiful grass to look at and not use too much, 'Meyer' zoysia is hard to beat. The other varieties such as 'Emerald' aren't as good.

Native Grasses

Texas' only native lawn grass, buffalograss, is my favorite choice for full sun and should be used more often. Here are some other native grasses that should be preserved and introduced more often.

Native Grasses

Common Name	Scientific Name
Big Bluestem	*Andropogon gerardii*
Blue Grama	*Bouteloua gracilis*
Bushy Bluestem	*A. glomeratus*
Eastern Gamagrass	*Tripsacum dactyloides*
Little Bluestem	*Schizachyrium scoparium*
Indiangrass	*Sorghastrum nutans*
Sand Lovegrass	*Eragrostis trichodes*
Sea-oats	*Uniola paniculata*
Longspike Silver Bluestem	*Bothriochioa saccharoides* var. *longipaniculata*
Sideoats Gramagrass	*Bouteloua curtipendula*
Switchgrass	*Panicum virgatum*
Coastal Muhly	*Muhlenbergia filipes*
Lindheimer's Muhly	*Muhlenbergia lindheimeri*
Canada Wildrye	*Elymus canadensis*
Texas Bluegrass	*Poa arachnifera*
Inland Seaoats	*Chaemanthium latifolium*

Texas Cover Crops

Cover crops are used, usually in winter months, to add nutrients and organic matter to the soil. Turning cover crops into the soil is called green manuring.

Winter	
Elbon rye	Plant in October at 25 to 50 lbs/acre as a winter cover crop and deterrent of harmful nematodes.
Oats	Plant in October at 30 to 40 lbs/acre. Works well as a winter crop especially when used along with hairy vetch.
Hairy vetch	Plant at 20 to 30 lbs/ acre as an attractive winter cover crop. Higher rates can be used on home vegetable gardens.
Clover	Plant a mix of clovers at total rate of 30 lbs/acre. White, crimson, and red are good choices.

Summer	
Black-eyed peas	Plant at 20 lbs/acre after the last killing frost date in spring.
Buckwheat	Plant at 30 lbs/acre after the last killing frost date in spring.

White clover, mistakenly considered a weed by some, is an excellent nitrogen-fixing legume cover crop.

CHAPTER 3

The Living Soil

Balanced Soil—The Basis of Organics

Whether you're starting with the acidic, sandy soils of East Texas, alkaline clay soils of North Texas, or rocky soils of Central Texas, the basis of organics is to establish and maintain healthy, balanced soil.

Dirt is an inert planting medium that holds up plants. Soil is a wonderfully dynamic, ever changing, complex, living system of life, energy, and minerals. Soil, like everything else in the environment, is fragile and difficult to repair once damaged. Unfortunately, most conventional landscape and agriculture procedures have damaged and are continuing to damage the soil. The purpose of the organic program is to stop the damage by starting to use management techniques, soil amendments, fertilizers, and pest-control products that benefit soil health.

The soil is made up of minerals, organic matter, living organisms, water, air, and energy. It contains approximately 25 percent air, 25 percent water, 45 percent minerals, 3 to 5 percent humus, and less than 1 percent living organisms. Under healthy conditions, the soil is loose and friable, rich in organic matter, alive with insects, earthworms, microscopic plants and animals. It is well-drained, sweet smelling, moist, and rich in a wide variety of minerals and nutrients.

The importance of air and water in the soil cannot be overemphasized. Air and water must be able to move freely through the soil. Soil with a natural balance of all ingredients will have good aggregation, drainage, aeration, and water retention ability.

The mineral portion of the soil includes decaying rock material, sand, silt, and clay, which are the natural sources of potash, phosphorus, and many trace elements. Minerals in the soil provide food for microorganisms and a slow-release supply of nutrients for plants.

Microorganisms make up a small but critical percentage of healthy soil. These tiny plants and animals are born, live, and die in the soil. Microscopic flora and fauna include bacteria, fungi, actinomycetes, algae, protozoa, yeast, nematodes, germs, and other tiny critters. Yes, there are good and bad microorganisms, but if nature's systems are not fouled up with toxic materials, the beneficial microbes will prevail.

A healthy soil has a dynamically active population of microbes, about 50 billion in a single tablespoon of soil. There are approximately 900,000,000,000, that's nine hundred billion, of these life forms in every one pound of healthy soil. There are also macroorganisms such as earthworms and insects.

Solid materials make up about half of the soil's volume; the rest is com-

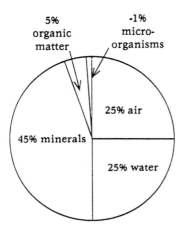

Soil is composed of minerals, organic matter, living organisms, water, air, and energy.

Soil erosion like this is often caused by overuse of chemicals, compaction, and loss of biodiversity.

posed of pores filled with air and water. Clay soils have tiny clay particles and small air pores. Sandy soils have large pores, but the total quantity of pore space is less than in soils with fine particles. Unbalanced sandy soils drain too fast, and unbalanced clay soils hold too much water and drain poorly.

Organic matter and microorganisms are usually lacking in sick soils. Microorganisms are a vital part of soil balance and are encouraged by the use of organic products and techniques. Microorganisms feed on organic matter and form glue-like material called *polysaccharides*. These complex sugars weld individual soil particles together creating larger particles or aggregates. This process gives soil its wonderful soft, crumbly tilth and its pleasant forest-floor fragrance.

Soil compaction is a common problem related to soil structure. Compaction prevents the proper transfer of soil gases and the normal growth of roots. Compaction results from chemical overuse, poor irrigation practices, mechanical or foot traffic, and other poor cultural practices. Compacted soil puts at least one-half of the fertility cycle out of action. Without oxygen in the soil, humus formation doesn't happen. The organic program alone will correct compaction in time, but to speed the process, heal damaged turf or farm land, and possibly save endangered plant materials, mechanical aeration is often needed.

Mineral Nutrients

Some Texas soils are sandy, some are silt, some are clay, some are a mixture. In parts of Texas, the soil base is iron ore, in other parts it's granite, and in a large part of the state, the base rock is limestone. The soil's most plentiful component is this mineral matter. In the top 6 inches of healthy soil, the mineral fraction will be approximately 45 percent. It is the principal determinant of the soil's character. Minerals exist as a result of the physical and chemical action of the parent rock near the surface of the soil. They also occur as a result of the mineralization of organic matter in the soil. As organic matter breaks down, mineral matter is all that's left.

Plants depend on three essential nutrients from carbon dioxide and water: carbon, hydrogen, and oxygen. Plants also depend on 13 essential nutrients from inorganic mineral salts—iron, potassium, calcium, magnesium, nitrogen, phosphorus, sulfur, manganese, chlorine, boron, zinc, copper, and molybdenum. The other 70 or so trace minerals are not fully understood but are important to the soil and to nature's whole. We know that because they are present in all plants.

Do Plants Need N-P-K Fertilizer?

Organic fertilizers do not have very high amounts of nitrogen, phosphorus, and potassium (N-P-K). Aren't these elements important? They aren't as important as the balance of all the mineral nutrients in the soil. In fact, the importance of N-P-K has been greatly exaggerated. Healthy soils and plants have a balance of all elements. A proper fertilization program avoids an overkill of N-P-K to help keep that balance intact. Too much N-P-K fouls up the availability of the other mineral nutrients.

A common error in the management of nutrient elements is the excess of nitrogen and calcium. Excess nitrogen is added in an attempt to stimulate leaf growth. Excess calcium is added under the false information that the pH of soil must be 6.8–7.0. The correct pH range is 6.2 to 6.5. The most common limiting factor of plant growth presently is the excess of these two elements and the deficiency of magnesium.

When buying fertilizer, remember how relatively unimportant nitrogen, phosphorus, and potassium are. Think in terms of providing to the soil all the elements that will help maintain the natural balance. If the soil is in a healthy, balanced condition (which includes organic matter and air), nitrogen, potassium, and phosphorus will be made available naturally by the feeding of microorganisms and relatively little of these elements will need to be added.

Boron

Boron exists in all cell membranes and is important for nitrogen efficiency and disease resistance. Boron is a strong disease fighter. Deficiencies show up as purple leaves, reduced sugar content, bitter taste, cracks in root crops, and corkiness. Boron works closely with calcium and contributes significantly to the quality of food crops and ornamental plants. Deficiency symptoms include tip growth dieback, buds turning light green, roots brown in the center, and poor forming flowers. Sources include fish products, Solubor, borax, and compost.

Calcium

Calcium is king of the nutrients. It is the most critical in low humus soils. Calcium is needed to feed microorganisms and affects the permeability of plant cell walls and thickness of stems. Sources include lime, bone meal, colloidal phosphate, gypsum, and marl. Deficiency characteristics include stunted roots, dieback of growth tips, and increased susceptibility to disease. Calcium is best known for its effect on causing high pH. Although some Texas soils have a calcium deficiency, most have too much calcium, which blocks other nutrients and makes them unavailable.

Carbon

Carbon is the key to life. It is essential for the availability of nitrogen and phosphate and is an important food source for microorganisms. Between 45 to 56 percent of a plant's compounds contain carbon. Carbon is also a significant source of soil and plant energy. Sources of carbon include plant residue, compost, leonardite, humate, coal, and carbon dioxide. Carbon dioxide is the major source of carbon and 95 percent of the world's CO_2 is produced in the oceans. Carbon is rarely deficient unless too much nitrogen is used. A deficiency symptom is inefficient decay of organic matter.

Chlorine

Chlorine is needed in balanced soils, although excessive amounts can be a great problem. It is needed for crop stimulation and is seldom deficient in Texas. Sources include city-treated water, organic fertilizers, and compost.

Copper

Copper is an important micronutrient for strong stalks and disease resis-tance. Most soils in Texas are deficient in copper. Excess calcium or excess nitrogen ties up copper, making it unavailable to plants. Common sources are copper sulfate and Bordeaux mixture. Copper exists in most organic fertilizers.

Hydrogen

Hydrogen is a nonmetallic element that is the simplest and lightest of all elements. It is the third most plentiful element in plants, being present in 6 percent of a plant's compounds. It is flammable and the most abundant element in the universe. The most common sources result when hydrogen combines with oxygen to form water, H_2O, and hydrogen peroxide, H_2O_2.

Iron

Iron is an essential element for the process of photosynthesis and the formation of chlorophyll. It is important for the green color in plants. Deficiency shows up as yellow leaves on the youngest growth and on top growth; veins, margins, and leaf tips stay green. Iron is often tied up in high calcium soils. Sources include copperas (iron sulfate), chelated iron, and most organic fertilizers.

Magnesium

Magnesium is important for photosynthesis, helps hold the soil together, aids in phosphate metabolism, and has more effect on pH than does calcium. Plants will show a deficiency if there is too much or too little magnesium. Deficiency will cause thin leaves and yellowing between veins from the bottom of the plant up. Sources include Sul-Po-Mag (a mineral

Minerals Essential to Healthy Plants

Mineral	Symbol	Sources
Boron	B	Solubor, Borax, compost
Calcium	Ca	Lime, bone meal, colloidal phosphate, gypsum, marl
Carbon	C	Plant residue, compost leonardite, humate, coal, carbon dioxide
Chlorine	Cl	City-treated water, compost
Copper	Cu	Copper sulfate, Bordeaux mixture
Hydrogen	H	Water, air
Iron	Fe	Copperas (ferrous sulfate), chelated iron, some organic fertilizers
Magnesium	Mg	Sul-Po-Mag, Epsom salts (Magnesium sulfate), plant residues, compost, Pro Mag 36
Manganese	Mn	Manganese sulfates, chelates
Molybdenum	Mo	Most organic fertilizers and compost
Nitrogen	N	Organic matter, released by microorganisms, most fertilizers
Oxygen	O	Mechanical aeration, water, hydrogen peroxide, biostimulants
Phosphorus	P	Colloidal phosphate, rock phosphate, compost, phosphoric acid
Potassium (Potash)	K	Granite, greensand, potassium sulfate, Sul-Po-Mag, molasses, plant residues, compost
Sodium	Na	Most manures and compost
Sulfur	S	Compost, molasses, sulfates, elemental sulfur, plant residues, gypsum
Zinc	Zn	Kelp meal, liquid seaweed, zinc sulfate

Role	Signs of Deficiencies	Signs of Toxicity
Disease resistance; quality and taste of food crops	Purple leaves; bitter taste; cracks in root crops; corkiness	Leaves turn yellowish red. Plant death
Feeds microorganisms; affects permeability of cell walls; affects soil pH	Stunted roots; dieback of growth tips; increased disease susceptibility	Reduces the intake of K and Mg and ties up trace minerals
Essential for nitrogen and phosphate availability; microorganisms food source	Plant stress; low yields	Not known
Crop stimulation	Seldom deficient	Streaks leaves
Disease resistance; strong stalks	Diseased; poor food crop taste	Prevents uptake of iron.Causes stunted roots. Plant death
Metabolic activities	Wilting	Root damage. Death
Chlorophyll formation and photosynthesis; green color	Yellow new growth with green veins, margins, and tips	Can limit availability of other trace minerals
Component of chlorophyll; helps hold soil together; aids phosphate metabolism, effects soil pH	Thin leaves and yellowing between veins from bottom of plant up	Reduces absorption of Ca and K and ties up trace minerals
Helps enzyme system	White leaf tissue between green veins; dwarfed leaves with dead spots	Small dead areas in leaves surrounded by yellow
Aids nitrogen fixation; health of microorganisms; other roles are a mystery	Usually unavailable in acid soils	Causes plant toxicity. Poisonous to livestock
Component of proteins; vital to general plant functions and growth	Lack of vigor and yellowing of the oldest leaves	Adverse effects on plant growth, fruiting and storage life; lowers insect and disease resistance
Most over-looked element, critical for biological processes in soil	Lack of vigor; plant stress; pest problems; low yields	Loss of soil moisture
Helps transfer plant energy; color and vitality of plants; increases seed and flower size	Weak flower and fruit production	Ties up other essential elements
Metabolic regulator; produces winter and summer hardiness; root and shoot balance; movement of plant foods	Early winter kill; poor survival of perennials; increased disease occurrence	Coarse, poor colored fruit.Poor absorption of Mg and Ca
Improves taste of food crops; increases protein content and seed production; assists legume nodule development	Yellow new growth	Foliage burn. Limits other nutrients
Sweet taste in vegetables and fruit	Dead areas on leaves; poor bud formation and small terminal leaves	Stunted growth and plant death

containing sulfur, potash, and magnesium), Epsom salts (magnesium sulfate), magnesium oxide, plant residues, and compost. Sulfates are fast acting; oxides are very slow.

Manganese

Manganese deficiency is similar to iron deficiency. It shows up as white leaf tissue between green veins. Plants will be dwarfed and leaves will have dead spots. If sodium plus potassium equals 10 percent or more of the available nutrients, no manganese will get to the plant. Sources include compost, manganese sulfates, and chelates.

Molybdenum

Molybdenum is important in natural nitrogen fixation, but is usually unavailable in acidic soils. Healthy plants will contain between .01 and 10 ppm. It is important for the health of certain microorganisms, but there is much mystery about the importance of molybdenum to plants. Sources include most all organic fertilizers and compost.

Nitrogen

Nitrogen is the most misused fertilizer element, but is an essential constituent of proteins and is vital to plant health. Texas soils require less nitrogen than soils anywhere in the United States. Excessive nitrogen can cause an imbalance in plant metabolism and hurt plant growth, fruiting, and storage life. Its overuse is a major cause of insect and disease infestations. Most of the useful soil nitrogen is found in organic matter and released through microbial activity.

Nitrogen accounts for 16 to 18 percent of a plant's proteins and distin-guishes them from carbohydrates. Nitrogen does not originate from the soil as other nutrients do, but instead from the air. The air is approximately 78 percent nitrogen. It enters the soil through rain or by being fixed (transformed into a plant-usable form) by living organisms associated with legumes such as clover, peas, beans, vetch, or alfalfa. Some organisms such as blue-green algae can fix nitrogen without an association with plants. Nitrogen deficiency shows by lack of vigor and yellowing of the oldest leaves.

Oxygen

Even though oxygen exists in about 45 percent of the compounds in plants, it is an often overlooked element. Adding oxygen to most soils can cause an immediate response in plants, as if high nitrogen fertilizers have been applied. Oxygen can be added to the soil by mechanical means such as aerifying, or tilling, or by using organic fertilizers and soil conditioners. Deeply rooted plants, with their extensive root systems, can be very beneficial in introducing oxygen into the all-important top 12 inches of soil. Liquid biostimulants and hydrogen peroxide help to add oxygen to the soil.

Phosphorus

Phosphorus is the soil's catalyst. Without adequate amounts, nitrogen is unavailable to plants. Its most important function is to help transfer the energy in plants from one point to another. Adequate phosphorus is needed for color and vitality of the plant at bloom time and at maturity. It also increases seed and flower size. Soils must have high levels of phosphates to ensure the formation of sugars. Sources include colloidal phosphate, rock phosphate, compost, and phosphoric acid. Deficiency characteristics are weak flower and fruit production as well as overall poor plant health.

Potassium

Potash is a metabolic regulator and is essential to the balance between leaf and root growth and is necessary for winter and summer hardiness. It is also important in the translocation of sugars. This element exists in ample quantities in many soils, but is often unavailable to plants because of mineral and biological imbalance. Healthy soil microbes will increase the availability of potash. Sources include granite dust, greensand, potassium sulfate, Sul-Po-Mag, molasses, plant residues, and compost. Deficiency characteristics include early winter kill, poor survival of perennials, and increased susceptibility to disease.

Chemically Balanced Soil

	Desired Saturation %	LBS. Per Acre	PPM	Notes
Organic matter	2.5–5%			5% is ideal
Calcium	60–70%*	Varies with EC		68% is ideal
Magnesium	12–20%*	Varies with EC		12% is ideal
Potassium	3–7.5%	Varies with EC		5% is ideal
Sodium	0.5–3.0%	Varies with EC		Must be lower than % K
Phosphate	.025%	500–750 lbs/acre	250–375	
Sulfate		40–50 lbs/acre	20–25	
Nitrogen		40 lbs/acre (Nitrate Form)	20	
Chlorides		160–240 lbs/acre	80–120	
Boron		4 lbs/acre	0.8–1.0	1.0 is ideal
Iron		400 lbs/acre	200	
Manganese		270 lbs/acre	50–125	Should be 2/3 of iron level
Copper		10–15 lbs/acre	2–5	Can be as high as 7.5
Zinc		20–40 lbs/acre	10–20	

PPM = Parts per million
PPM × 2 = lbs/acre
EC = Exchange Capacity
*Sandy soils will require different levels (TEC 2-6)
See appendix for additional soil testing information.

Sodium

Sodium is most important in its relationship with potassium. The available potassium must be higher than the available sodium or a "salt" problem will exist in the soil. Sources include most manures and compost. Sodium is rarely deficient in Texas soils.

Sulfur

Sulfur is called a secondary element and sometimes even a minor element, but it is actually a major element. As with nitrogen, a deficiency causes yellow leaves, but a sulfur deficiency turns the newest leaves yellow. It is the easiest leached of all minerals. Sulfur improves the taste of food, increases protein content and seed production, and helps legume nodule development. Sources include compost, molasses, sulfates, elemental sulfur, plant residues, and gypsum.

Zinc

Zinc is important for the sweet taste in vegetables and fruit. Its availability requires well-drained soil. Deficiency shows in leaves with dead areas, poor bud formation, and small terminal leaves. Weed pressure is greater in soils where zinc is deficient. Sources include compost, kelp meal, liquid seaweed, and zinc sulfate.

Healthy Soil Is Well Balanced

The health, balance, and productivity of the soil depends on three basic pieces being in place: chemistry, biology, and physics. All three are dependent upon each other, but the chemi-cal balance of the soil must be present for the biology and physics to be correct. The living portion of the soil must be active and healthy for the tilth and drainage to work properly,

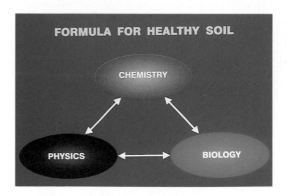

Healthy soil is a balance of chemistry (mineral nutrients), biology (living organisms), and physics (soil structure and energy).

and the physical properties of the soil must be correct for the living organisms to thrive. Nature will balance the soil for you over time if a few basic ingredients are added: organic matter, air, and moisture. To help nature speed up the process, you can correct the serious deficiencies and imbalances by amending the soil with those elements that show in a soil test to be limiting factors.

For example, if the soil test shows a deficiency of magnesium, add magnesium. If it shows a deficiency of iron, add iron. In general, the imbalances of minerals in Texas soils will be in two categories. In most black clay soils, calcium will be too high and magnesium will be too low. This imbalance causes potash, phosphorus, and most trace minerals to be unavailable. Correct this condition by adding granulated sulfur to the soil in spring and fall at the rate of 5 lbs per 1,000 sq ft or approximately 220 lbs per acre. The other common condition is acid, sandy soil with low calcium and high magnesium. For this imbalance, add high calcium lime (not dolomitic) at 40 lbs per 1,000 sq ft in sandy soil and up to 80 lbs per 1,000 sq ft in clay soils.

Soil Microorganisms

You don't hear much about soil microorganisms from conventional horticulturists and farmers. That's because traditional chemical agriculture and horticulture ignore the importance of soil biology. Microorganisms are microscopic plants and animals living in the soil. They include bacteria, fungi, actinomycetes, algae, protozoa, yeast, germs, ground pearls, and nematodes. There are about 50 billion microbes in one tablespoon of healthy soil. There are approximately 900,000,000,000 (nine hundred billion) microorganisms per pound of healthy soil.

To give you a clear idea of the population of these vital microbes, the estimated numbers of common organisms found in one gram of reasonably healthy agricultural soils are as follows:

Common Organisms Found in One Gram of Soil

Bacteria	3,000,000	to	500,000,000
Actinomycetes	1,000,000	to	20,000,000
Fungi	5,000	to	1,000,000
Yeast	1,000	to	1,000,000
Protozoa	1,000	to	500,000
Algae	1,000	to	500,000
Nematodes	10	to	5,000

Note: one gram is the approximate weight of a standard paper clip.

The primary job of microorganisms is to break down organic matter—first into humus, then various acids, enzymes and compounds, and ultimately into basic mineral elements (a process known as mineralization). Microbes must have a constant supply of organic matter or they will be reduced in population and weaken the soil. Certain microorganisms have the ability to fix nitrogen from the air, which is 78 percent nitrogen. Healthy soils produce food through microbial feeding. Microbes are constantly being born, living, and dying. The dead bodies of microbes create an important source of organic matter and humus in healthy soil.

Beneficial microbes thrive in moist soil that is about as wet as a squeezed-out sponge. Healthy organic soil can save as much as 50 percent of the water normally used for irrigation where large quantities of harsh pesticides and synthetic fertilizers are used.

Actinomycetes

Actinomycetes are a higher form of bacteria and similar to fungi and molds. They generally thrive in neutral to alkaline aerated soils and are less active in acid or waterlogged soils. They are extremely important to the decay of organic matter in dry regions. They can be seen as the white fungus-like threads on decaying organic matter. The earthy smell of newly plowed soil or the forest floor is courtesy of actinomycetes. They work at various depths in

the soil to help form humus. While they are decomposing animal and vegetable matter, actinomycetes liberate carbon, nitrogen, and ammonia, making mineral nutrients available for higher plants.

Algae

Algae account for the majority of the photosynthetic microflora in the soil. They thrive primarily on or near the soil surface where moisture and light are adequate, although some live

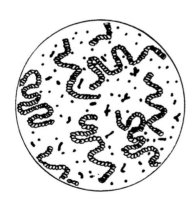

in the subsoil. Algae produce organic matter by taking carbon dioxide from the air and energy from sunlight to create new cells. Fungi and bacteria reduce the net amount of organic matter, but algae increase the volume. They are much less numerous than bacteria, fungi, and actinomycetes.

Blue-green algae (also called cyanobacteria) are able to fix or grab nitrogen directly from the air.

Bacteria

Bacteria are the most plentiful soil microorganisms and can thrive under a wide variety of conditions—from acid to alkaline soils and from aerobic (with free oxygen) to anaerobic (lack of free oxygen) conditions. Bacteria

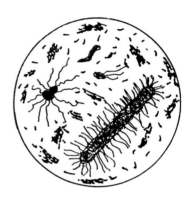

feed on organic matter and encourage organic and inorganic chemical reactions that have a strong effect on plant growth. Some bacteria fix nitrogen from the air in the soil. Most bacteria are found in the top one foot of soil.

Fungi

Fungi are multicelled, filamentous or single-celled primitive plants. They lack chlorophyll, and therefore lack the ability to make their own carbohydrates. Their primary function is to help break down organic matter. Fungi thrive mainly in well-drained, neutral to acidic, oxygenated soils. Mycorrhizal fungi grow on plant roots and effectively enlarge the plant's root system. These fungi are visible as

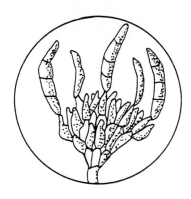

white cobweb-like threads that actually enter the cells of the root hairs and become part of the root.

Nematodes

Nematodes are probably the most numerous multicellular creatures on earth. They are active, tubular, microscopic animals living on moist surfaces or in liquid environments like the films of water in the soil. Destructive and beneficial nematodes exist in

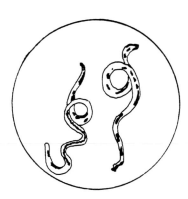

almost all soils. Some enter the soil through lesions to feed on roots. Some nematodes cause knots on roots; some don't. Some nematodes feed only on nematodes or other animals in the soil. Some species of beneficial nematodes are being used to control termites, grubworms, and other soil inhabiting pests.

Protozoa

Protozoa are the simplest form of animals. They are single-celled and microscopic in size and the earth's

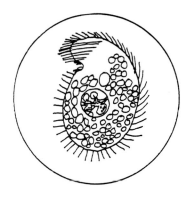

most abundant invertebrates. They obtain their food from organic matter and serve to regulate the size of the bacterial community.

Yeasts

Yeasts are fungi that exist as single-celled organisms that are larger than bacteria and more developed. They multiply by budding or fission. Yeasts

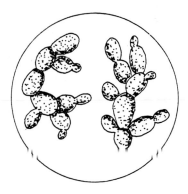

make up a small percentage of the total microbe population. Their function is not clearly understood, but yeasts are found to exist in all soils in all parts of the world. Large concentrations are often found in the root systems of plants.

Microorganism	Location, Living Conditions	Function
Actinomycetes	Thrive in neutral to alkaline soils; high oxygen requirement; prevalent in dry regions located at various depths in soil.	Liberate carbon, nitrogen, and ammonia during decomposition of organic matter; help form humus.
Algae	On or near soil surface; need adequate moisture and light.	Use CO_2 from air and energy from sunlight to create new cells; blue-green algae fix nitrogen directly from air.
Bacteria	Thrive under most conditions; usually found in top one foot of soil.	Feed on organic matter; encourage organic and inorganic chemical reactions that affect plant growth; fix nitrogen from air in soil.
Fungi	Thrive in well-drained, neutral to acidic, oxygenated soils.	Help break down organic matter. Mycorrhizal fungi help develop healthy root systems by growing on plant roots.
Nematodes	Exist in almost all moist soils.	Beneficial: control termites, grubworms, and other soil inhabiting pests. Destructive: feed on roots; cause root knots.
Protozoa	Present in almost all soils.	Regulate size of bacterial community.
Yeasts	Exist in all soils in all parts of the world. Often concentrated in plant root systems.	Not clearly understood yet.

Soil Macroorganisms

Healthy soil will also have larger living organisms. Macroorganisms can be seen with the naked eye. They range from tiny mites to large rodents, and all have a specific function in the soil. The most famous soil macroorganism is the earthworm.

Macroorganisms can be divided into three major subgroups: herbivores, detritivores, and carnivores, although some may fall into more than one subgroup. Herbivores feed on living plants, detritivores feed on dead and decaying plant tissues, and carnivores feed on other living animals. Herbivores (plant eaters) include snails, slugs, insect larvae, termites, beetle larvae, woodchucks, mice, and grubs. Detritivores (decaying matter eaters) include mites,

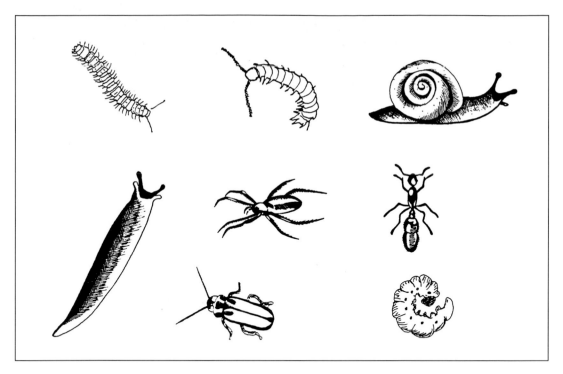

Macroorganisms—Millipede—Centipede—snail—slug—spider—ant—beetle—cut worm

snails, beetles, millipedes, woodlice, springtails, earthworms, enchytraeid worms, spiders, scorpions, centipedes, earwigs, crickets, termites, slugs, and ants. Carnivores (animal eaters) include mites, springtails, enchytraeds, centipedes, snails, slugs, flies, moles, ants, spiders, centipedes, scorpions, and beetles.

Macroorganisms loosen the soil by burrowing and digging; help decompose plant tissue for use by microorganisms; and through their waste, help create beneficial compounds for plant use.

The World's Best Soil Builders

Earthworms—long neglected and even killed as a nuisance—have been "rediscovered" as the world's best soil builders. These "Intestines of the Soil" as Aristotle called them, break up soil

Earthworms are probably the most beneficial macroorganism in the soil.

hardpans, drill miles of burrows that soak up fast-falling rains, help plants root more deeply into the soil, and help balance nutrients and loosen compaction.

Our earthworm friends enrich soil and improve its productivity in many ways, while at the same time, help to balance the natural systems in the earth. Here are some of the earthworm's specific contributions.

Water absorption. Earthworms dig pencil-sized vertical tunnels that allow rainfall to flow deep into subsoil so that even hard rains can soak in rather than runoff and erode the ground.

Water runs through the worm tunnels and seeps slowly from these underground conduits into surrounding soil so the entire root zone is evenly watered. This is a particularly important factor in heavy clay soils. Earthworm tunnels help prevent waterlogged, anaerobic soils by removing excess water from the root zone.

Aeration. From the surface to a depth of 3 to 5 feet, earthworms bring oxygen down by way of their tunnels to stimulate microbial conversion of minerals into plant nutrients. The aerobic depth of the soil is increased and carbon dioxide is more effectively moved up to the soil surface and released. The linings of tunnels are rich with glue-like nutrient sugars or polysaccharides that help the tunnels remain in place for years. The oxygen, nutrients, and rich bacterial life associated with the tunnels encourage plant root growth down into subsoil moisture.

Root growth stimulation. Another function of earthworms is the creation of a horizontal network of tunnels that enables roots to grow 6 or 7 inches a day through otherwise compacted soil. As generations of root residue fill these tunnels, deep moisture also moves by osmosis up through the "pipelines" to feed roots nearer the surface.

Tilling. Earthworms pull scraps of decaying organic matter from the ground surface down into the network of underground passages. They also bring minerals from the subsoil up to the topsoil. They mix the debris thoroughly into the topsoil and then help to digest the raw residue and convert it to nutrient-rich humus and other compounds beneficial to plants.

Hormones. Earthworms break down crop growth inhibitors, such as phenols and formaldehyde, from decaying residue and add plant growth stimulants containing auxins and cytokinins. Earthworms can treat 50 tons of topsoil per acre each year. Earthworms place deposits of nutrient-laden castings through the soil, encouraging vigorous root growth.

Minerals. Earthworms help convert minerals into water-soluble, plant-available forms. This action increases soil test results for calcium, nitrate and ammonium nitrogen, phosphorus, and potassium. Worms help chelate such minerals as zinc, boron, and iron, linking them chemically with other nutrients so roots can absorb them. Processed deposits, called castings, left by earthworms contain 5 to 10 times the amount of soluble plant nutrients as the original soil. Under good working conditions, worms can process and bring to the surface a half-inch of finely textured, stone-free mineral soil each year.

Microorganisms. Earthworm bodies contain compartments that multiply microorganisms, distribute them along the passageways, and spread them on the surface to help decompose organic matter. Earthworms create soil conditions that discourage populations of nematodes and other pathogens harmful to plants.

Thatch. Earthworms help to eliminate thatch problems by fragmenting and digesting plant debris and helping the microorganisms convert the organic matter into humus.

The way to have more earthworms is to feed them organic foods and manures, avoid over tilling, mulch all bare soil, and avoid high nitrogen fertilizers and chemical pesticides. Earthworms will repopulate naturally if they aren't poisoned.

Earthworms are especially active early in the spring when the temperature rises and the soil is moist. They stay deep in the soil during the heat of the summer, then come back up when it starts getting wet and cool in the fall.

And you thought worms were just good for fishing.

While some macroorganisms, such as grubs, can be considered harmful or destructive to plant roots, their presence may also be valuable to the health of the soil. They are an important food source for other organisms. The principles of organics teach us that helping all components of nature work in harmony is essential. If we try to kill all the macroorganisms that are detrimental, we will certainly kill the beneficial ones as well. Balance is the goal. When the balance is disrupted, the symptoms of insects and diseases occur.

Soil Structure and Energy

Healthy soil has aggregated soil particles, lots of air space in between the particles, positive drainage, good moisture holding ability, and high energy.

Soil texture relates to particle size. Most soils are made up of a mixture of sand, silt, and clay. Clay particles are microscopic, sand the largest, and silt in-between. Sandy soils have larger air spaces and less surface tension than clay soils. That's why clay soils hold water longer than sandy soils. The tiny clay particles have more surface area than sand particles and can hold more nutrients. A mix of soil particles is best.

Soil structure is also determined by other factors. Chemistry and biology influence the physical structure. If the chemical nutrients are relatively balanced, the microorganisms will aggregate the small soil particles into larger particles.

The other physical part of the soil that's rarely discussed is energy. Everything on earth is energy—air, animals, insects, rocks, water, people, and everything else. Energy is simply manifest in different forms, and it radiates in different wave lengths.

Healthy soils and healthy plants have high levels of energy. Energy

Rich soil is composed of soil particles, air spaces between the particles, water, and energy.

systems in the soil and in plants have a definite order. That order will naturally be in place if the soil chemistry, biology, and physical structure are balanced. Problems related to energy usually occur when energy is too low. N-P-K fertilizers increase the energy, but it's a temporary increase—it doesn't hold long. Substances that increase and sustain energy levels in soil and plants include fish products, seaweed, humates, sugars, vitamins, trace minerals, Epsom salts, calcium, baking soda, hydrogen peroxide, and vinegar. You'll read more about these materials throughout the book.

Plants are electrical systems. So are insects. Within these two simple facts lies the answer to why insects do not attack healthy plants. Sick plants radiate energy patterns that say "come and get me." And the insects do.

Organic Matter

Organic matter is related to all three components of a balanced soil: chemistry, biology, and physics. It supplies mineral nutrients for plants, provides food for microorganisms, and improves soil structure by increasing pore spaces. Organic matter in the soil comes from many sources including plant and animal wastes and the dead bodies of small animals, insects, and microorganisms. Organic matter sources include leaves, sawdust, bark, roots of plants, root exudates, weeds, algae, cover crops, animal urine and manure, agricultural waste, nut hulls, dead animals, trash, and water plants. Organic matter decomposes primarily by the feeding of microorganisms. This natural process creates humus.

Humus is the decomposed remains of organic matter. Humus is a soft, sweet smelling, shapeless, dark brown to black crumbly substance that is the heart of healthy soil. Humus is nearly insoluble and contains about 30 percent each of lignin, protein, and complex sugars. It contains 3 to 5 percent nitrogen and 55 to 60 percent carbon and has a carbon to nitrogen ratio of 10 to 1.

Humus is never static but is constantly transformed by natural processes into various acids, enzymes, and minerals. Humus is the food source and energy for microorganism development and is the stage of organic matter decomposition that provides slow-release food for plants.

Our Texas soils are usually deficient in humus. A proper soil test will show most soils having less than 2 percent organic matter. Healthy soil should have 3.5 to 5 percent.

Humus is constantly used up and depleted unless additional matter is recycled into the soil. The constant tilling of the soil, growth of plants, and the removal of plants and organic matter without replenishment will ultimately reduce the soil to an inorganic state, rendering it useless for healthy plant growth. The use of high nitrogen fertilizer speeds this degrading process.

Aeration

If I could get new organic gardeners to do just one thing different, it would be to get more air in the ground. Air in the soil is extremely important, but it's lacking in most soils. Punching holes in the ground and rototilling are the most common techniques of aeration.

Various companies make machine aerators that can be rented or purchased.

Hand-held aerators with long tines are excellent tools for loosening the soil.

By using a metal or PVC pipe with one end cut off at an angle and the other fitted with a hose connection, you can aerate and water at the same time.

Mechanical aeration can be done with hand tools, gasoline powered machines, plows, rippers, disks, or the hoofs of grazing animals. When soil is healthy, the earthworms and microorganisms will till and aerate the ground and keep it in good shape if high nitrogen fertilizers and pesticides cease to be used. Until that time the most important gardening activity is the physical addition of air to the soil. Oxygen is a critical nutrient but not the only important part of the composition of air. Carbon dioxide and nitrogen, both essential to soil and plant health, exist in large quantities in the air. Many other mineral elements such as copper, boron, iron, and sulfur are in the air. These nutrients are available to plant roots and microorganisms if there is enough pore space in the soil. Oxygen gives the most noticeable response. It stimulates microbial activity and helps make other soil nutrients available to plant roots. In fact, good aeration gives the same greening effect as that of applying nitrogen fertilizer to the ground. Look at the tall green grass around fire ant mounds. That response is primarily due to the aeration of the ants in the ground.

To mechanically aerate simply punch holes heavily throughout the turf and bed areas. Core aerators and devices that tear the soil under the surface are the best choices but any kind of holes punched in the soil will help.

Mechanical aerators include hand held devices such as the Soil Digger from Gardener's Supply. Smith and

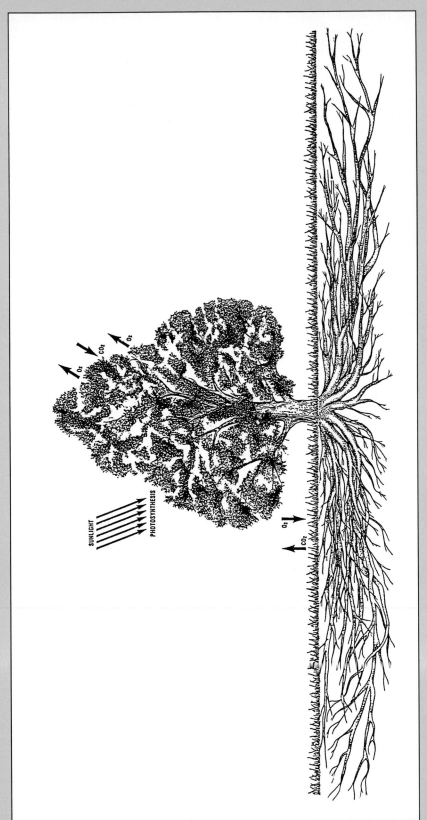

Whether the plant is a bluebonnet, bur oak, or bluegrass, its growth process is the same. It requires air, water, sunshine, and minerals to be healthy.

Hawkin's catalog device is the Broadfork. A Dallas company makes a similar device called the Aero-Till. Large hand tools are the best aerators on the market. They have very long tines, do a wonderful job breaking and aerating compacted soil, and they are very rugged.

Machine aerators are expensive, but they work wonders. They are all beneficial to soil health. Buy or rent one that fits your needs and budget. Landscape contractors can provide the equipment and do the work for you.

My favorite aerator for large scale properties is the Air-Way which is a tractor attachment. Units are available from 6 feet wide to 24 feet. It punches and tears large holes in the ground without destroying the turf. Other good aerators include Ryan, Hahn, Olathe, Jacobsen, and Torro.

How Plants Grow

Nature creates plant life using air, water, sunshine, and earth minerals. Most plants are about 95 percent air, water, and sunshine and only 5 percent minerals.

Sunlight is the source of all energy, as far as we know, and the green leaves are nature's instruments for gathering in the sunlight. Sunlight energy and the gas called carbon dioxide (CO_2) enter the foliage of plants to combine with water and chlorophyll to form sugars, proteins, fats, and carbohydrates—the foodstuff of plants. This process is *photosynthesis*. These naturally created foods are transferred from the foliage through the stems and limbs, down through the trunk into the roots, and out into the soil in the form of exudates that leave the roots through the root hairs and enter the rhizosphere.

The rhizosphere is the soil area immediately adjacent to the roots and the location of the heaviest concentration of microbiotic activity. Soil microorganisms include mycorrhizal fungi, nitrogen-fixing bacteria, yeasts, algae, cyanobacteria, actinomycetes, protozoa, mites, nematodes, and other small animals. It's here that the roots and soil are working together to produce and release nutrients from the soil to feed the plant and to stimulate other processes in the soil.

Microorganisms of all sorts feed on the soil's energy-rich substances, primarily humus and rock dust, to release a vast array of minerals, vitamins, antibiotics, regulators, enzymes, and other compounds that can be absorbed back into the roots and move through the plant to produce strong growth and increased insect and disease resistance.

Whether the plant is a bluebonnet, bur oak or blue grass, the process is the same. This natural process only works at its full potential and efficiency if the soil is healthy and balanced.

CHAPTER 4

Getting the
Soil Ready

Creating the Forest Floor

A good way to understand how to prepare beds properly is to go into a forest and dig a hole large enough to get down into. Then look at the wall of the hole, especially the top 7 inches. The layering of material there teaches a simple but extremely important lesson.

The top 2 to 4 inches is mulch—leaves, twigs, bark, dead plants, dead bodies of animals, and animal manure. Next is the organic matter that's beginning to decay. White fungus-like matter is visible. Below that is 1 to 2 inches of one-year-old organic matter that is broken down into humus. Below that is a mixture of humus and the native rock matter. Below that is the subsoil. Earthworms, insects, and plant roots are mixed throughout the layers. The top 7 inches of the forest floor is well aerated and is the host of a huge population of living organisms. That layered structure, transitioning down from rough mulch to subsoil, is exactly what we want to create in the vegetable garden and in the ornamental garden.

Creation of the ideal "Forest Floor" would be something like this:

Step 1	Till 4 to 6 inches compost into existing soil.
Step 2	Spray soil with fish emulsion, seaweed, or some other biological stimulator.
Step 3	Plant.
Step 4	Apply a light coating of earthworm castings—just enough to barely cover the soil.
Step 5	Apply a 1½-inch layer of finished compost.
Step 6	Apply a 2-inch layer of partially finished compost.
Step 7	Apply a 2-inch layer of hardwood bark mulch or wood chips.

We'll never be able to do as good a job as Mother Nature in creating the forest floor, but we can come pretty close.

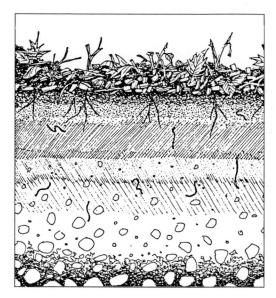

The forest floor is a wonderfully alive and dynamic community of plants and animals.

Key Points to Remember About Nature

- Nature never attempts to grow plants without animals.
- Nature always grows mixed crops and never allows a monoculture.
- Nature takes careful steps to cover the soil to prevent parching and erosion.
- Mixed animal and vegetable debris are converted to humus.
- There is no waste in nature.
- The process of growth and the process of decay balance one another.
- Large fertility reserves (humus) are always maintained in nature.
- Healthy soil stores moisture.
- Plants and animals are left to protect themselves against insects and diseases.

Compost—Mother Nature's Fertilizer

What is compost? How do you make compost? Is compost a fertilizer? How do I use compost? Is composted manure in a bag really compost? Do I need bark, peat moss, and compost?

To answer all these questions, let's go through the entire composting process. For starters, everything on earth that's alive, dies, and everything that dies, rots; and completely rotted, once-living material is compost. Yes, compost is a fertilizer. In fact, it is the best fertilizer—being nature's own. Compost is not only a great fertilizer but also an excellent way to recycle waste. The word compost comes from two Latin words meaning "bring together."

What is Compost?

The best composts are those that are made from several ingredients. The ideal mixture is 80 percent vegetative matter and 20 percent animal waste. The best materials are those that you have on your own property. The second-best materials are those that are locally available.

Even though there are many recipes for compost, it's almost impossible to foul up the compost-making process. For new gardens or planting beds, the composting can be done in the ground by tilling raw organic matter into the soil and covering the surface with mulch. To use this method effectively, it's best to do the work at least six months prior to planting. Composting in the ground, as the forest does, takes longer than composting in a pile. Remember that composting is more of an art than a science, and a little experimenting is good. There are many acceptable ways to build compost piles, but I find that the simplest systems are usually the best.

If space permits, containers are not needed to make a compost pile.

When needed, hay bales work well to contain the compost and to help maintain the moisture level.

How is Compost Made?

The best time to compost is whenever the raw materials are available. It's ideal to have compost piles working year round. Choose a convenient site—some easily accessible utility area such as behind the garage or in the dog run. The compost pile can be located in sun or shade, and covers are not necessary. The most effective compost piles are made on a paved surface so that the liquid leachate can be caught and used as a fertilizer. When the pile is on the ground, the leachate is wasted, but the earthworms can enter the pile and help complete the natural degradation of the material. So both methods work.

Next, decide what kind of a container to use. I don't use a container at all, but instead, just pile the material on the ground or on a concrete slab. If you choose to use a container, buy some hog wire, lumber, wooden pal-

lets, cinder blocks, or any materials that will hold a volume of about 4 feet × 4 feet with a height of at least 3 feet. A minimum compost pile should be 3 feet × 3 feet × 3 feet.

Hay or wheat straw bales make an excellent container for compost. Build a 2- or 3-sided container by stacking the bales to make the sides. At the end of the composting process, the hay bale sides can be pulled into the mix to become part of the compost.

Many materials can be used to make compost: grass clippings, leaves of all kinds, sawdust, spent plants, weeds (don't worry about the weed seed), tree chips, coffee grounds, feather meal, seaweed, peanut hulls, pecan hulls and other nut shells, fish scraps, brewery waste, slaughterhouse waste, pine needles, wool, silk, cotton, granite dust, uncooked vegetable scraps, fruit peelings and waste, pet hair, household dust, and animal manures. It's controversial whether dog and cat manure should be used in the compost pile. I don't have cats, but I do use dog manure. You should make your own decision on this point. I do not recommend using greasy or cooked foods, newspaper or other dyed or printed materials, synthetic fabrics, burned charcoal, plastics, or rubber.

The materials should be chopped into various size pieces and thoroughly mixed together. Compost piles that contain nothing but one particle size will not breathe properly. Layering the ingredients, as most books recommend, is unnecessary unless it will help to get the proportions right. After the first turning, the layers are gone. Green plant material contains water and nitrogen and will break down faster than dry, withered materials. Add some native soil (a couple of shovelfuls) to each pile to inoculate the pile with native soil microorganisms. To thrive, microorganisms need (1) an energy source, which is any carbon material such as leaves or wood

(2) a nitrogen source, such as manure, green foliage, or organic fertilizers, and (3) vitamins, which are stored in most living tissue.

Watering the pile thoroughly is important and best done while mixing the original ingredients. The proper moisture level is between 40 to 50 percent, similar to the wetness of a squeezed-out sponge. Piles that are too wet will be anaerobic and not decay properly. Piles that are too dry won't compost properly or fast enough. Once you have gotten the pile evenly moist, it's easy to maintain. Add a little water during dry periods. If you have ants or other insects in your compost pile, it's usually too dry or sloppy wet.

Turning the pile is important. It keeps the mixture aerobic by helping oxygen penetrate the material. Turning also ensures that all the ingredients are exposed to the beneficial fungi, bacteria, and other microorganisms that work to decay the raw material into humus. It also assures that all

Making compost is simple—just mix vegetative and animal waste together and keep moist.

the ingredients are exposed to the cleansing heat at the center of the pile. In a properly "cooking" compost pile, the heat of approximately 150° kills the weed seed and harmful pathogens but stimulates the beneficial microorganisms. Don't be concerned if your pile heats for a while and then cools off—that's natural. The entire process takes anywhere from two months to a year, depending on how often the pile is turned. Piles with high levels of nitrogen will compost faster. If the ingredients contain a high percentage of wood chips, the process may take even longer. It's interesting that softwood sawdust or chips break down slower than hardwood.

Compost activators help the pile heat up and cook faster. Many specific products exist and work, although almost any organic fertilizer can be used as a compost activator at the rate of 3 to 4 lbs/cu yd of compost.

How is Compost Used?

Compost has many uses. Partially completed compost makes an effective top-dressing mulch for ornamental plants and food crops. It's easy to tell when the compost is finished and ready to use as a fertilizer and soil amendment. The original material will no longer be identifiable, the texture will be soft and crumbly, and the fragrance will be rich and earthy.

Compost can be used to fertilize grass areas, planting beds, vegetable gardens, and potted plants. It is the only material I recommend for the preparation of new planting beds. Why is compost better than pine bark or peat moss? Because it's alive, it contains mineral nutrients and is loaded with beneficial microorganisms. Peat moss and pine bark are lifeless and have little nutrient value.

Is Bagged Composted Manure Really Compost?

It can be or it can just be a bag full of bark, sand, dried manure, sawdust, and other fillers. Quality compost contains no fillers and it is 100 percent composted organic matter.

Mulch—Mother Nature's Blanket

After planting any kind of plant—tree, shrub, groundcover, flower, herb, or vegetable, cover all bare soil with at least 3 inches of mulch. Mulch is not a soil amendment to be mixed into the soil—it's a covering placed on top of the soil after the plants have been installed. It helps conserve moisture, buffers the soil from temperature extremes, shades out weeds, looks nice, increases the tilth of the soil, and supplies food for the microorganisms and nutrients for the soil.

Not all mulches are created equal. There are many acceptable mulches, but they vary in quality and effectiveness. One of the best top-dressing mulches is partially decomposed compost. I discovered this at home as a result of being too impatient to wait for my own compost pile to finish its decomposition. The not-quite-finished compost has larger particles and does a good job of mulching and letting oxygen breathe through to the soil surface.

Nature doesn't allow bare soil to exist—neither should you.

Do Grass Clippings Make Good Mulches?

Grass clippings make a fair mulch, but only if mixed with leaves and other debris. I don't recommend lawn grass clippings as a mulch by themselves because the flat blades plate and seal off the soil's gas exchange.

What are Some Good Mulches?

Straw and hay make excellent mulch, even though they are coarse in appearance. Alfalfa is the best hay mulch because of its nutrient value and presence of *triacontanol*, a growth regulator.

Another excellent mulch is shredded hardwood bark. This good-looking material comes from the lumber industry in places like East Texas. It is tree bark that has been run through a hammer mill. This smashing action gives the bark its fibrous texture. It's that texture that helps to hold it in place in your beds, even on slopes, but still allows air to circulate down to the soil.

Shredded hardwood bark mulch is the best choice for ornamental beds.

Tree chips are coarse textured but are an effective and inexpensive mulch choice.

Organic Mulches	Rating	Application	Remarks
Coffee grounds	Poor	Best to use in compost pile.	Slightly acid. Will blow and wash away.
Compost	Excellent	Use partially decomposed material 3 to 5 inches thick.	Save the more decomposed material to till directly in the soil.
Corncobs (ground)	Good	Apply 3 inches deep.	Availability may be a problem.
Cornstalks (chopped)	Fair	Apply 4 to 6 inches deep in vegetable gardens.	Very coarse texture.
Cottonseed hulls	Fair	Apply 3 to 4 inches deep.	Have fertilizer value similar to cottonseed meal. Very light and tends to blow around.
Cypress chips	Good	Apply 3 inches deep.	Can seal off oxygen. Expensive.
Grass clippings	Poor	Not recommended.	Best to leave on the lawn or mix with other materials in the compost pile.
Gravel	Poor	Best used at 3 to 6 inches in utility areas.	Large decorative stones are good for use in shady landscape areas.
Hay	Excellent	Apply 4 to 5 inches deep in ornamental beds 8 to 10 inches deep in vegetable garden.	Use for winter protection. Alfalfa is the best. Bermuda grass is the worst. Can be a fire hazard. Chopping makes it more attractive and easier to handle.
Lava rock	Fair	Apply 3 to 5 inches deep.	Avoid using in large areas - too harsh.
Leaves	Good	Best to run through a chipper and mix with other material before applying 3 inches deep.	Blowing and washing can be a problem. Contains many trace minerals; best food for earthworms.
Manure	Fair	Apply only after composting.	Fresh manure can burn plants and can contain salts and weed seeds.
Peat moss	Terrible	Don't use; the worst mulch choice.	Expensive; blows and washes away. Water won't penetrate well. Adds little to no nutrients to the soil.
Pecan shells, Peanut shells, Rice hulls	Good	Apply 3 inches deep. Better to compost first with other materials.	Inexpensive; becoming more available; high in nitrogen.
Pine bark (large size)	Good	3 inches deep.	Works well, but some people don't like the look. Best to use on top of a layer of compost.

(continued)

Organic Mulches	Rating	Application	Remarks
Pine bark (small to medium)	Poor	Use as a last resort only.	Washes and blows around. Flat pieces tend to seal off oxygen from the soil.
Pine needles	Excellent	Apply 3 to 5 inches thick on vegetable gardens and ornamental beds.	Looks best when used in association with pine trees. Does not pack down.
Sawdust	Poor	Use in the compost pile, not as a mulch.	Small pieces seal off oxygen exchange when used as a mulch.
Seaweed	Fair	Not readily available but, works well.	Watch for salt content. Decomposes slowly.
Shredded hardwood bark	Excellent	Apply 3 to 4 inches deep in ornamental beds.	Best mulch of all for sloped areas.
Straw	Good	Apply 4 to 5 inches deep in ornamental beds. 8 to 10 inches deep in vegetable garden.	Use for winter protection. Can be a fire hazard. Chopping makes it more attractive and easier to handle.

Not all bark makes a good top-dressing mulch. For example, the fine-to-medium grades of pine bark make, at best, a second-rate mulch. Pine bark consists of flat pieces that plate together and seal off the oxygen from the soil. Pine bark often washes or blows away. The tars and resins in pine bark can also be a problem for the proper aerobic degradation. The only pine bark that makes a decent mulch is the large, nugget-size because it will at least hold in place well. The large nuggets don't fit together tightly, so air can still circulate around the pieces down to the soil.

Pine needles have some of the same resin problems if mixed into the soil but are a good choice when used as a top-dressing mulch. Pine needles and other forest floor debris make effective mulches, especially when used in parts of the state where pine trees are native. There's an economic advantage when the material is locally available and can be gathered from the forest floor, although care should be taken to never deplete the organic matter in any natural setting.

Walnut should not be used as a mulch until fully composted. The raw material has strong growth retarding properties.

Another good mulch for large areas is tree chips. This mulch material is the by-product of the tree care industry. Pruned limbs are ground into coarse-textured chips and often quite green. They make a good natural-looking mulch, especially after they have aged a while and have become gray in color. Some tree chipping machines have the ability to grind tree chips into a finer texture, and the resulting product makes an excellent top-dressing mulch.

Hay mulch is the best choice for vegetable gardens. Alfalfa is the best hay choice.

Sawdust is sometimes used as a mulch, but I don't recommend it unless it has been mixed with coarser materials and composted for a while. Sawdust does make an excellent ingredient for the compost pile.

Pecan shells make a good top-dressing mulch but are much better if composted first with other vegetative materials.

Shredded cypress chips make another good mulch but tend to mat and seal off oxygen a little more than I would like. They break down very slowly and are more expensive than most other mulches.

I do not recommend the artificial mulches such as plastics and fabrics, nor do I recommend gravel as a mulch. The non-organic mulches don't biodegrade and don't return anything to the soil. Real mulches of organic matter, when applied in appropriately thick layers will shade out weeds, eliminate the need to cultivate, eliminate soil compaction, preserve

soil moisture, preserve and stimulate the soil microorganisms, and maintain the ideal soil temperature. In the heat of summer, the soil surface under a proper layer of mulch will be around 82° to 85°. The temperature of bare soil can be in excess of 120°.

Some experts say that whenever a highly carbonaceous mulch such as bark mulch is used, decomposition organisms will steal nitrogen from the soil unless a fertilizer that supplies 1 lb of nitrogen for each 100 lbs of mulch is added. Not true! For years I have mulched with hay, bark, tree chips, etc., without supplying extra nitrogen and have never observed any symptoms of nitrogen deficiency as long as the mulch stays on the top of the soil. When raw organic matter is tilled into the soil, there usually is nitrogen draft. Finished compost *only* should be tilled into the soil.

Conclusion: use compost to prepare planting beds and use a coarse-textured mulch on the surface of the soil.

Organic Fertilizers—
Mother Nature's Food

Organic fertilizers nourish and improve the soil. As opposed to synthetic fertilizers, they help the soil because they do not create high levels of salts and nitrates in the soil, which kill or repel beneficial soil organisms. By composition, organic fertilizers release nutrients slowly and naturally according to nature's blueprint. All components in an organic fertilizer are usable by the soil and the plants, because there are no useless fillers as there are in synthetic fertilizers. Organic fertilizers add organic matter to the soil—synthetic fertilizers do not. In fact, they don't do anything good for the soil.

The nitrogen-phosphorus-potassium analysis (N-P-K), which is required to be printed on bags of fertilizer by law, is basically irrelevant in an organic program. Feeding the soil and plants with nothing but nitrogen, phosphorus, and potassium is like feeding your kids nothing but cheese. Soil, like people, needs a balance of nutrients. For some unknown reason, fertilizer recommendations continue to emphasize these three nutrients, with special emphasis on high levels of nitrogen. The standard recommendation is a ratio of 3-1-2 or 4-1-2, such as 15-5-10 or 16-4-8. These recommendations are based on forced crop production instead of on soil needs.

Studies at the Department of Agronomy at Alabama Polytechnic University show that as much as 50 percent of all synthetic nitrogen applied to the soil will be leached out, and the half that does reach the plant may be hurting it. Other studies show that an excess of chemical fertilizer slows or even stops the activity of microflora and microfauna, such as beneficial bacteria, algae, fungi, and other microorganisms. Harsh fertilizers also cause damage to macroorganisms, such as earthworms, millipedes, and centipedes, which are extremely important to the natural processes in the soil.

High nitrogen fertilizers also can cause severe thatch buildup in lawns by forcing unnatural flushes of green growth. That's why mechanical thatch removal programs are often recommended for chemically maintained lawns. Organic lawn care programs take care of thatch problems naturally, as the living microorganisms feed on the grass clippings and other dead organic matter.

High nitrogen fertilizers such as 24-8-16, 15-5-10 (or even higher) are still being recommended by many in the landscaping business. I've made the same recommendations myself in the past, but those amounts of nitrogen, phosphorus, and potassium are unnecessary and even damaging to soil health.

Organic fertilizers are better because they are the derivatives of plants, and therefore, contain all the trace elements that exist in growing plants. Organic fertilizers are naturally slow-release and provide nutrients to plants when they need the nutrients. Synthetic fertilizers glut the plants with nutrients and usually at the wrong time. Organic fertilizers work within nature's laws and systems while synthetic fertilizers try to control nature. It can't be done.

Fertilizer Chart

	N	P	K	Comments
Alfalfa	3	1	2	Vitamin A, folic acid, trace minerals & growth hormone "tricontanol."
Bat guano	10	3	1	High in nitrogen, phosphorus, and trace minerals.
Blood meal	12	1	1	Good nitrogen source but smelly.
Bone meal	2	12	0	Raises pH but good calcium and phosphorus source.
Cow manure	2	1	1	Best to use in composted form to avoid weed seed and odor.
Compost	1	1	1	Best all around organic fertilizer.
Cottonseed meal	7	2	2	Acid pH, lots of trace minerals; stinks; possible pesticide residue.
Earthworm castings	1	.1	.1	Beneficial bacteria, trace minerals, humus, earthworm eggs.
Fish Emulsion	5	2	2	Foliar plant food; helps with insect control; stinks!
Fish meal	7	13	3	Nitrogen, phosphorus, and lots of vitamins and minerals but smelly.
Granite sand	0	0	5	Low cost source of minerals, especially potash.
Greensand	0	2	5	Natural source of phosphorus, potash, and trace minerals.
Kelp meal	1	0	2	Dried seaweed; source of enzymes, nutrients, and hormones.
Molasses	1	0	5	Food for microorganisms and source of sulfur and potash.
Rabbit manure	3	2	1	Not used enough; excellent source of natural nutrition.
Pig manure	.5	.3	.5	Good source of humus and microorganisms.
Poultry manure	5	3	2	High nitrogen organic fertilizer; best to compost first.
Sheep manure	.5	.3	5	Good natural fertilizer.
Seaweed, liquid	1	0	1	Same as dry but can be used as a foliar spray.
Sludge compost	5	3	0	OK in the lawn, but don't use on the veggie garden.
Sul-Po-Mag	0	0	0	Mined source of sulfur, potassium, and magnesium.
Tankage	6	8	0	Slaughter house by-product.

Manufactured Fertilizer

	N	P	K	Comments
Agrispon	0	0	0	Cytokinin growth stimulator; increases all plant and soil processes.
Bioform	4	2	4	Fish emulsion, seaweed, molasses, and soil penetrant.
Earth Safe	4	1	5	Feather meal, alfalfa, molasses, meat and bone meal
GreenSense	3	1	2	Composted manure, activated charcoal, alfalfa, molasses, iron sulfate.
Maestro-Gro	6	2	4	Fish meal, bone meal, and other natural ingredients.
Old Farmers Almanac	3	1	2	Composted manure, activated charcoal, alfalfa, molasses, iron sulfate.
Orgro	4	2	4	Composted chicken and turkey manure.
Tomas	8	2	8	Feather meal, bone meal, and other natural ingredients.
Ringer	9	4	4	Feather meal, fish meal, and other natural ingredients.
Sustane	5	2	4	Composted turkey manure.

For more detail see Chapter 7.

Step-By-Step Bed Preparation

Bed preparation includes native soil and compost tilled together. Rear tined tillers are the easiest to use.

One of the great benefits of organics is the fact that basically all plants can be planted in the same kind of beds. Flowers, trees, shrubs, and grasses all need "healthy" beds that are created by mixing compost into the existing soil. Even better beds can be made by adding minerals and organic fertilizers.

Most of the soils in Texas have three basic problems: (1) lack of humus, (2) lack of oxygen, and (3) lack of biological activity. In order to help overcome these problems, the following soil preparations are recommended for planting landscape plants and, in general, all food crops.

Remove Weeds and Grass

Scrape away all weeds and grasses. Deep excavation is unnecessary. Usually about 2 to 3 inches deep is enough to remove the regenerative part of the plants. Do not use synthetic herbicides to kill grass and weeds. Undesirable plants must be dug out whether they are green or brown, so save the money and avoid the chemicals. Remember that our purpose is to create a healthy soil. Herbicides kill plants—large ones as well as the microscopic varieties in the soil. If the soil is bare, build the bed up on top of the existing soil to create a raised bed. Excavating the bed area and then backfilling with foreign soil creates a big pot in the ground and wastes a lot of money.

Add Topsoil for Proper Grade

If the area to be planted is low, bring it to grade with native soil. Do not use a different kind of soil. Remember to allow for the addition of compost and root balls but the final condition of the bed should be a raised level.

Add Compost

Cover the areas to be planted in shrubs and trees with a 6-inch depth of a properly made, multi-ingredient compost. Use 8 inches of compost for vegetable gardens and only 4 inches for groundcover beds. You may have heard somewhere that pine bark, sharp sand, and synthetic fertilizers are needed. Not true! These ingredients are a waste of money and can be detrimental to the soil balance. Compost is all that's needed.

Add Minerals

Most of the Texas clay soils have plenty of minerals, although they may be unavailable due to a calcium/magnesium imbalance. Minerals are released as soil health improves, but in many soils a deficiency will still exist unless new minerals are added. Sandy soils are harder to balance than clay soils because they don't have many mineral nutrients.

A balance of minerals is critical. The only way to determine what's needed is from a cation exchange capacity (CEC) or total exchange capacity (TEC) soil test. The high calcium clay soils in Texas will start to release some of the "locked-up" minerals after the application of elemental sulfur. Sulfur applied at 5 lbs/1,000 sq ft in the spring and fall will help to balance the calcium and magnesium. Sandy soils, on the other hand, lack nutrient minerals because they have little holding capacity. The deficiencies may be calcium, potassium, and phosphorus. High calcium lime applications will help. A proper soil test is the only way to know for sure. (See Appendix). In general, the addition of oxygen and organic matter will set the natural process of mineral release in motion.

Add Fertilizer

Broadcast a light application (10 lbs per 1,000 sq ft) of a 100 percent organic fertilizer onto the planting bed prior to tilling. See Chapter 7 for options.

Till Compost Together With Native Soil

Till the compost and the existing topsoil and supplements together until the depth of the compost/soil mixture is 10 to 12 inches. Tilling deeper is a waste of money and can be detrimental. A 6-to 8-inch depth is all that is needed for ground cover.

Raise the Beds

The top surface of the beds should be flat and higher than surrounding grades. The edges of the beds should be sloped down for drainage. A small trench at the base of the bed edge helps hold the mulch in place and improves drainage.

Moisten Beds Before Planting

Beds should be moistened before planting begins. Do not plant in dry soil because the young roots can dehydrate quickly. Avoid planting in sloppy wet soil as well. A key to plant health is to avoid stressful conditions from the very beginning.

Set the Plant Properly

Loosen pot bound roots by hand or with a knife and set new plants so that the top of the rootball is even with or slightly higher than the surrounding soil. Setting the plant too low causes oxygen starvation and drowning. Planting too high can cause the upper roots to dry out. For quick root development spray or soak the roots of plants with a 1 percent solution of a

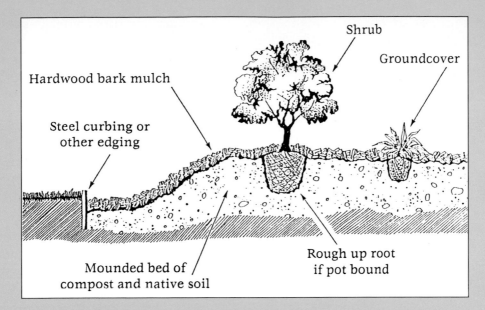

The top of the finished raised bed should be flat and higher than surrounding grades with sloped edges for drainage.

Planting holes should be dug exactly the same depth as the height of the earth ball. The top of the ball should be flush with the soil surface or even slightly higher.

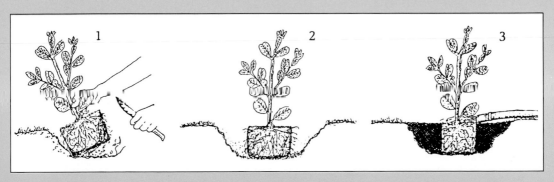

Here's how to install a plant properly: 1) Cut or tear pot-bound roots from the outside edge of the ball. 2) Dig a dish-shaped hole and set the plant so that the bottom is on firm existing soil and the top of the plant ball is flush or slightly higher than the existing grade. 3) Backfill with the prepared bed soil. Settle the soil around the plant by watering slowly to remove all mulch up against the trunk of the plant.

biostimulator. If possible, avoid the compaction caused by walking on freshly prepared beds. Soil should be settled around plants by watering thoroughly. Do not tamp.

Mulch the Bare Soil

After planting, mulch all bare ground. Mulch should be at least 2 inches deep on top of planting beds, 3 to 4 inches is better. Mulching prevents erosion, helps hold moisture in the beds, controls weeds, and keeps the soil temperature cooler in summer and warmer in winter.

Do not use plastic sheets as a mulch. The plant's root system will cook from the summer heat buildup. Plastic eliminates the oxygen/carbon dioxide transfer at the soil's surface. I also do not recommend fabrics or gravel as mulches. They don't provide the natural decay of organic matter at the soil surface. Nothing compares to a thick layer of organic material—just as nature intended

Drainage Solutions

Proper drainage isn't an option. It's a *must* for ornamentals, vegetables, fruits, herbs, and grasses. If a site doesn't drain, it won't work; it won't grow plants properly. Biological activity and chemical exchange will be slowed or stopped and plant roots will suffocate—it's that simple. Drainage can be accomplished with surface and/or underground solutions. Any system that works is a good system. There are many organic products that will improve the physical structure and the drainage of any soil, but it's still a great benefit to start any project with proper grades, drainage devices, and mechanical aeration that will get rid of excess water as quickly as possible.

In residential and commercial projects, I recommend and use underground drain lines (perforated PVC pipe) set in gravel for hard-to-drain areas. Using pipe and gravel to drain tree holes can often be the difference between success and failure. Drainage ditches can solve many problems. Trenches filled with gravel can serve as interceptions, drain lines, or both.

Organic techniques and organic products will improve the soil's drainage over time by increasing earthworm and microorganism activity. As microorganisms flourish, they create a glue-like material that welds small soil particles together to form aggregates. The aggregated soils drain away excess water but hold just the right amount of water for a longer time. Earthworm tunneling creates physical drain tubes and stimulates microbial activity. Biological activity is not only healthy for root growth, it saves money on water bills and preserves two of our most important natural resources—topsoil and water.

Any drainage technique that works is a good one. This is one way to physically improve drainage.

CHAPTER 5

*Gardening the
Organic Way*

People don't grow trees! Trees grow in spite of people. In some cases, people allow trees to grow, and in a few rare cases, people actually help trees to grow. If we people-types give trees half a chance, they will grow well for us and be quite healthy.

There are a few fundamental secrets that I have stumbled upon through the years that seem bluntly apparent but have been seldom used. Putting those theories in a nutshell looks like this: Choose a tree well-suited to the particular soil and climate and plant it in a way that most closely resembles how it would naturally exist and grow.

Sounds simple doesn't it? It is!

Dig an Ugly Hole

Dig a wide, rough-sided hole exactly the same depth as the height of the ball. Don't guess. Measure the ball and the hole as it's dug. The width of the hole should be at least three times wider than the ball, especially at the top. The width of the bottom of the hole is not important. The sides of the hole should be rough and jagged, never slick or glazed such as those caused by a tree spade or auger. Holes with glazed sides greatly restrict root penetration into the surrounding soil and limit proper root development.

Run a Perk Test

Fill the hole with water and wait until the next day. If the water level doesn't drop substantially overnight, the tree needs to be moved to another location or have drainage added. Tree holes must drain well for proper root development and overall health of the tree. It's ideal if the water drains completely out of the hole overnight.

If the water level in the hole remains stationary overnight, you have a drainage problem. There are three possible solutions.

1. Add a drainline (PVC pipe) set in gravel running from the bottom of the tree hole to a lower point on the site.
2. Dig a sump or pier hole from the bottom of the hole down into a different soil type or break into rock. A sump from the top of the ball down to the bottom of the ball does little if any good.
3. Move the tree to a new location.

Positive drainage is critical, so don't shortcut this step.

Backfill with Existing Soil

Place the tree in the center of the hole and make sure the top of the ball is flush with the surrounding grade. Slightly higher is okay, slightly lower is the kiss of death. Backfill only with the soil that came from the hole. Let me repeat: **backfill only with the soil that came from the hole.** The soil from the top 7 to 12 inches of the ground is best because it will have more biological life. Adding amenities to the backfill such as peatmoss, pine bark, sand, or foreign soils wastes money and is detrimental to the tree. Putting gravel in the bottom of the hole is a total waste of money.

When the hole is dug in solid rock, topsoil from the same area should be used. Some rock mixed into the soil is beneficial. Topsoil rather than subsoil should be used for the top 6 to 12 inches of backfill if possible. Mixing some compost into the top 6 inches of backfill is okay, but don't overdo it.

On field-dug trees, remove the burlap from the top of the ball as well as all nylon, plastic string, and even wire mesh. Burlap can be left on the sides of the ball. Container trees will usually be pot bound. Cut and tear the outer roots away from the ball. This loosening of the roots is a critical step in the planting procedures of container trees but should not be done to field-collected trees. After backfilling, water thoroughly to remove all air pockets but do not hard tamp the backfill.

Bare-rooted, balled and burlapped, and container plants should all be planted the same way. When planting bare-rooted plants, it is important to protect the roots from drying during the planting process.

Do Not Wrap or Stake

Wrapping tree trunks with paper or burlap is a waste of money, looks unattractive, harbors insects, and leaves the bark weak when removed. Tree wrapping creates a problem similar to leaving a bandage on your finger too long. If trunk sunburn is a worry, paint the tree trunk with a white wash made from latex paint and water. As the white wash wears off, the bark will slowly adjust to the sunlight.

Staking and guying are usually unnecessary if the tree has been planted properly and are a waste of money and detrimental to the proper trunk development. Staking should only be done as a last resort and never left in place more than one growing season. Temporary staking, if needed, should be attached as low on the tree as possible with strong wire, metal or wooden stakes, and eye-bolts screwed into the tree trunk. Pieces of garden hose wrapped around the trunk are acceptable if they are removed after a few months. Staking is unsightly, expensive, adds to mowing and trimming costs, and restricts the tree's ability to develop tensile strength in the trunk. When the tree is allowed to move slightly with the wind, strong trunk flair is developed at the lower trunk.

Do Not Overprune

It's an old wive's tale that limb pruning must be done to compensate for the loss of roots during transplanting or planting. Most trees fare much better if all the limbs and foliage are left intact. Even lower limbs should be left. They help develop trunk strength. The more foliage, the more food can be produced to help build the root system. The health of the root system is the key to the overall health of the tree. The only trees that seem to respond positively to thinning at the time of transplanting are densely foliated evergreen trees such as live oak and yaupon holly collected from the wild. However, magnolia needs no pruning. Plants purchased in containers definitely need no pruning, and there is no evidence that severely pruning bare-rooted plants is beneficial. Deciduous trees such as oak, elm, ash, bald cypress certainly need no pruning when planted.

Mulch the Top of Ball

If the new trees are planted in lawns, do not plant grass up to the trunks. Leave the area above the top of the ball unplanted and mulch with 1 inch of compost followed by 4 inches of shredded hardwood bark. Native tree chips or hay can be used in place of the bark. The purpose of the layering is to recreate the forest floor. Don't pile the mulch against the trunk of the tree. The reason to avoid grass above

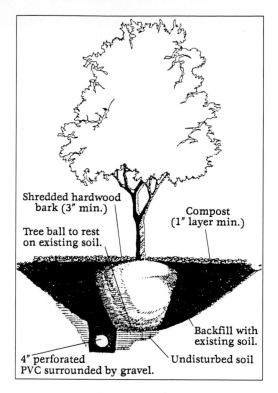

Shredded hardwood
bark (3" min.)

Tree ball to rest
on existing soil.

Compost
(1" layer min.)

Backfill with
existing soil.

4" perforated
PVC surrounded by gravel.

Undisturbed soil

How to plant a tree the right way.

frame good ones, improve the soil, and offer up a source of fuel and building supplies. Try asking that of a gardenia.

Trees are also the first consideration of the garden design. They create the framework for all that happens in the landscape. Trees are the only home improvement that can return as much as ten times the original investment provided they are chosen, planted, and maintained correctly. Unfortunately, this is where I see the most expensive mistakes. Maybe I can help a little.

Proper maintenance is important to the health of any plant.

the tree ball is to eliminate the competition for water and nutrients, especially oxygen. As the tree establishes, it's okay for the grass to grow in toward the trunk, although maintaining a mulched area around the trunk of the tree is healthy and helps keep the weed eaters and mowers away. Adding some organic fertilizer to the surface of the soil after planting is beneficial.

After It's Planted

Trees are the best investment in the landscape.

If soil is the soul of a garden, trees are the heart. Besides providing beauty, grace, color and shade, trees help children learn to climb, provide the atmosphere and structure for swings and hammocks, produce food for animals and people, screen bad views and

Aerating

Oxygen is the most important fertilizer for trees. Mechanical hole punching is a good way to get oxygen into clay or other tight soils. Oxygen helps trees by stimulating soil microbes and roots. Once the soil is soft and rich with humus and living organisms, hole punching is no longer needed, but until that time, aerate the root zone at least twice a year. Spring and fall are the ideal times, but a shot of oxygen is welcome at any time of the year. Aeration can also be done with a garden hose and a piece of PVC or steel pipe. Using this technique after spreading a 3-to 5-inch layer of compost on the soil is an excellent way to revitalize a sick fruit or shade tree.

A pipe injector connected to the garden hose is an excellent way to aerate and fertilize by washing compost down into the root system.

Fertilizing

The easiest way to fertilize a tree is to fertilize the grass and planting beds underneath. Feeder roots will grab the nutrients in the top few inches of soil.

Remember that over 80 percent of a tree's root system is in the top 3 feet of soil and 90 percent of the nutrient and water gathering roots are in the top 12 inches.

General organic fertilizers should be applied to the soil surface two or three times a year, while fertilizing the lawns and other plantings. Spreading a ¼-inch to 1-inch layer of compost over the entire root zone of trees is an excellent way to feed the soil and plants. Monthly applications of foliar food through sprays are also beneficial. Good products for Texas trees in all soils include fish emulsion, seaweed, and other biostimulants. In alkaline clay soils, Epsom salts, chelated iron products, and vinegar are good additional ingredients.

Pruning

Few trees need major pruning every year, but most trees need fine tuning yearly. Good pruning is not noticeable after the work is done.

Wound dressings and wraps are wasteful and detrimental. After the freeze of 1983, a great deal of time, effort, and money was spent on wrapping damaged tree trunks. The wrapping didn't help any, but it did cause a lot of problems. Trunk wrapping with burlap or paper only gives insects and diseases a good home. Remove the loose, broken bark and leave the damaged spot exposed to the air. Keep the wound clean and uncovered for the natural healing process to work quickly and efficiently.

Shade and ornamental trees can be pruned any time of the year, but the best time is from fall to spring. Fruit trees should be pruned from midwinter up until bud break in late winter.

Certain fruit trees are especially sensitive to this timing. Peach trees, for example, should only be pruned just before bud break because pruning induces bud break and flowering.

Wrapping tree trunks with paper or cloth is silly. It harbors insects, makes the bark weak, and wastes money.

Before cutting a tree, stand back and look at it carefully. The overall character and shape of the tree should be preserved. It's a mistake to try to change the character and overall, long-term shape of a tree. Do not indiscriminately remove lower limbs to raise the canopy. Low sweeping limbs add to the grace and beauty of the tree and help maintain the tree's balance. Remove all dead, diseased, broken or damaged limbs and the weakest of crossing limbs. Remove limbs that grow into the center of the tree and limbs that are dangerous or interfere

with buildings or activities. Removing limbs just to eliminate a certain percentage of the foliage is a mistake. Heavy thinning and severe opening of a tree's canopy throws the plant out-of-balance, inviting pests and ice storm damage. This is called "gutting" and should never be done.

Pruning cuts should be made with sharp tools. Hand tools such as bow saws, Japanese pruning saws, loppers, and pole pruners are good for small limbs. Chain saws can be used for larger limbs, but only with great care and a thorough understanding of the equipment.

Over pruning trees not only wastes money and looks bad, it is detrimental to plant health.

Pruning cuts should be made at the point where the branch meets the trunk, just outside the *branch collar*.

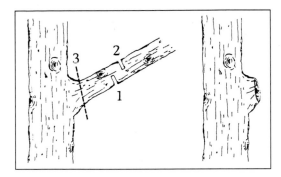

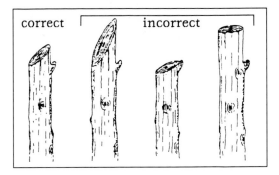

Proper pruning cuts use a three-step process on limbs larger than 2 inches. 1) Make the first cut under the limb about a foot from the trunk. 2) Make the second cut on top of the limb outside the first cut to remove the bulk on the limb. 3) Make the final cut just outside the branch collar to protect the tree's healing zone. 4) Do not paint the cuts with wound dressing.

Small pruning cuts should not be done in a sloppy manner.

Incorrect cuts are made flush with trunks. These cuts are too large, encourage disease, and slow the healing process.

The branch collar will have the appearance of a small stub after pruning. The *branch bark ridge* should also be left intact on the tree. It is the scar-looking tissue that angles down from above the branch collar.

Flush cuts should never be made. It's scientific fact that cutting into or removing the branch bark ridge or the branch collar causes problems. Flush cuts create large, oval-shaped wounds and encourage decay and the start of cavities. They also destroy the natural protective zone between the trunk and the branch and can cause several serious tree problems including discolored wood, decayed wood, wet wood, resin pockets, cracks, sun injury, cankers, and slowed growth of new wood near the improper cut. Proper cuts are round, smaller, and heal much faster. Peach, plum, apricot, and other fruit trees are particularly sensitive to flush cuts. Fruit tree insects and disease problems are often related to improper

Correct pruning cuts leave a small stub, the branch collar, and preserve nature's healing device.

pruning cuts. Long stubs are also detrimental and should be avoided.

Topping trees, climbing trees wearing boot spikes and cutting away lower limbs for no reason, has no place in good tree care.

Research by Alex Shigo, Carl Whitcomb, and the U.S. Forest Service has shown that pruning paint or wound dressings have no benefit and can in some cases be harmful. They can often slow down the healing process because healthy tissue needed for callus is killed by pruning paint or dressings. Trees have built-in defenses, much like white blood cells in mammals. Lignin cells are produced on the backside of a wound to naturally prevent diseases from entering fresh cuts. Pruning paint interferes with this natural process. Just as a cut finger heals faster when exposed to the air, so does a tree wound.

Cavities in trees are voids where fungi have rotted healthy material. They are usually started from injury to the bark. Removing the decayed material is the remedy. Fillers such as concrete and foam are only cosmetic and not recommended. When removing decayed matter from cavities, be careful not to cut or punch into the living tissue. These injuries can introduce decay further into the healthy wood. When cavities hold water, drain tubes are sometimes inserted to release water. That's another bad idea. Drain tubes puncture the protective barrier between the rotted and healthy wood and allow decay to expand. I don't recommend injector systems for fertilizer and insect control because of their puncture wounds.

Cabling and bolting are sometimes effective to prevent trees with weak crotches from splitting, but cabling should not be used to hold up low growing limbs. If cables are to be used, they should be installed horizontal to the ground so the natural movement of the tree is not completely prohibited. Cabling can be very dangerous and should only be done by professional arborists.

When pruning has been completed, the large pieces should be used for firewood and the limbs and foliage should be shredded and used as mulch under trees or mixed into a compost pile. Pruned material should always be recycled and never hauled to the landfill.

Pest Control

Aphids can be a persistent pest for trees during the cooler months. Aphids damage plants by sucking plant juices from the tender growth. They can be controlled by water blasts followed by the release of beneficial insects—ladybugs or green lacewings. The same technique works for spider mites and other small pests.

Web worms and other caterpillars can be controlled with Bt (*Bacillus thuringiensis*), elm leaf beetle with Bt 'San Diego,' and unusual outbreaks of insect pests can be controlled with a pyrethrum/rotenone product called Pyrellin E.C., which does not contain petroleum distillates. Products containing Neem are effective insect repellants and do not hurt beneficial insects. Fungus problems such as black spot, powdery mildew, and sooty mold can be stopped with baking soda spray (4 teaspoons per gallon of water with 1 teaspoon of liquid soap). See Chapter 6, *How to Control Pests the Natural Way*, and Chapter 7, *Organic Solutions*, for more complete details on pest control.

How to Grow Shrubs, Vines, and Groundcovers

Groundcover, like this sedum, is an attractive addition to any landscape.

Planting Shrubs, Vines, and Groundcovers

These plants should be planted in soil rich with compost and mounded or raised to ensure good positive drainage. Shrubs and vines should be planted from containers for best results. Larger specimens can be balled and burlapped, but even the larger plants are best grown in containers. If the shrubs are balled and burlapped, use the planting instructions for trees. If container plants are

Cut or tear the tightly bound roots that are found against the container.

used, remove the plants from the containers, cut or pull the bound roots loose, remove the fertilizer pellets from the ball, and set the plant in a wide, rough-sided hole with the top of the root ball flush with the soil surface. Backfill with the soil in the bed. Settle the backfill by watering thoroughly. Cover all bare soil after planting with at least 3 inches of mulch. Groundcover is planted the same way from 2¼-inch or 4-inch pots. Be sure to moisten the beds prior to planting.

Don't worry about hurting the plant. Without this step the new roots can't break away into the soil.

Azaleas, Camellias, Dogwoods, and Rhododendrons

These acid-loving plants don't like most of Texas. Unless you live in East Texas here's what to do if you insist on trying to grow these high-maintenance plants:

- Scrape away existing grass or weeds and till or fork the existing soil. The width of the bed should be at least 24 inches for each row of plants, a minimum of 36 inches for one row of plants.
- Build the beds with a pre-moistened mixture of 50 percent compost, 50 percent shredded hard-

wood bark, copperas at 2 lbs/cubic yard and granulated sulfur at 1 lb/cubic yard. Place the pre-moistened mix in the bed area to a depth of 16 inches. Be sure to thoroughly saturate this mixture in a tub or wheelbarrow prior to placing it in the bed.
- The raised bed you have created should have excellent drainage; however, if the planting area is in a low place, add drain lines from the beds to a lower point on the site.
- Tear or cut the pot-bound roots of new plants before planting and remove the fertilizer pellets from the ball. This is a critical procedure.

Note: If you live in an acid soil area, simply till 6 inches of quality compost into the existing soil and correct the mineral deficiencies that show up on the soil test.

Shrubs are easy to maintain if proper plant selections have been made. The general information in the tree section applies to shrubs, vines, and groundcover, but here is some specific advice.

Aerating

Aerify bare or compacted soil with hand tools such as a turning fork or hand aerator. This work is especially important in and around stressed or sick plants.

Mulching

Maintain a 3-inch minimum mulch layer over the bare soil in all planting beds. No bare soil should be exposed. A thinner layer is sometimes needed for newly planted groundcover.

Pruning

Shrubs can be maintained at a given height and spread for years by pick pruning. This method is done with

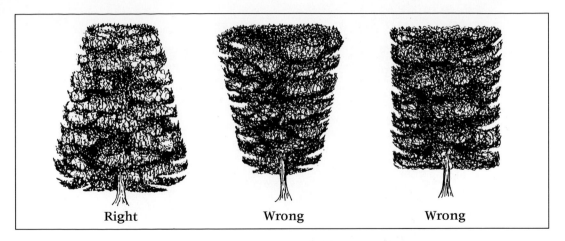

How to prune shrubs.

hand pruning shears, not hedge shears, by cutting off a branch where it is attached to the main stem or trunk. Blooming shrubs or vines can be lightly sheared after blooming to maintain a more compact size. Shrubs should be pruned so that the plants are wider at the bottom than at the top.

Become familiar with the natural character of the shrub or vine species being pruned and try to preserve that character. Remove all dead, dying, diseased, objectionable wood and weak branches as needed.

Mow most groundcover, except English ivy, each year in late February to maintain a vigorous and manicured appearance. Mow the purple wintercreeper, Asian jasmine, and other similar goundcovers to a 5 inch height. Prune English ivy from any tree trunks.

Fertilizing

Fertilize shrubs, groundcovers, and vines by applying fertilizer to the entire soil surface. Use a 100 percent organic fertilizer at 20 lbs/1,000 sq ft twice per year. When first starting your organic program it's best to fertilize three times—early spring, early summer, and late fall. Once the soil is balanced and healthy, an annual application may be all that's needed.

Weeding

Mulch all bare soil and hand remove weeds as necessary. Throwing mulch down on top of most annual weeds will eliminate them in beds.

Organic herbicides can be used if needed. Spray 10 or 20 percent food-grade vinegar during a hot, sunny day, but remember that it's non-selective and will burn good plants too.

Watering

Water deeply and infrequently to attempt to imitate natural rainfall.

Pest Control

Work to improve soil health by aerating and using organic fertilizers, release beneficial insects, and use the least toxic pesticide as a last resort. See Pest Remedies Chart in Chapter 6.

How to Grow Annuals, Perennials, and Bulbs

Annuals and perennials add interest, color, and beauty.

Annuals and perennials are planted in the same manner as most other plants, but the timing is more important. Annuals are seasonal and must be planted at the proper time each year. Plant summer annuals like lantana in May, fall annual color like mums in late summer, and winter color like pansies in October.

Perennials are planted opposite the season they bloom. Fall-blooming perennials are planted in the spring, and spring bloomers are planted in the fall. Dividing perennials is also done on the same schedule.

Flowers are a little bit harder to maintain, but they basically need the same kind of care as shrubs and trees. Here are some specific tips.

Aerating

Aerifying is usually unnecessary unless compaction has occurred in the beds after the flowers have been planted. If needed, aerify with a hand aerator in compacted areas.

Mulching

All bare soil should be mulched with a minimum of 2-inch shredded hardwood bark. If the plants are large enough to accept it, use 3 inches. Avoid piling mulch up onto the stems of succulent flowers like impatiens and begonias.

Pruning

Remove spent flowers regularly and cut all perennials back severely after major flushes of color have faded. Hard trimming will force a new flush of flower color.

Fertilizing

Annuals and perennials should be fertilized along with trees and shrubs two or three times per year with a 100 percent organic fertilizer. They should

Liquid fertilizers enter plants through the foliage very efficiently, especially when sprayed late in the day.

also be fertilized four times per year with earthworm castings at 10 lbs/ 1,000 sq ft and a natural fertilizer like bat guano or kelp meal at 10 lbs/1,000 sq ft. Spray monthly with mixture of seaweed and fish emulsion. In alkaline soil areas, add vinegar and Epsom salts to the spray (1 tablespoon per gallon of each).

Weeding

Weeds should be removed by hand and additional mulch should be added as needed. Covering weeds with mulch will usually eliminate them.

Watering

Amend the normal watering schedule and water by hand if necessary to keep flower beds moist but not soaking wet. Water deeply and infrequently as possible to imitate natural rainfall.

Pest Control

Regular inspections of annuals and newly planted perennials are necessary to spot early infestations of insects and diseases. Water blasts are normally all that's necessary to eliminate bug problems if beneficial insects are being released.

Most disease outbreaks can be stopped with the baking soda spray, although plants growing in healthy soil with organic feeding will have very few outbreaks.

How to Plant and Care for Roses

Yes, you can grow organic roses. First of all, select those varieties that are the most resistant to problems and avoid buying roses that develop severe cases of black spot or powdery mildew.

There are tough hybrid choices, and almost all of the antique roses are easy to grow.

Plant roses in well-prepared soil that is a mixture of native soil and compost. The top 8 to 10 inches of the finished bed should be at least 80 percent compost and no more than 20 percent native soil. Raised beds are also a great help. The positive drainage that results is the main benefit.

If you already have roses planted, apply 3 to 4 inches of compost on the beds and then inject water into the ground around the rose bushes. Use a piece of PVC pipe attached to the end of a garden hose. Be careful not to wash the roots too heavily. This water injection will both aerify the poorly prepared soil and wash some of the compost down into the ground. Landscape contractors can provide this service if you don't want to fool with it.

After you have finished the deep root injection, apply a 100 percent organic fertilizer and water with a watering can containing Epsom salt (magnesium sulfate) at 1 tablespoon per gallon, alfalfa meal at ¼ cup per gallon, and a biostimulant. If you use any one of these materials, there will be improvement. If you use all—stand back!

Next, mulch the bare soil with a thick blanket of alfalfa hay or shredded hardwood bark. Do not use pine bark mulch or synthetic fabrics. Pine bark won't stay in place and synthetic materials eliminate the natural decay process.

For on-going maintenance, spray the foliage every two weeks with a mix of fish emulsion and seaweed. Spray a mixture of Epsom salts and chelated iron occasionally to darken the foliage color and increase bloom production.

At the first sign of black spot or powdery mildew, spray with baking soda at four teaspoons per gallon with one teaspoon of liquid soap per gallon. Spray lightly on the foliage every three days until the problem is under control.

Antique roses are easier to grow and are prettier plants than the hybrids.

How to Grow Bulbs

When you are waiting for spring, the first bulbs to bloom can be a welcome sight.

Bulb plants, like tulips and daffodils, should be planted in prepared beds for best results. As always, the beds should be prepared by tilling or hand forking large amounts of compost into the native soil. Bulbs will give a showier flower display if a handful of earthworm castings or colloidal phosphate is tossed into the bottom of each hole. Plants will be larger and more consistent if sprayed or dipped in a 1 percent solution of a biostimulator prior to planting.

Bulb Planting Dates

Anemone	November–December
Spring crocus	November–December
Fall crocus	March
Daylilies	Spring or fall
Grape hyacinths	November–December
Hyacinths	December
Iris	October–November
Narcissus	November–December
Tulips	December

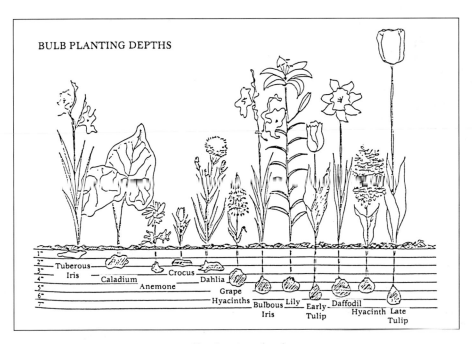

Bulb planting depths.

How to Grow Herbs

Herbs provide color, texture, and fragrance to your garden.

Herbs can be grown from seed or transplants. It's best to do some of both, so you can get into production as soon as possible. I would plant transplants of thyme, salad burnet, bay, lamb's ear, lemongrass, lemon verbena, Mexican mint marigold, rosemary, and tansy. Others can be grown easily from seed. Some herbs like ginger, comfrey, and elderberry can be grown from fleshy roots.

The traditional definition of a herb is a herbaceous plant that is used to flavor foods, provide medicinal properties, and offer up fragrances. Herbs have many other benefits, not the least of which is that they are easy to grow. Here's how to plant them.

Herbs can be planted either in containers or in well-prepared, well-drained beds. Prepare beds by mixing 6 inches of compost into the native soil. Then mix in earthworm castings at the rate of 20 pounds per 1,000 square feet. Top-dress beds after planting with mulch, especially during the hot months. Apply organic fertilizer in the spring, summer, and fall until beds are healthy and balanced. Control any serious pests with garlic/pepper "tea" (See Chapter 7 for recipe). Control caterpillars with *Bacillus thuringiensis* or remove by hand.

Herbs are very easy to maintain because they don't have many pest problems. Overwatering is the most common culprit of herb problems.

During rare outbreaks of disease or insect attack, organic pesticides can be used. Diseases can be controlled with copper and sulphur sprays or baking soda spray. Insects can be controlled with water blasts for aphids and spider mites and Bt (*Bacillus thuringiensis*) for caterpillars. For more horsepower, pyrethrum, rotenone, and sabadilla can be used. A foliar spray of liquid seaweed and fish emulsion every one to two weeks will help control most pests and feed the plants at the same time. For easier, more longer-lasting control, release beneficial insects regularly until healthy natural populations are established. Water regularly to maintain an even moisture level and, as always, mulch bare soil under the plants with compost or shredded hardwood bark mulch.

How to Grow Wildflowers

In the past, most wildflower planting was done by scattering the seeds over bare ground and hoping something would come up. This often made wildflower establishment frustrating and a waste of money.

In the wild, the beauty of wildflowers seems effortless. The secret is to duplicate nature's techniques. Here's how to do it.

Timing

The time to plant is midsummer through fall. Sowing the seeds from July through October is best in Texas. Some seeds need the hot weather of late summer for germination.

Soil preparation

Rake or till bare soil to a depth of about 1 inch. Deep tilling is not only a waste of money but can actually damage the soil and encourage weeds. If grass exists in the planting site you've chosen, set the mower on its lowest setting and scalp the area down to bare soil before tilling.

Planting

Mist or soak the seeds with a biostimulant solution prior to planting. After they have dried, distribute the seeds uniformly over the area at the recommended rate and rake lightly into the soil to assure good soil/seed contact. It's not essential, but ideal, to broadcast a thin (¼-inch) layer of compost over the seeded area.

Watering

Water the seeded area thoroughly but avoid overwatering, which will erode

With a little care, it's easy to duplicate nature's exuberance and beauty by planting wildflowers in your own garden.

the loose soil and displace the seed. Many wildflower varieties will germinate in the fall, and the small plants will be visible all winter. Others will only start to be visible the next spring.

Maintenance

The most critical step in wildflower planting is to help nature with the watering if needed. Be sure to provide irrigation (it can be temporary irrigation) the first fall, if it is a dry season, and again in March and April, if it's an unusually dry spring. This is a critical step. The tiny plants need moisture as they germinate and start to grow. They will survive in low water settings once established, but they need moisture to get started.

Fertilizing

Broadcast a light application of earthworm castings, compost, or other 100% organic fertilizer after the seeds germinate and begin to grow in the the spring. This is optional.

Selection

Some wildflowers are easier to grow than others. Refer to the list in Chapter 2 for the ones I would recommend for the beginner. This list will provide a long display and a wide variety of colors.

How to Grow a Vegetable Garden

You can produce delicious vegetables in your own garden by using simple organic methods.

Most vegetables are not native to Texas, so we have to make the soil as good as we can for best results. The goal is high production of delicious, nutritious whole food. The basic concept is the same—a balanced soil of minerals, living organisms, and proper soil structure is needed. The process can be accelerated by adding lots of high quality compost, raising the planting beds or rows, and amending the soil with lacking minerals.

Starting in the Spring

Remove existing grass and add 8 inches of compost to the entire garden area. Till to a depth of 10 inches.

Build wide beds, 2 feet at least, but 4 feet is better. That way, 2 feet of the bed can be worked from each side. The space between rows should be narrow, 12 to 18 inches, to preserve planting space. If time allows, plant a cover crop of oats and hairy vetch in September and till it into the soil two to three weeks prior to planting in the spring. Elbon rye can also be used, and it also helps with nematode infestations.

Starting in the Fall

Prepare the garden soil the same as for spring planting. Use lots of compost, 8 inches at least, and till into the native soil.

Plant from Seed	Plant from Transplants	Plant from Roots and Stems
Beans	Broccoli	Asparagus
Beets	Cabbage	Garlic
Carrots	Eggplant	Ginger
Corn	Greens	Horseradish
Cucumber	Lettuce	Jerusalem artichoke
Melons	Peppers	Onions
Mustard	Spinach	Potatoes
Okra	Tomatoes	
Onions		
Peas		
Pumpkins		
Squash		
Turnips		

If time allows, both spring and fall gardens should be prepared at least six months prior to planting.

Some plants should be planted directly into the garden from seed, other more tender plants should be started in flats or small pots and then transplanted in the garden. Here are some guidelines.

If your soil isn't completely balanced yet, it's a good idea to toss a small handful of colloidal phosphate and earthworm castings into each planting hole. Plant tomatoes deep because they have the ability to sprout roots from the stem, which will make the plants more stable. Tall transplants can be laid sideways in a trench-type planting. Cut or tear roots that are pot bound.

For an added boost, soak or mist the root system of transplants with an organic root stimulator or liquid seaweed prior to setting out.

Structures for Climbing Vegetable Plants

A unique planting device for vegetable plants is the Japanese ring. The ring can be made of welded wire or reinforcing wire. Some people even use wooden barrels with no bottoms for the ring. The ring should be placed on well-prepared and raised soil, should be 3 to 5 feet tall, and filled with compost. Tomato, squash, pepper, or other plants should be planted in additional rings attached to the outside of the big ring and spaced approximately 24 inches on center. The diameter of the ring can range from 2 feet to 4 feet. The plants can be staked, wired to the Japanese ring, or have their own individual rings. The plants are irrigated by watering the compost in the center ring. The water traveling through the compost carries natural fertilizer to the plants at each watering. The ring can also be recessed into the soil and filled with compost.

Vegetables are heavy feeders and do best when extra amounts of humus are available. High quality compost, that is at least 20 percent manure, and earthworm castings are the best sources of humus in this case. Raise the planting area by building flat topped hills or rows. The raised bed created by either technique improves drainage and soil aeration. Don't forget how important oxygen is to the root system.

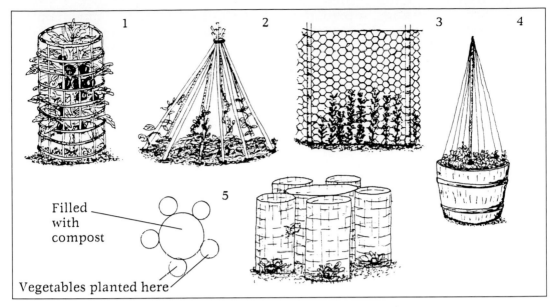

Vegetable planting structures. 1) Concrete reinforcing wire mesh is the best material for making tomato cages. Many other vegetables can also be grown vertically in these structures. 2) Tepee trellises can be made from bamboo poles or metal rods. This structure is particularly good for growing beans, peas, cucumbers, and other climbing vegetables. 3) Chicken wire, chainlink fence, or welded wire fabric mounted vertically and attached to metal or wooden stakes is another good structure for climbing peas and beans. 4) A barrel trellis is made using a single metal rod or bamboo pole in the center with string or wire connecting the top of the pole to the inside edge of the barrel. 5) The Japanese ring is made by filling the center ring with compost and manure. Outer rings contain the vegetable plants. Watering is done through the compost ring to provide a continuous slow feeding of liquid manure.

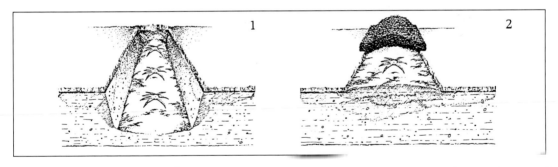

How to plant asparagus. Technique #1: Dig a trench. Put the roots 8 to 10 inches underground and slowly fill with a mix of soil and manure. Technique #2: Place the roots on top of healthy soil and cover with 10 to 12 inches of alfalfa hay mulch.

Asparagus Bed Preparation

Asparagus beds can be planted two ways.

Trench method. Dig a trench, 2 feet wide and 8 inches deep. Spread the asparagus crowns across the bottom of the trench after mixing compost into the soil in the bottom of the trench. Cover the crowns with a two-inch layer of 50 percent soil and 50 percent compost by adding a layer every two weeks.

Ruth Stout method. Spread the crowns on the soil and cover with compost and then 10 inches of hay. Alfalfa is the best. This method only works if the soil is healthy and balanced.

Daily Inspections

The most important ingredient in maintaining a garden is you. Daily inspections are not only important for spotting early signs of insects and disease pests, they are the best way to enjoy the garden. Inspections any time of the day are beneficial, but looking at the plants closely at night with a flashlight is one of the most important gardening activities. It's during the night that many of the pests are active and doing their mischief.

Vegetable Planting

Plant	How Deep to Plant	From Planting Seeds to Picking
Beans, Pole	2"	60 days
Beans, Bush	2"	60 days
Beans, Lima	1"	60–80 days
Beets	1"	60 days
Broccoli	1/2"	70 days
Brussel Sprouts	1/2"	90 days
Cabbage	1/2"	50–100 days
Cauliflower	1/2"	45–70 days
Celery	1/2"	110 days
Collard Greens	1/2"	50–60 days
Corn	2"	70–100 days
Carrots	1/2"	70 days
Cucumbers	1"	50–60 days
Eggplants	1/2"	50–80 days
Lettuce	1/2"	40–60 days
Melons	1"	60–90 days
Mustard Greens	1/2"	30–35 days
Onion	1"	40–50 days
Parsnips	1/2"	90–100 days
Peas	1"	60–90 days
Peppers	1/2"	60–90 days
Radishes	1/2"	20–25 days
Spinach	1/2"	40–50 days
Squash, Summer	1"	40–60 days
Squash, Winter	1"	50–100 days
Tomatoes	1/2"	50–80 days
Turnip Greens	1/2"	40–50 days

How to Grow Fruits, Nuts, and Berries

Fruits, nuts, and berries should be given tender loving care for best production.

A peach tree or any other fruit tree should be planted just like an oak. Even bare-rooted trees should be planted in a wide, ugly hole and back-filled with the native soil from the hole, and mulched with a thin (one-inch) layer of compost followed by 4 inches of mulch.

Cutting the top of the tree back, as is often recommended, is not needed. Staking is an unnecessary and possibly harmful procedure, and wrapping the trunk with cloth or paper is a very bad idea. If trunk sunburn is a worry, paint the trunk with a whitewash made from half white latex paint and half water. If borers are a concern, paint the trunk with a soupy mixture of one-third manure, one-third colloidal phosphate, and one-third diatomaceous earth. The tree will shed the material as it grows.

Fruit and nut trees should be planted in the late fall or winter on a day when the soil is not sopping wet. See the beginning of this chapter for specific instructions.

Berries should be planted during late fall through winter, although the ideal time is a few weeks before spring flowers break.

Strawberries should be planted from transplants. A fall planting is ideal. Blackberries and dewberries should be planted from roots, and blueberries should be planted from bare-rooted transplants or containers.

Fruit crops have a biological clock/thermostat that measures the dormant season exposure to cold weather. It's called the "chilling requirement." It is the number of hours between freezing and 45°. Each fruit variety has its own specific needs and will have its own minimum number of hours that it must receive before it can break bud and bloom. Choose varieties that have chilling hour requirements for your part of Texas.

Fruits, nuts, and berries should be given tender loving care for best production, but the basic maintenance program is the same as for ornamental plants. The soil must be balanced. It must be well-aerified, have positive drainage, and be covered with either mulch or green manure cover crops.

Aerating

Mechanical aeration should be done to the root systems of any plants in compacted or imbalanced soil. Spray the soil with a biostimulant and make sure the planting area drains well. Liquid soil penetrants can be used in lieu of mechanical aeration. The best aeration, however, is done by physically washing compost down into the soil with a root injector.

Mulching

All bare soil around fruit and nut plants should be mulched or covered with a green manure cover crop. In large orchards and gardens, the native grasses and weeds can be used but should not be allowed to grow over 2 feet tall. Taller plants can sap soil moisture. Don't mow all cover crops at one time. Always preserve some habitat for beneficial insects.

How to Prune

Fruits	
Apples	Prune to create limbs growing at 45 degree angles for best production. Do not remove large amounts of structure.
Apricots	Remove dead, diseased, inward-growing and crossing limbs only.
Plums	Prune to allow for as many 45 degree-angled limbs as possible and remove 20 to 30 percent of the total branching.
Peaches	Prune to create 3 main branches grown out of 45 degree angles to the ground. Remove about 40 to 50 percent of the total branching including all gray 2-year-old shoots. Fruit only bears on 1-year-old red shoots.
Pears	Prune to create 45 degree-angled limbs. Remove dead, diseased, and inward-growing branches. Do not remove more than 20 percent of the bearing wood.

Berries	
Blackberries	Remove fruiting canes to the ground immediately after harvest. Keep other canes pruned to 36 to 48 inches.
Blueberries	Prune away low limbs near the soil and vigorous upright shoots. Keep the center of bushes open.
Grapes	Train grape vines to horizontal wire trellises and remove 80 to 90 percent of the top growth of mature vines each winter. To avoid over-cropping, thin 3-year-old vines to 10 to 12 clusters, 5-year-old vines to 15 to 25 clusters, and mature vines to 40 to 80 clusters.

Nuts	
Pecans and walnuts do not need to be thinned. Remove dead wood, limbs that are rubbing, and limbs that are a physical problem.	

Pruning

Fruit and nut trees should be pruned late in the winter just before bud break. Pruning earlier in the winter can encourage early flowering and damage by late freeze. Use the chart on page 128 as a guideline.

Fertilizing

Fruits, nuts, and berries should be fertilized with organic fertilizers in the spring and in the fall at 20 lbs/1,000 sq ft. Spray foliage with fish emulsion/seaweed mixture once per month in growing season. The fertilization requirement should be based on a cation exchange soil test. In the beginning, two applications (spring and fall) are usually needed, but as the soil health improves, less fertilizer will be needed. Only one application a year is needed after the soil balance has been improved.

Pecan trees can be fertilized by annually broadcasting a 100 percent organic fertilizer to the root zone at 20 lbs/1,000 sq ft or by broadcasting manure or compost at 2 to 5 tons/acre. This rate can be reduced as soil health improves.

For additional nut production, spray the foliage with a mixture of fish emulsion, seaweed, and a biostimu-lant. A monthly application is ideal but not essential. Foliar sprays have the greatest effect if done early morning or around dusk. Zinc or other micronutrients should be added to the mix but only if the soil test shows a deficiency in those nutrients.

Weeding

In large-scale orchards, weeds can be used as a management tool. Let the weeds grow to 2 to 2½ feet and mow every other row each time always leaving some 2-feet weeds for beneficial insect habitat. In home settings, use legume cover crops or mulch under the plants. In all cases, avoid bare soil.

Watering

Water deep and infrequently to try to imitate natural rainfall. Two inches of water weekly is ideal if drainage is good.

Pest Control

Basic pest control results from healthy soil, good plant choices, and good cultural practices such as beneficial insect release. See the Pest Remedies Chart in Chapter 6 for control of specific insects.

How to Plant and Maintain Lawns

Lawns can be planted from seed, sprigs, spot sod, and solid sod. Seed and sprigs can be planted by hydromulching.

Grass Planting

Solid Sod. Loosen any compacted soil and rake smooth. Apply a 100 percent organic fertilizer at 10 lbs/ 1,000 sq ft and lay the sod joint to joint. Fill joints if necessary with compost. Do not use a roller to level grass.

Hydromulch. Lightly cultivate compacted soil and spray seed with a biostimulant before planting. Never mix seed into the hydromulch. Broadcast seed directly onto bare soil and then cover seed with the hydromulch spray.

A lush, healthy lawn is easy to maintain with organic techniques.

Mulching mowers are the future—grass catchers are the past. Mowers specifically designed for mulching are convenient, time-saving, and good for the soil.

Seeding. Lightly cultivate compacted soil and rake the soil smooth. Spray a biostimulant, fish emulsion, and seaweed over area to be planted.

Organic fertilizer should be applied to the soil at 10 lbs/1,000 sq ft prior to any of the three planting procedures.

Aerating

Until soil is healthy, all grass areas should be aerified two times per year (March and June). The holes should be punched in a crisscross pattern. Aeration should be done immediately prior to the granular fertilizer applications. Once the soil is relatively healthy and balanced, this procedure can be eliminated. Lawns that receive a lot of foot traffic or other forms of compaction should be aerified every year. Liquid soil penetrants can be used to aerify soil where mechanical aerator use is impractical.

Mowing

Lawns should be cut frequently enough (normally weekly) to maintain a neat appearance, and clippings should be left on the ground. Mowing height for Bermuda and St. Augustine should start in the spring at $2\frac{1}{2}$ inches and steadily be raised throughout the growing season to a height of $3\frac{1}{2}$ inches or higher. If the time between cuttings should be extended for any reason, causing an excessive amount of clippings on the lawn, the clippings should be removed and put into the compost pile. Wet and matted clippings should always be removed from lawns. Buffalograss, unless used as a groundcover, should be mowed six times per year during the growing season at a height of at least 3 inches. Frequency of mowing should be adjusted to the growth rate of the turf. Wildflowers and native grasses should be mowed one time in the fall at 6 to 8 inches.

Hand trim or mulch around trees in lawn areas. Do not use weed eaters around trees.

Do not scalp turf in spring. This goofy procedure is messy, exposes bare soil to the air, encourages weed seed germination, and wastes precious organic matter that should be left in the ground.

Change mowing patterns regularly to prevent rutting of turf areas. Check, adjust, and sharpen blades and cutting height before each mowing.

Edging and Trimming

Edge along walks and curbs weekly. Use monofilament trimmers along steel edging, curbs, and other hard surfaces but **never** around trees or shrubs. Do not scalp grass while using line trimmers. Edge around turf irrigation heads where tall grass is disrupting the irrigation coverage.

Weeding

Reprogram your attitude on weeds. A few weeds are acceptable. Primary control will come from improved soil health through organic fertilizers, aeration, and mineral balancing. Preferred treatment is hand removal of noxious weeds and improved cultural practices such as proper watering, mowing, fertilizing, and hand weeding. Pre-emergent herbicides are **never** to be used. Organic herbicides should be used as needed. Twenty percent food-grade vinegar during a hot, sunny day is the best choice.

Fertilizing

Apply a 100 percent organic fertilizer at 20 lbs/1,000 sq ft March 1 and at 10 lbs/1,000 sq ft June 1. This work should immediately follow mechanical aeration. Apply mineral supplements that the soil test shows are lacking. For example, if the base saturation of calcium is above 80, apply sulfur at 5 to 10 lbs/1,000 sq ft. If the base saturation of calcium is below 60, apply high calcium lime at 20 to 30 lbs/1,000 sq ft. If magnesium is shown to be below 10, apply a magnesium product such as Pro-Mag 36 at 10 to 20 lbs/1,000 sq ft.

Watering

Water deeply and infrequently. Attempt to copy natural rainfall. Avoid watering so heavily that runoff occurs, especially on slopes. Several short applications may be needed until the soil is healthy enough to absorb the water easily. Try to moisten the soil to a depth of 7 inches or more at each watering. Light, frequent waterings should be avoided.

Pest Control

Disease and insect pests are rare in organically maintained lawns. I don't recommend any preventative measures, other than building healthy soil, or any calendar applications of pesticides. For occasional specific outbreaks use the suggestions in the Pest Remedies Chart in Chapter 6.

Basic Maintenance Program for Lawns and Planting Beds

March	Apply 100 percent organic granular fertilizer @ 20 lbs/1,000 sq ft, Sulfur @ 5 to 10 lbs/1,000 sq ft, and in alkaline soils and high calcium, lime @ 20 to 30 lbs/1,000 sq ft in acid soils.
April	Liquid spray: fish emulsion, seaweed, molasses and biostimulant.
June	Apply 100 percent organic fertilizer @ 10 lbs/1,000 sq ft.
August	Liquid spray: fish emulsion, seaweed, molasses, and hydrogen peroxide.
September	Liquid spray: fish emulsion, seaweed, and biostimulant.
October	Apply 100 percent organic fertilizer @ 10 lbs/1,000 sq ft.

Note: See Rate Chart in Chapter 7 for specific mixing instructions.

How to Grow Container Plants

Container soil needs to be healthy and alive just like garden beds.

To grow flowers or any other plants organically in pots, use normal pots and a living potting soil. Many of the potting soils on the market are basically sterile, containing only inert materials such as peat moss, perlite, vermiculite, and chemical fertilizers. Organic potting soil will have some inert materials but also a high percentage of living compost and earthworm castings. Be sure to look for brands that contain these ingredients.

To decrease watering requirements, try the following technique:

- Select two containers, one about two-thirds the size of the other.
- Fill the smaller container with sandy loam.
- Carefully pour this core of soil into the center of the larger container.
- Pour organic potting mix around column of soil until container is full.
- Plant.

Here are three good homemade potting soil recipes:

Recipe 1

 5 parts compost (homemade or store bought)
 4 parts sand (lava is best, granite sand is next best)
 3 parts earthworm castings
 2 parts colloidal phosphate
 1 part greensand

Recipe 2
 5 parts compost
 4 parts Isolite
 3 parts earthworm castings
 2 parts greensand
 1 part fishmeal

A similar recipe that's almost as good but will need more fertilizer is as follows:

Recipe 3
 3 parts compost
 2 parts colloidal phosphate
 1 part sand or Isolite

How to Transplant Existing Plants

Transplanted plants need the same or better care than new plants. Plants in general should be moved during the fall and winter.

Established plants should be relocated during the dormant periods—that's usually in the fall or winter, although some plants go dormant in the summer. The larger the plant, the more difficult the transplant. Smaller plants that have not developed extensive root systems can be moved during their growing season if moved quickly and watered-in immediately. Transplanted plants should be installed with the same techniques used for new plants as explained previously.

If plants must be transported to their new home, be sure to keep them moist and cover them with tarps or shade cloth. Even in the cooler parts of the year, damage from drying can happen quickly. This is obviously more critical during the growing season.

How to Plant by the Moon

Gardening by the moon is not a religious activity nor is it opposed by any religion. It is science. The earth's gravitational forces and the energy forces of the moon and planets are very real. If astrological events can move the level of tides by 30 or more feet, imagine the power involved. Why then wouldn't it make sense that the moon phases could affect the moisture levels in plants and, in fact, the moisture pressure in every cell of every plant.

Plants that produce above ground should be planted in the increasing light of the moon (first and second quarters or phases). Plants that produce under ground should be planted during the decreasing light of the moon (third and fourth quarters or phases).

People who garden by the moon strongly believe that the same gravitational force that moved the tides, also has significant influence on plant growth. Most moon gardeners believe that the period of increasing light up to the full moon benefits those plants that bear fruit above the ground. Conversely, they believe that when the moon is on the wane, and its light and gravitational pull are on the decrease, the earth's gravity kicks in again, and the plants that produce below the

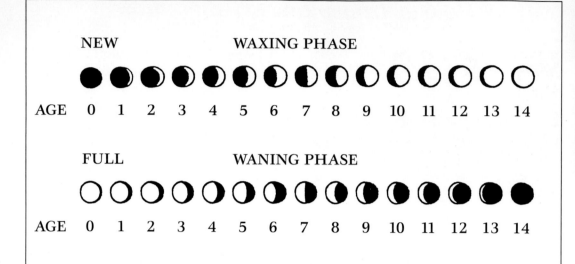

NEW   WAXING PHASE

AGE 0 1 2 3 4 5 6 7 8 9 10 11 12 13 14

FULL   WANING PHASE

AGE 0 1 2 3 4 5 6 7 8 9 10 11 12 13 14

On the first day of the lunar month, the moon is dark. It is called the new moon. It increases in light until full moon on the 15th day. Then the moon decreases in light until the 30th day when it is the dark new moon again.

ground are benefited. The *Old Farmer's Almanac* agrees, saying that flowering bulbs and vegetables that bear crops below ground should be planted during the dark of the moon; that is, the time from the day after the full moon to the day before the new moon. Anything like radishes, onions, potatoes that grows underneath the ground, will grow larger and produce better. If you plant these vegetables and bulbs on the new moon, while the light is increasing, the plants will grow tall and bloom, but they won't be as good. Planting should not be done when the moon is absolutely dark because that's when plants should rest. The new moon (increasing light) seems to be a good time to kill weeds because they won't grow back as readily.

CHAPTER 6

*How to Control Pests
the Natural Way*

Working With Nature

Ever wonder how insects were kept under control or why plants weren't devoured by destructive insects before man started to "control" the environment? The answer lies in the fact that nature has a balanced, natural order and a system of checks and balances.

With the proliferation of chemicals during the twentieth century, many beneficial insects have been killed along with the harmful insects. Generally, the harmful bugs will re-establish quicker than the beneficials, and plant loss accelerates. Encouraging the beneficial insects to be established again is a primary goal of an organic program. However, there are many natural or low-toxic products available to make the transition from a chemical program to an organic program. These products will reduce the harmful effects on beneficial insect populations, wildlife, pets, man, and the environment in general.

A report by the scientific journal *Bioscience* says that a mere 1 percent of the pesticides applied to plants ever reaches its ultimate destination—the pest insects. The other 99 percent pollute and poison the air, soil, water, good insects, animals, and man.

This section is divided into two parts—harmful insects and beneficial insects. First, the major harmful insects are discussed, along with ways to control them with biological and/or organic pesticides. Then beneficial insects are described, along with ways to use them to help keep the harmful insects under control. After all, keeping them under control is all that is really needed, because the ones that are not killed will serve as a lure to the beneficial insects. This chapter will also show you how to control the other pests: diseases, weeds, and other critters.

For a more complete description of many of the organic pesticides recommended in this section, see Chapter 7, *Organic Solutions.*

Harmful Insects

Most insects are beneficial, but the harmful ones, like these aphids, can cause serious damage.

Aphids

Aphids are sucking insects that attack tender growth of plants, cause stunted and curled leaves, and leave a honeydew deposit. High levels of nitrogen in plant tissue stimulate aphid reproduction. They can be controlled by using biodegradable soap and water or fish emulsion or just strong blasts of water. They are the favorite food of green lacewings and ladybugs. Protecting and encouraging beneficial insects and promoting soil health and biodiversity is the best control for these indicator pests. The most effective control is through regular releases of beneficial insects.

Ants

There are many different ants such as carpenter ants, fire ants, and pharaoh ants. Some solutions for ants indoors include diatomaceous earth, (See Chapter 7) silica aerogel, boric acid, diacide, and pyrethrum. Pyrethrum is especially effective for ants indoors. *Logic* works for large-scale infestations of fire ants. Boiling water will kill individual mounds as will vinegar or garlic tea poured directly into the center of the mound. Both liquids work better if 2 tablespoons of diatomaceous earth are added to each gallon of liquid. Pyrethrum/rotenone products are excellent for knocking out individual mounds. The herb tansy, when crushed or chopped, repels household ants quite well.

Bagworms

Bagworms are a common pest of ornamental trees and some shrubs. They will prey on many different species of plants such as cedar, juniper, and cypress. In the larval stage they can defoliate trees. They can be controlled at this stage by *Bacillus thuringiensis* (*Bt*). Hand picking the bags in winter is also beneficial for control. Trichogramma wasps can help to control problem infestations.

Beetles

Many adult beetles eat plant foliage and can destroy plants. Rotenone and sabadilla are effective solutions for destructive beetles. Garlic tea is a less toxic repellent. Make sure the beetle in question is destructive—many are beneficial. Colorado potato beetle and elm leaf beetle can be controlled with the biological product M-One (*Bt*/'San Diego').

Bees

Bees are beneficial and should be protected. For the proper environmental control, contact the beekeeper club or society in your area. They will usually come and get the bees or give you advice on control.

Borers

Borers attack trees in stress. Adult beetles will eat tender terminal growth and then deposit their eggs at the base of trees. Once the eggs reach the larval stage, they bore into the tree and continue to tunnel through the

wood until the tree is weakened. Active tunneling larvae can be killed by running a stiff wire into the holes. Rotenone and pyrethrum applied full strength directly in holes with putty to seal in the fumes will usually kill active larvae; however, keeping trees healthy and out of stress is the best prevention. Quinine placed in holes will also work. Nicotine sulfate will also work but is very dangerous to handle. A generous amount of diatomaceous earth at the base of susceptible trees will also help. Lye soap rubbed on the trunk is an old organic technique. Painting a mud made of manure, colloidal phosphate, and diatomaceous earth, one-third of each on tree trunks, is a good preventative.

Canker Worms

The canker worm hangs on a silk thread from trees. He or she doesn't do a lot of damage. Wasps will usually control them. If not, use *Bt* sprays for heavy infestations.

Casebearers

The pecan nut casebearer is a small insect that enters the pecan on the stem end of the small fruit. A generation usually appears in early May and a second generation about 42 days later. Careful release of trichogramma wasps and green lacewings will control this pest. Releases should generally start in late March.

Cabbage Loopers

Cabbage loopers are the larvae of moths. They can be killed with *Bt* sprayed when the insects are young. Use soap as a surfactant and spray late in the day because these guys feed at night. Trichogramma wasps as well as the native wasps will also help control these critters. It's interesting that even the chemical "pushers" admit that the chemical insecticides are ineffective at controlling loopers.

Caterpillars

Caterpillars are best known for their ability to defoliate trees and vegetables. *Bacillus thuringiensis* (*Bt*) is an excellent biological control. Wasps are also a great help in controlling caterpillars of all kinds. Remember that many caterpillars grow up to be beautiful butterflies, so don't kill them all.

Chiggers

Chiggers are known for their very annoying bite. The itching usually starts the day after you are bitten and lasts two to four days. Sulfur will help prevent bites; diatomaceous earth and sulfur will help control the critters. Vinegar or comfrey juice rubbed on bites will eliminate the itch.

Chinch Bugs

Chinch bugs are tiny, black, pinhead-size or smaller bugs. During hot, dry weather, they can destroy lawns. The lawns will look yellow, turn brown, then die. Control with diatomaceous earth or pyrethrum/rotenone products. This insect hardly ever attacks healthy, well-maintained grass.

Crickets

Crickets live in and out of doors, destroy fabrics such as wool, cotton, synthetics, and silk and also attack plants, especially the tender sprouts of wildflowers and vegetables. Solutions include diatomaceous earth, pyrethrum, and rotenone outdoors — boric acid for indoor use. *Nosema locustae* products are the best control for outdoors.

Cutworms

Cutworms are soft-bodied worms about 1¼ inches long, gray to black, usually found curled up just below the soil surface. They feed at night on small sprouts primarily and are fond of tomatoes, peppers, beans, cabbage, and many flowers. Dusting diatomaceous earth or colloidal phosphate generously around new transplants or sprouts will control them. Products containing *Bt* are also effective.

Elm Leaf Beetles

These beetles can usually be found in American elm, cedar elm, and especially Siberian elm trees. The elm leaf beetle will eat and damage lots of foliage, then move to the next tree. Trees can die from defoliation, but only unhealthy trees are seriously attacked by elm leaf beetles. Solutions include diatomaceous earth, soap spray, and fish emulsion/seaweed spray. Strong populations of beneficial insects will also help. The 'San Diego' *Bt* product is effective on elm leaf beetle.

Fire Ants

Field tests by the Texas Department of Agriculture have shown that *Logic* fire ant bait can provide control for an entire year, while the other bait

products may need to be reapplied in late summer or fall. Although *Logic* may provide the longest control, it is also the slowest to take effect, requiring several weeks to completely eliminate colonies. The active ingredient in *Logic* (fenoxycarb) is an insect growth regulator that prevents young ants from maturing. The colony is slowly eliminated as worker ants die and are not replaced.

The active ingredients in *Amdro* (hydramethylnon) and *Affirm* (avermectin) are slow toxins that kill all ants, immature and adult. Because they are slow-acting, they are passed to all members of the colony, including the queens, before they take effect. They are effective, although they are more toxic. Applying instant grits or Malt-O-Meal to dry soil around mounds is reported to have impressive results.

Fleas

Fleas are nasty little things, and it's curious why they were created. Fleas can live for many months without food. They generally invade a house by hitching a ride on a pet, rodent, or person. While not destructive to plants, they are a nuisance for pets and their owners. Control with diatomaceous earth and pyrethrum dusted or sprayed around pets' favorite resting spot and bedding. Insect growth regulators such as *Precor* are a helpful control of problem infestations inside the house. Bathing the pets regularly with mild soapy

water, brushing them, and feeding them garlic and brewer's yeast is helpful. Plant repellents include rue, wormwood, and pennyroyal mint. Stronger controls include *Demize*, a citrus oil extract, for use indoors, and pyrethrum/rotenone outdoors.

Flies

Flies can be repelled with tansy or garlic. They can also be killed with fly swatters. On the farm they can be greatly reduced by feeding the animals small amounts of diatomaceous earth. Release of trichogramma and other predatory wasps and fly parasites are effective natural controls.

Forest Tent Caterpillars

These caterpillars will sometimes do some damage in early spring, but if pesticides are avoided, the beneficial wasps will usually keep these guys under control. *Bt* can be used if they get out of hand. At worst they are only a temporary problem.

Fungus Gnats

Fungus gnats are present when the soil surface is too wet. They do little, if any, damage but can be eliminated by drying the soil. Baking soda sprayed lightly on soil will quickly solve the problem.

Galls

Galls are fuzzy or hard-shelled growths on leaves. They are usually caused by insect stings and do little damage. Even phylloxera gall on pecans is worse-looking than damaging, and no sprays are really effective. Soil health is the best control.

Grasshoppers

Grasshoppers feed on numerous plants. They are usually kept in check by natural predators such as birds, but on occasion, the conditions can be right for them to destroy plants. They may be controlled by sabadilla dust or pyrethrum/rotenone mix. A soap spray will help by making the foliage less tasty. Garlic/pepper tea will also discourage them. *Nosema locustae* sold as Grasshopper Attach, Nolo Bait, or Semispore is an effective, long-term, biological control.

Grubworms

Adult June beetles will chew leaves and subterranean grubs will eat roots of grass and garden plants. Solutions include Grub Attack, BioSafe, and other beneficial nematode products. Some experts say that milky spore dis-

ease will not control white grubs, but many organic gardeners say that it will. You be the judge. Grubs are rarely a problem in healthy, biologically active, well-drained soil. If you find any gigantic grubs, they are probably the larvae of the rhinocerous beetle and not very harmful.

Lacebugs

Lacebugs attack various deciduous trees and broad-leafed evergreens. The lacebug is flat and oval and sucks the sap from the underside of the leaf. A quick solution for this pest is biodegradable soap and water, or pyrethrum/rotenone mix. Garlic tea with vegetable oil is also effective. Healthy biodiversity in the garden will eliminate a destructive population of this pest.

Leafhoppers

Leafhoppers excrete honeydew and damage leaves by stripping them, causing stunted, dwarfed, and yellow foliage. They can be controlled with pyrethrum or simply by the encouragement of diverse populations of beneficial insects.

Leaf Miners

Leaf miners will cause brown foliage tips often continuing over the entire leaf. Solutions include products containing Neem extract. A fish emul-

sion/seaweed mix will also help. They cause minor damage only, so treatment is rarely needed.

Loopers (See Caterpillar)

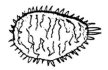

Mealybugs

Mealybugs are sucking insects that look like cotton on plant stems. Mealybugs suck sap from the foliage and stems and can destroy the plant. Mealybugs like warm weather and often attack houseplants. Helpful controls include soap and water, predator insects, diatomaceous earth, pyrethrum, and lizards. For houseplant problems, dab alcohol on bugs with a Q-tip. Crytolemus is a beneficial insect that looks like a big ladybug and is sometimes used to control mealybugs. Green lacewings are less expensive and more effective.

Mosquitoes

A liquid spray containing vitamin B complex is helpful. Bactimos briquettes in stagnant water are very effective. The best solution is to eliminate all standing stagnant water.

There are other solutions such as pyrethrum, purple martins, frogs, toads, and bats. *Bacillus thuringiensis* 'Israelensis' will kill mosquitoes in decorative ponds without harming fish or aquatic plants. Encouraging birds, especially purple martins, is extremely helpful. Bats are also great friends in controlling mosquitoes. Diatomaceous earth and garlic tea can be sprayed before a party or outside event to lessen the problem. Citronella candles will also help to repel these miserable pests. Citrosa, a cross between citronella grass and scented geranium, will help some.

Mites (See Red spider mites)

Moths

Moths are the adults of certain caterpillars. They are controlled naturally by wasps and with sprays containing *Bt*.

Nematodes

Actually microscopic round worms, many nematodes are beneficial, but there are those that will attack ornamental trees, garden plants, and lawn grass. Controls include increasing the organic level and living organisms in the soil, using organic fertilizers, and applying products that increase microbial activity. Increasing the organic level in the soil, using Clandesan, Agrispon, Medina, and other biostimulants will help by increasing microbial activity. Cedar flakes applied to the soil surface will also help. Beneficial nematode products are also very helpful. Planting ceral rye (elbon rye) also gives effective control.

Pecan Nut Casebearers (See Casebearers)

Pill Bugs

Pill bugs, (sow bugs or roly-poly bugs) are crustaceans and related to shrimp, crabs, and crawfish. They are found beneath objects where it is damp and feed on organic matter, but when abundant will also eat plants. Controls include rotenone, pyrethrum, and sabadilla. Beer in a trap is still one of the best solutions. Colorado State University found that the beer liked most by slugs and pillbugs is Kingsbury Malt beverage (non-alcoholic). Michelob and Budweiser were the favorites of the regular beers and Pabst was the least favorite. Pill bugs don't like evening primrose, and sabadilla will knock 'em out. Banana peels attract them so you can then drop them into a soapy water solution. For serious infestations, 5 percent rotenone is effective.

Plum Curculios

Rotenone/pyrethrum at 75 percent flower petal fall is the organic version

of the extension service control. However, it's better to approach control from a health standpoint. Thick mulch, at least 4 inches of compost, rough bark, or tree chips is important. Six to eight inches is even better. If raw mulch or chips are used, put a 1-inch layer of compost on the ground first to serve as a buffer. Regular spraying of fish and seaweed is the best organic preventative. Biodiversity is critical for control of this pest. For sick soil and sick trees, use a root injector and wash compost, water, and air into the root system of the tree.

Red Spider Mites

Tiny red spider mites feed on garden plants and ornamental trees. They are identified by the webbing that accompanies them. Controls include spraying water or garlic/pepper tea on the underside of the infected leaves every three days for nine days. Strong blasts of water followed by the release of ladybugs and lacewings is the best control. A spray of $1/2$ percent solution (1 oz/gal) of blackstrap molasses is also effective.

Roaches

There are many species of cockroaches, but only a few really pose a problem. Cockroaches usually live

out of doors and feed at night. Roaches will enter a home or building through any crack or crevice. They will infest homes or office buildings and chew on cloth, books, cardboard, and food scraps. Some solutions are: a shoe, newspaper, diatomaceous earth, keeping your house clean, eliminating standing water, sealing all openings, caulking all cracks, and eliminating cardboard boxes and other hiding places. Boric acid indoors gives effective control. Silica gel is another roach control product. Boric balls—1 cup boric acid, 1 cup flour, ½ cup sugar, mix, add water, roll into cakes and place behind appliances. It's best to put them in bait stations and always keep away from pets and children.

little slime balls! Effective controls include garlic tea with diatomaceous earth, pyrethrum or beer traps. Sabadilla and rotenone are very powerful if all else fails. Sprays made from the juices of dead slugs are effective preventatives.

Sowbugs (See Pill bugs)

Spider Mites (See Red spider mites)

Squash Bugs

Squash bugs are difficult to control. They attack squash, cucumbers, pumpkins, cucurbits, and a few ornamentals. Control by smashing the eggs on the backs of leaves, dusting the adults with sabadilla, and planting lemon balm in between plants. Dusting young plants regularly with cheap flour will also help.

Scale

Scale insects attach to stems, branches, and trunks and suck sap from the plants. Controls include lime sulfur spray, ladybugs, pyrethrum, vegetable oil, and dormant oil. Use mild soap and water with seaweed on interior plants. The native black, scale-eating ladybug is very helpful.

Slugs

Slugs and snails must be kept moist at all times to live and will go anywhere there is moisture. I hate these

Squash Vine Borers

The squash vine borer is an insect whose larva is a worm that bores into the base stem of squash, cucumber, melon, gourd, and pumpkin. Cut the stem open, remove the worms, and cover the wounded area with soil. Inject *Bt* into the base of the stem with a syringe. Spraying with *Bt* will also help.

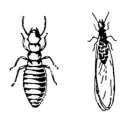

Termites

Tim-Bor is a new wood treatment boric acid product that is effective. Using a 16-grit sand barrier on the inside and outside of grade beams works well. New construction can use the sand under the slab. Be careful not to create drainage problems. Pyrethrum/rotenone will kill the pests on contact.

Thrips

Thrips attack tight petaled flowers such as the buds of roses, mums, and peonies. Thrips are not visible to the naked eye but will rasp the plant tissue and drain the sap. When there is an infestation, they can kill a plant. Thrips are general eaters and will attack flowers or field crops. Controls include liquid kelp as a repellent, pyrethrum, and green lacewings. Nicotine sulfate can be used as a last resort.

Ticks

Ticks are difficult to control, but the diatomaceous earth/pyrethrum/rotenone sprays work quite well. Bathing pets regularly will also help considerably. *Demize* sprayed in the pet's sleeping area will also help.

Tobacco Horn Worms (See Caterpillars)

Whitefly

Whiteflies are very small and resemble little white moths. Whiteflies are impossible to control with synthetic pesticides and will suck the juices from several kinds of plants. They will attack vegetables and ornamental plants outdoors and indoors. Controls include biological soap, garlic/ pepper tea, pyrethrum, or yellow sticky traps. Encarsia formosa is effective in greenhouses. Seaweed and garlic/pepper tea have been my most effective controls. Sweet potato whitefly has proven to be immune to chemical controls but can be effectively controlled by releasing green lacewings and allowing natural enemies to repopulate.

Beneficial Insects

The green lacewing is the most helpful of all the beneficial insects.

Ground Beetles

One third of all animals and 40 percent of all insects are beetles. All beetles have hard, opaque wing covers that meet in a straight line down the middle of their backs. Ground beetles (*Calosoma scrutator*) are important predators of plant-eating insects. They usually feed at night on soft-bodied larvae like cankerworms and caterpillars. They also eat many kinds of slugs and snails. Soldier beetles (*Poadabrus tomentosus*) are also beneficial. They feed on aphids, grasshopper eggs, cucumber beetles, and various caterpillars.

Ladybugs

The ladybug or ladybird beetle is the most popular and most universally known beneficial insect. There are several hundred different kinds in North America and all are beneficial. The most common native varieties are the (*Lindorus lophantae*), black with red spots and the (*Olla abdominalis*), gray with black spots. The imported variety (*Hippodamia convergens*), orange with black spots, is the most available commercially.

Yellow ladybug eggs are visible in the winter and early spring in clusters on the backs of leaves and on the trunks of trees. Both the larvae and adult beetles eat large quantities of aphids and other small, soft-bodied insects such as scale, thrips, and mealy bugs.

To release ladybugs, open the container at dusk and scatter them on infested plants after watering the foliage. Ladybugs will store in the refrigerator for a few days (35° to 45° is best for storage). They will remain dormant and alive under these cool temperatures, although storage tends to dry them out, and a few will die.

Release ladybugs during the cool part of the day after wetting the foliage.

For ladybugs to mature and lay eggs, they need a nectar and pollen source, such as flowering plants. Legumes such as peas, beans, clover, and alfalfa are especially good. To make an artificial food, dilute a little honey with a small amount of water and a little brewer's yeast or bee pollen. Streak tiny amounts of this mixture on small pieces of waxed paper, and fasten to plants. Replace these every five to six days, or when they become moldy. Keep any extra food refrigerated between feedings. The ladybug's favorite real food is aphids.

If ladybugs are released indoors or in a greenhouse, screen off any openings to prevent their escape.

Fireflies (Lightning bugs)

The firefly (*Photinus pyralis*) is a fascinating insect that produces a light by releasing luciferin from its abdomen to combine with oxygen. When conditions are right, the male flashes his light every six seconds to be answered by the female two seconds later. Firefly larvae feed on snails, slugs, cutworms, and mites.

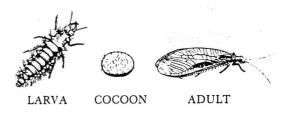

LARVA   COCOON   ADULT

Green Lacewings

The green lacewing (*Chrysopa carnea*) is a beautiful, fragile, light-green or brown insect with lustrous yellow eyes. The adult is about a half-inch long, holds its wings up tent-like when at rest, and feeds on honeydew, nectar, and pollen. The adults really aren't terribly beneficial. They just fly around, look pretty, and mate. The larvae, on the other hand, are voracious eaters of aphids, red spider mites, thrips, mealybugs, cottony cushion scale, and many worms.

The lacewing larvae (also known as "aphid lions") emerge from the eggs, which appear on the end of thin filaments attached to leaves or stems. The larvae pupate by spinning cocoons with silken thread. The adult emerges in about five days by cutting a hole in the cocoon.

Green lacewing eggs.

half-inch in length in two to three weeks. Biweekly releases are ideal.

Nematodes

Beneficial nematodes are microscopic roundworms used to control cutworms, armyworms, corn rootworms, cabbage loopers, Colorado potato beetles, turf grass grubs, termites, and other soil pests. Nematodes enter the insect pest through the mouth or other body openings. Once inside the host, nematodes feed and reproduce until the food supply is gone, then emerge in search of new victims. Sounds pretty gross, doesn't it? Nematodes are purchased on sponges.

If it is inconvenient to release the lacewing immediately after purchase, the eggs or larvae may be refrigerated for a few days, but be careful **not to freeze**. Temperatures of 38° to 45°F will delay development but not hurt the eggs.

Eggs and larvae can be hand sprinkled wherever harmful insects exist. Even if you put them in the wrong place, they will search almost 100 feet for their first meal. One of the best ways to distribute lacewing eggs and larvae is with a pill bottle with a fourth-inch hole in the cap. A salt shaker will work, but you have to increase the size of the holes. A thimble will hold about 10,000 eggs. Releasing the green lacewing from a card or cup mounted above the ground can help to protect them from ants.

The gray lacewing larvae look like tiny alligators and grow to almost a

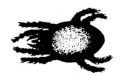

Predatory Mites

The predatory mite (*Phyoseiulus persimilis*) is orange in the adult stage and pale salmon in its immature stage. It can be differentiated from the "red" two-spotted spider mite by the lack of spots on either side. The body is pear-shaped, and the front legs are longer than those of pest mites. Predatory mites move about quickly when disturbed or exposed to bright light and multiply twice as fast as pest mites. Females lay about 50 eggs. Each mite eats from 5 to 20 eggs or mites per day.

Release predatory mites at the first sign of spider mite damage. If there is more than an average of one mite per leaf, you will probably need to reduce the populations of pest mites with organic sprays such as insecticidal soaps or garlic/pepper tea and seaweed. Strong water blasts are effective prior to release.

Praying Mantids

These fierce looking but friendly critters (*Mantis religiosa*) will eat almost any insect, especially caterpillars, grasshoppers, beetles, and other damaging pests. They will also eat roaches. Be careful not to confuse the egg case with the asp, which is a soft hairy insect with a powerful sting. The praying mantid's egg case looks very similar to an asp but is hard like papier-mache. The only negative about praying mantids is that they also eat beneficial insects. They don't usually eat ladybugs, however, because they're bitter.

Spiders

Not technically insects, most spiders are beneficial and harmless, with the exceptions of the black widow and the brown recluse. Although very dangerous, the brown recluse is rarely seen because it seeks out dark corners in closets and wood piles and moves about at night. The female black widow is easy to identify by the red

hourglass on her abdomen. Beware of her because her venomous sting is very powerful and causes illness or even death. The puny little male isn't much trouble; in fact, the female devours the male after mating.

Wasps

All wasps and mud daubers are beneficial. One of their favorite foods is the tent caterpillar that often disfigures pecan trees. When the wasp eggs hatch, the larvae feed on the eggs of the pest. By the way, the wasps will sting only if you threaten them, and the mud dauber will if you grab it! Trichogramma wasps don't sting at all. The mud dauber's favorite food is the black widow spider. It's also good for controlling flies in horse stables. Braconid wasps kill pests by laying their eggs in hosts like hornworms, codling moths, and aphids.

Trichogramma Wasps

Trichogramma wasps or "moth egg parasites" are used to control pecan casebearers, cabbage worms, tomato horn worms, corn earworms, and apple orchard pests. They are gnat-like parasitic wasps that attack over 200 types of worm pests. The trichogramma wasp stings the pest worm egg and deposits its own egg

Most wasps, even the stinging kind, are beneficial.

parasite of the whitefly. It is about the size of a spider mite. It attacks the whitefly in the immature stages, laying eggs in the third and fourth stages, while feeding off the first and second stages. Early application of *Encarsia formosa* prior to heavy infestations is

recommended. Parasites should be released at the first sign of whitefly to avoid damage to tomatoes, cucumbers, and ornamental plants. Sweet potato whitefly is not controlled well by this bug, but green lacewings do work.

inside. The egg hatches and feeds on and kills the pest.

Early application of trichogramma before a problem has been diagnosed is the ideal way to begin a pest control program. Weekly or biweekly releases during the early part of the growing season are ideal.

Whitefly Parasites

The whitefly parasite can help prevent serious damage to tomatoes, cucumbers, and ornamental plants. *Encarsia formosa* is a small, efficient

Other beneficial insects include pirate bug, big-eyed bug, assassin bug, dragonfly, syrphid fly, giant wheel bug, and many others.

Of course, whenever you use beneficial insects, you'll want to avoid spraying pesticides.

How to Use Beneficial Insects

Although the praying mantid is a strange looking critter, it is one of the best pest controlers you can have in your garden.

Springtime is the key time to release beneficial insects. Soft, succulent new

growth on plants attracts aphids and other critters especially if you are still using high nitrogen fertilizers and encouraging unhealthy fast growth. Releasing beneficial insects on a regular schedule and fertilizing with soil improving materials will provide excellent control. The best bugs to buy and release are ladybugs, green lacewings, and trichogramma wasps. For a simpler program, stick with lady bugs and green lacewings. Keep them cool and watered and don't spray anything that will kill them, including organic insecticides. Their favorite food is juicy bad bugs. If you don't have bad bugs, there's no reason to buy and release good bugs.

Aphids are the most common insect pest during the cool spring weather. Ladybugs can be purchased in mesh bags or in small boxes that contain anywhere from 1,500 bugs in a pint up to 70,000 bugs in gallon containers. The best way to release ladybugs for the control of aphids is to sprinkle the foliage with water and release the bugs directly on the infested plants at dusk.

Green lacewings are even better beneficial insects because they control so many different kinds of pests. Containers of eggs or larvae mixed in sawdust can be purchased for release to control aphids, spider mites, thrips, caterpillars, and other pests. It's again best to release them in the cooler part of the day. These insects are very small but aggressive and voracious. The adult is about a half inch long and feeds on honeydew and nectar. However, it's the ferocious larvae that actually do the insect control. It's a good idea to release green lacewings throughout the spring and summer in a series of releases until natural populations are established.

Trichogramma wasps should be released from small containers or cards attached to plants that are having problems with pecan casebearer, cabbage worms, tomato hornworms, corn earworms, and many orchard pests. These beneficial insects are very tiny gnat-like parasitic wasps. They should also be released in a succession of releases.

Praying mantids, predatory mites, and beneficial nematodes can also be used to provide natural control of bothersome bugs.

There are three ways to purchase and distribute beneficial insects. The first is to buy empty boxes from the garden shop. The customer pays the nursery for the empty box of insects and then sends in the order form that's in the box. The insectory then delivers the beneficial insects directly to the customer. This eliminates delay in shipping and storage and the risk of high temperatures or other environmental changes that might destroy the animals. Several nurseries in Texas are now using this service. It takes about 10 days to receive the bugs. The second method is to order them directly from the insectories. The third method is to buy them directly from you local nursery or feed store.

Here's a schedule for insect release. This is a suggested starting point and should be adjusted to fit each specific site. Your garden or farm may need more or fewer insects. The exact program should be based on the existing populations of insects.

Beneficial Insect Release Schedule
(Per acre or per residential lot)

March–April	• Release trichogramma wasps @ 10,000 eggs to 20,000 weekly for six weeks.
	• Release green lacewings @ 4,000 eggs weekly for four weeks.
	• Release ladybugs as needed on aphid infested plants.
May–September	• Release green lacewings @ 2,000 eggs every two weeks.

Biofac	P.O. Box 87, Mathis, TX 78368	800-233-4914
Bio Insect Control	710 S. Columbia, Plainview, TX 79072	806-293-5861
Biome	P.O. Box 6707, Katy, TX 76706	800-998-1701
Gardens Alive	5100 Schenley Place, Lawrencebury, IN 47025	812-537-8650
Integrated Pest Management	305 Agostino Road, San Gabriel, CA 91776	818-287-1101
M&R Durango	P.O. Box 886, Bayfield CO 81122	800-526-4075
Natural Gardening Research	P.O. Box 149, Sunman, IN 47041	812-623-3800
Nature's Control	P.O. Box 35, Medford, OR 97501	503-899-8318
Necessary Trading Co.	P.O. Box 603, New Castle, VA 24127	703-864-5103
OrCon, Inc.	5132 Venice Blvd., Los Angeles, CA 90019	213-937-7444
Organic Pest Management	P.O. Box 55267, Seattle, WA 98155	206-367-7007
Pest Management Services	Rt. 12 Box 346-31, Lubbock, TX 79424	806-794-4567
Rincon-Vitova Insectaries	P.O. Box 95, Oak View, CA 93022	800-248-BUGS

Best Source: Your local neighborhood nursery or feed store.

Herbs to Ward Off Pests

In addition to beneficial insects, some herbs are also helpful with pest control. Here is a guide showing the best.

Basil	Flies and mosquitoes
Borage	Tomato worm
Datura	Beetles
Chives	Many fruit tree and tomato pests
Garlic	Aphids, beetles, weevils, borers, spider mites
Henbit	Most insects
Lamium	Potato bugs
Lavender	Ants
Marigold	Many insects
Nasturtium	Aphids, squash bugs, white fly
Onion	Cabbage moths
Pennyroyal	Ants, aphids, ticks, fleas
Peppermint	Ants
Pyrethrum	Most insects
Rosemary	Cabbage moths, beetles, mosquitoes, slugs
Rue	Beetles
Sage	Moths
Spearmint	Ants, aphids
Thyme	Cabbage worms and many other insects
Tansy	Ants

Insect Control—The Natural Way

Of the millions of kinds of insects in the world, less than two percent are really harmful. The rest are beneficial. Even those we classify as harmful such as aphids are beneficial in the overall balance of nature. Aphids, for example, are constantly identifying, attacking, and removing unhealthy plants. They are an important link in the survival of the fittest and have been providing their services for millions of years.

The best way to control troublesome insects is to allow them to control themselves. Nature provides beautiful checks and balances if we allow them to function.

The following products and techniques are a guide for controlling insects with the least damage to nature's balances. Organic pesticides are favored over chemical pesticides, but I hope you can learn to only use them as a last resort because even the organic pesticides can't tell the difference between a good bug and a bad one.

Organic Pest Remedies

Insect	Controls	Application
Aphids	• Water blast • Soap and water • Garlic/pepper tea • Beneficial insects	• Use hose nozzle or a strong thumb. • 1 tsp per gal. • Spray as needed or biweekly as a preventative. • Release ladybugs and green lacewings.
Ants Fire Ants	• *Logic* fire ant control • Vinegar, garlic tea, hot water or pyrethrum/rotenone • D-E/pyrethrum products	• 1 lb/acre on dry soil when ants are foraging. • ¼-gallon poured in center of mound. Mix ¼ cup of diatomaceous earth into liquid for extra strength. • Stir dry into mounds.
Carpenter Ants Sugar Ants	• Boric acid • Boric acid, flour, and sugar • Pyrethrum • Tansy	• Wood treatment or dusting indoors. • Use in bait stations. • Dust problem areas. • Sprinkle bits of tansy leaf in problem area.
Bagworms **Caterpillars** **Corn Borers** **Cabbageworms** **Armyworms**	• *Bt (Bacillus thuringiensis)* • Beneficial insects	• Spray with 1 tsp soap per gal at dusk. • Encourage and protect native wasps. Release green lacewings and trichogramma wasps.
Beetles Elm leaf beetle Flea beetle Borer beetle	• Pyrethrum, *Bt* 'San Diego' • Rotenone • Sabadilla • D-E/pyrethrum products	• Make sure beetle in question is harmful—many are beneficial. • Encourage biodiversity of insects, birds, plants, and small animals. • Use all per label instructions.
Borers, Tree	• Pyrethrum/rotenone products • Rotenone • Sabadilla	• Run stiff wire into borer holes. • Put insecticide into holes full strength and seal holes with putty. • Mulch root system area of trees.
Casebearers	• Trichogramma wasp	• Release eggs at least every two weeks starting with first warm weather, usually mid-March.
Crickets **Chiggers** **Chinch Bugs**	• Diatomaceous earth (D-E) • Pyrethrum • Mix diatomaceous earth and pyrethrum • D-E/pyrethrum products • Nolo Bait (crickets—outside)	• Dust infested area @ 2 Tbs/1,000 sq ft. • Per label instructions. • Mix with water at 2 Tbs/gal and spray infested area. • Per label instructions. • *Nosema locustae* (also sold as Semisporc Bait and Grasshopper Attack). Broadcast on infested area.

(continued on next page)

Organic Pest Remedies Continued

Insect	Controls	Application
Chinch Bugs *(cont.)*	• Dusting sulfur (outside use)	• Dust on legs for chigger bites.
Colorado Potato beetle	• M-One (*Bt*/'San Diego') • Garlic/pepper tea and diatomaceous earth	• Spray late in the day per label instructions. • Spray liquid mix as needed.
Cutworms	• Diatomaceous earth • Bone meal or colloidal phosphate • *Bt (Bacillus thuringiensis)* • Collars	• Pour a ring of material around each plant. • Pour a ring of material around each plant. • Apply per label at dusk. Add 1 tsp soap per gal. • Wrap aluminum foil around vegetable stem.
Elm Leaf Beetle	• Insecticidal soap • Horticulture oil • Garlic tea with vegetable oil • *Bt* ('San Diego') • Diatomaceous earth/ pyrethrum products	• 1 tsp per gallon. • Spray per label for severe problems. • $^1/_4$-cup concentrate per gallon. • Spray per label at dusk. • Per label instructions.
Flies	• Garlic/pepper tea • Yellow sticky traps • Fly parasites • Diatomaceous earth	• Spray infested area. • Hang in infested area. • Release every two weeks when needed. • Feed to livestock and pets @ 1 percent of food volume.
Flea Beetles	• Pyrethrum/rotenone products • Garlic/pepper tea with diatomaceous earth	• Spray as needed on heavy infestations. • Spray at first sign of problem.
Fleas	• Pyrethrum/rotenone products • *Demize* and *Precor* (indoors) • Outdoors: Pyrethrum/ rotenone products or D-E/Pyrethrum products	• Spray as needed. • Label instructions. • 2 tsp per gal. Spray infested area. 1 tsp soap. • Bathe pets regularly in mild soapy water.
Fungus Gnats	• Baking soda spray • Water schedule	• Spray lightly on soil. • Allow soil to dry out.
Grasshoppers	• *Nosema locustae* products	• Broadcast per label instructions.
Grubworms	• Beneficial nematodes • Milky spore disease products • All products that stimulate soil biology	• Release per label instructions. • Apply per label instructions. • Compost, organic fertilizers, microbial stimulators.
Lacebugs	• Insecticidal soap • Horticultural oil • Pyrethrum/rotenone mix	• 1 tsp/gal. • Per label instructions. • Label instructions.

Organic Pest Remedies Continued

Insect	Controls	Application
Lacebugs *(cont.)*	• Beneficial insects	• Release praying mantids, ladybugs and green lacewings.
Leafhoppers	• Garlic/pepper tea • Pyrethrum/rotenone products • Praying mantids	• $1/4$ cup/gal as needed. • Label instructions. • Release as necessary.
Leafminers	• Neem products • Don't worry about 'em	• Label instructions. • Minor damage only, usually no need to treat.
Loopers	• Bt (*Bacillus thuringiensis*) • Beneficial insects	• Apply per label instructions at dusk. • Release regularly until healthy, native populations exist.
Mealybugs	• Horticulture oil • Mealybug predators • Pyrethrum/diatomaceous earth products • Rubbing alcohol • Lizards	• Label instructions. • Release as needed. • 2 Tbs/gal with 1 tsp soap. • Spot treat with cotton swab. • Protect native ones and introduce new ones.
Mosquitoes	• Bti (*Bacillus thuringiensis* 'Israelensis') • Encourage frogs, birds, bats • Garlic/pepper tea • Instant coffee	• Put briquettes in standing water. • Eliminate standing, stagnant water. • Spray as needed. • Sprinkle crystals in standing water.
Moths	• Bt (*Bacillus thuringiensis*) • Beneficial insects	• Spray per label instructions at dusk. • Release ladybugs and green lacewings every two weeks until natural control exists.
Nematodes	• Beneficial nematodes • Organic matter	• Release per instructions. • Stimulate soil biology with compost, organic fertilizers, and microbe stimulators.
Mites	• Garlic/pepper tea • Seaweed and soap spray • Bioform • Horticultural oil • Beneficial insects	• $1/4$ cup/gal. Spray every three days for nine days. • 1 Tbs/gal. Add 2 Tbs fish emulsion for extra effect. Soap optional @ 1 tsp/gal. • 3 Tbs/gal. • Per label instructions. • Release green lacewings and predatory mites every two weeks while infestations exist.
Pecan Casebearer	• Trichogramma wasps	• Release every two weeks during the spring. Start in mid-March or during first warm spell.
Pill Bugs (Sow bugs)	• Beer traps	• Pour beer into a recessed plastic ice tea glass, jar, or dish.

(continued on next page)

Organic Pest Remedies Continued

Insect	Controls	Application
Pill Bugs *(cont.)*	• Bone meal or colloidal phosphate	• Pour a ring around each plant.
	• Diatomaceous earth	• Pour a ring around each plant.
Plum Curculio	• Pyrethrum/rotenone	• Spray during petal fall.
	• Garlic/pepper tea	• Spray during petal fall.
	• Mulch	• Compost, shredded hardwood or hay.
	• Aerate	• Wash compost, air and water into soil with injector.
	• Imidan	• Spray per label instructions.
Roaches	• Diatomaceous earth/pyrethrum products	• Dust infested area lightly.
	• Boric acid	• Dust infested areas lightly (indoors only).
	• Boric balls	• Mix boric acid, flour, and sugar. Add water and roll into balls or cakes.
	• Eliminate food source	• Remove food and water sources daily.
Scale	• Dormant oil	• Label instructions in winter.
	• Horticultural oil	• Per label instructions.
	• Beneficial insects	• Release ladybugs and praying mantids.
Squash Bugs	• Flour	• Dust plants with cheap flour.
	• Sabadilla	• Per label on serious infestations.
	• Hand removal	• Destroy eggs from the back side of leaves.
	• Bee balm (lemon balm)	• Interplant with vegetables.
Squash Vine Borers	• Bt (*Bacillus thuringiensis*)	• Spray onto very young plants and inject into stem with syringe.
	• Beneficial insects	• Release trichogramma wasps and green lacewings.
Slugs Snails	• Beer traps	• Plastic jar or dish sunk into ground.
	• Garlic/pepper tea and D-E	• Spray as needed.
	• Diatomaceous earth	• Dust infested area.
	• Bone meal or colloidal phosphate	• Dust infested area or put ring around individual plants.
Spiders	• Physically remove	• No need to control spiders except black widow and brown recluse.
	• Encourage	• Most are beneficial.
	• Pyrethrum	• Label instructions.
	• Lizards	• Natural or introduced.
Sow Bugs (Pill bugs)	• Beer traps	• Pour beer into a recessed plastic ice tea glass, jar, or dish.
	• Bone meal or colloidal phosphate	• Pour a ring around each plant.
	• Diatomaceous earth	• Pour a ring around each plant.

Organic Pest Remedies Continued

Insect	Controls	Application
Spider Mites	• Beneficial insects	• Green lacewings and predatory.
	• Water blasts	• Spray as often as needed.
	• Liquid seaweed	• 2 Tbs/gal. Add fish emulsion for extra effect.
	• Garlic/pepper tea	• Spray every three days for nine days.
	• Horticultural oil	• Per label instructions. Last resort only.
Termites	• Sand barrier	• 16-grit sand placed on both sides of the grade beam or under the slab.
	• Tim-Bor	• Treat wood.
	• Boric acid	• Label instructions.
	• Nematodes	• Apply to soil as preventative
	• Rotenone/pyrethrum	• Spray on active infestations.
Ticks	• Diatomaceous earth	• 2 Tbs/gal. Spray infected area.
	• Pyrethrum	• 1 Tbs/gal. Spray infected area.
	• D-E/pyrethrum products	• 2 Tbs/gal. Spray infected area.
	• Pyrethrum/rotenone mix	• 2 Tbs/gal. Spray infected area.
	• Demize	• 1 oz/gal. (for inside use)
Thrips	• Beneficial insects	• Release green lacewings as needed.
	• Garlic/pepper tea	• Spray every two weeks or as needed.
Tobacco Horn Worms	• Bt (*Bacillus thuringiensis*)	• Label instructions at dusk.
	• Beneficial insects	• Release beneficial wasps every two weeks.
Tomato Pin Worms	• Garlic/pepper tea	• Spray every two weeks.
	• Pyrethrum/rotenone products	• Spray as needed.
	• Beneficial insects	• Release green lacewings and trichogramma wasps.
Treehoppers	• Pyrethrum/rotenone	• Spray for serious infestations per label instructions.
	• Garlic/pepper tea	• Spray every two weeks or as needed. They are seldom a problem.
Wasps	• Water blast	• Nests can be moved to new location and nailed in place after spraying wasps with water. Do not attempt if allergic to wasps.
	• Protect if possible	
Whiteflies	• Garlic/pepper tea	• 1/4 cup/gal. Spray as needed.
	• Vegetable oil	• 1 tsp/gal. Spray for severe infestations.
	• Yellow sticky traps	• Hang in infested area.
	• Green lacewings	• Release as needed.
Webworms	• Insecticidal soap	• 1 tsp per gal with diatomaceous earth.
	• Bt (*Bacillus thuringiensis*)	• Spray with 1 tsp soap per gal at dusk.
	• Wasps	• Introduce and protect trichogramma wasps and natives.

Disease Control

Brown patch in St. Augustine grass can be controlled with baking soda spray.

Disease control in an organic program is an interesting situation. Increased resistance to most diseases results as a nice side benefit from the use of organic products, especially those containing the cytokinin-type hormones. The best products include Bioform, Medina Plus, seaweed, and Agrispon. These products are root growth stimulators and help to control all sorts of pathogens through increased biological activity.

On the other hand, all organic products help control disease to some degree. When soil is healthy, there is a never-ending microscopic war being waged between the good and bad microorganisms, and the good guys usually win.

Drainage is also a key ingredient in the prevention of diseases. Beds or tree pits that hold water and don't drain properly are the ideal breeding places for many disease organisms.

As with insects, spraying for diseases is only treating the symptoms, not the major problem. The primary problem is usually related to the soil and the root system. Therefore it is critical to improve drainage, add organic material, and stimulate and protect the living organisms in the soil.

In general, fungi infestations are circular or oval in a random arrangement. They often look like a chlorotic halo with a black dot in the center. Bacteria stay within the cell walls and therefore show up as square shapes.

Anthracnose. A serious fungal problem in sycamore trees, beans, and ornamentals where the foliage turns a tan color overnight. Control is difficult other than by avoiding susceptible plants. Bordeaux or baking soda sprayed as leaves emerge in the spring will sometimes help.

Bacterial blight. A bacterial disease that causes dark green water spots that turn brown and may leave a hole in the leaf of tomatoes, plums, and several ornamental plants. Control includes healthy soil, baking soda spray, garlic tea, and bordeaux mix.

Bacterial leaf scorch. Causes drought stress and browning in foliage. Common problem in sycamores-often confused with anthracnose.

Black spot. More common name of fungal leaf spot. Black spot attacks the foliage of plants such as roses. There is usually a yellow halo around the dark spot. The entire leaf then turns yellow and ultimately dies. Best controls include selection of resistant plants and baking soda spray.

Blossom end rot. A physiological disorder showing a brown or black leathery area on the blossom end of tomatoes, peppers, and watermelon. The primary causes are moisture fluctuation and deficient calcium.

Brown patch. Cool weather fungal disease of St. Augustine. Brown leaves pull loose easily from the runners. Small spots in lawn grow into large circles that look bad and weaken the turf but rarely kill the grass. Baking soda spray is the best curative; soil health, drainage, and low nitrogen input are the best preventatives.

Canker. A disease of trees and shrubs causing decay of the bark and wood. Healthy soil and plants are the best solution.

Cotton root rot. A fungal disease common in alkaline soils that attacks poorly adapted plants. The best preventative is healthy soil with a balance of nutrients and soil organisms.

Damping off. Disease of emerging seedlings where tiny plants fall over as if severed at the ground line. Avoid by using living (not sterilized) soil and colloidal phosphate on the surface of planting media.

Downy mildew. A serious disease of the cucumber family causing yellow to brown spots on the upper leaf surface. Purplish mildew on lower surface. Prevent with healthy soil and food air circulation. Spray baking soda if needed.

Early blight. A common disease on tomatoes, potatoes, peppers, and other vegetables. Dark brown spots on lower foliage enlarge to kill entire leaves. Remove infected leaves and spray with baking soda spray.

Fireblight. Disease of plants in the rose family where twigs and limbs die back as if they've been burned. Leaves usually remain attached but often turn black or dark brown. Prune back into healthy tissue and disinfect pruning tools with 3 percent hydrogen peroxide. Spray plants at first sign of disease with Triple Action 20.

Gray leaf spot. A disease of St. Augustine grass that forms gray vertical spots on the grass blades. A light baking soda sprayf is the best curative.

Oak wilt. A disease of the vascular system of oak trees that is transmitted by insects and through the root system of neighboring trees. Biodiversity and soil health are the best deterrents.

Powdery mildew. White or gray powdery fungal growth on the leaf surface and flower buds of zinnias, crepe myrtles, and many vegetables. Best control is baking soda spray.

Diseases	Organic Solutions	Application
Anthracnose	• Liquid copper or Bordeaux	• Spray per label on new foliage in early spring.
	• Baking soda spray	• Spray emerging foliage at 4 tsp per gal.
	• Better soil health	• Use mulch, compost, biostimulants.
Bacterial Blight	• Baking soda spray	• Spray lightly as needed.
	• Garlic/pepper tea	• Spray as needed.
	• Better soil health	• Use mulch, compost, microbials.
Black Spot (Fungal leaf spot)	• Baking soda spray	• Spray lightly as needed.
	• Lime sulfur spray	• Use label directions.
	• Liquid copper	• Spray as needed.
	• Bordeaux mix	• Avoid irrigation water on foliage of susceptible plants, e.g., roses.
	• Better soil health	• Use mulch, compost, biostimulants.
Brown Patch	• Baking soda spray	• Spray lightly as needed.
	• Better soil health	• Avoid wet soil and high nitrogen fertilizer in late summer.
		• Mulch, compost, biostimulants, aerify.
Canker	• Increase drainage	• Change planting site, aerify soil, mulch.
	• Delay pruning until bud swell	• Never use flush cuts or pruning paint.
	• Paint tree trunks	• Paint tree trunks with white latex whitewash.
	• Better soil health	• Mulch, compost, biostimulants.
Crown Gall	• Avoid physical damage to trunk	• Keep trees and shrubs in beds rather than lawns.
Fireblight	• Triple Action 20	• Spray whenever problem arises.
	• Garlic/pepper tea	• Spray plants at 75 percent petal drop.
	• Better soil health	• Mulch, compost, biostimulants.
	• Limit use of nitrogen	• Cut off infected area.
Gray Leaf Spot	• Baking soda spray	• Light foliage spray as needed.
	• Better soil health	• Aerify and balance the soil nutrients.
Oak Wilt	• Maintain soil and plant health	• Fertilize with organic techniques and water regularly.
	• Alamo	• Inject per instructions as a last resort.
Peach Tree Curl	• Baking soda spray	• Spray in fall.
	• Garlic tea	• Spray in fall.
	• Liquid copper products	• Spray in fall.
	• Better soil health	• Use mulch, compost, and biostimulants.
Powdery Mildew	• Baking soda spray	• Light foliage spray as needed.
	• Better soil health	• Use mulch, compost, biostimulants.
Sooty Mold	• Baking soda spray	• Light spray as needed.
	• Beneficial insects	• Ladybugs and green lacewings will control aphids whose honeydew causes the sooty mold.

Rust. Causes small red to black blisters on the lower leaf surface and on pods. Leaves will later turn yellow and fall from plant. Control by planting resistant varieties and using sulfur fungicides.

Sooty mold. Black fungal growth on the foliage of gardenias, crepe myrtles and other plants infested with aphids, scale or whiteflies. It is caused by the honeydew (poop) of the insect pests. Best control is to release beneficial insects to control the pest bugs.

St. Augustine decline. Virus in common St. Augustine grass that causes a yellow mottling. The grass slowly dies away. The answer is to replace with a healthier grass. The best St. Augustine at the moment is 'Raleigh.' Texas bluegrass is also good in shady areas.

Virus. Most viruses cause stunted plants, mottled and distorted leaves, poor quality fruits, and the death of plants. Control by planting resistant varieties and removing infected plants. Soil health will prevent most infestations.

Weed Control

There are no known cases of weeds attacking children. Despite that fact, Americans have been convinced that weeds are dangerous, ugly social embarrassments and must be eliminated!

We need a new attitude about weeds. They really aren't such a big deal, and some so-called weeds should even be encouraged. It's amazing that clover is treated like a noxious weed. White Dutch clover and other varieties are beautiful evergreen plants that improve the soil by fixing nitrogen from the air. I plant white clover and encourage it on residential and commercial projects. Take a look at the beautiful stand of white clover on the berms in Carpenter Park near Central Expressway in downtown Dallas. Wild violets, moss, henbit, and various wildflowers are other examples of beautiful weeds.

The sound of the word *weed* causes people to automatically think about what should be sprayed to kill them. They rarely think of why the weeds are there in the first place.

Weeds don't happen accidentally. They are here on earth for very specific purposes. Different weeds have different jobs to do, but all provide some function. Some are here to cover bare soil and to shade and cool the ground. Others are here to prevent the erosion of bare soil. Others are here to help balance the minerals in the soil. Many weeds provide all these important functions. If you have lots of noxious weeds, you have sick soil.

Weeds germinate and spread to protect soil left bare by man's mismanagement of the land. In every cubic foot of soil lie millions of weed seeds waiting to germinate when needed. When man strips the natural vegetation off the land, weeds are needed. When hard winters freeze the ornamental lawn grasses, weeds are needed. When we mow too low and apply harsh chemicals to the soil, weeds are needed. If it weren't for weeds, the topsoil of the earth would have eroded away years ago.

Some people consider dandelions weeds—some don't.

Weeds help to build the soil with their strong and powerful roots that deeply penetrate to loosen hard packed ground. The deep roots bring minerals, especially trace elements, from the subsoil to the topsoil.

There are safe and nonpolluting weed control methods such as mechanical aerifying, mulching with organic materials, and using organic fertilizers to stimulate the growth of more desirable plants. The old reliable methods of hand weeding, hoeing, and timely cultivating are not yet against the law and provide good exer-cise. "The Weeder" and the "Weed Popper" are excellent mechanical tools for hand weeding. Do not scalp the lawn. Scalping is messy, hard on the mower, and encourages weeds. It exposes bare soil which weed seeds need for germination. Scalping also wastes valuable organic matter.

The best weed control in the lawn is the following: mechanically aerate the soil at least once each year until the soil is healthy and breathing naturally, fertilize with 100 percent organic fertilizers, water deeply but infrequently, mow at a higher setting—2½ to 3 inches, and leave the clippings on the ground. Easy and effective weed control in the ornamental and vegetable beds is done by keeping a thick blanket of mulch on the bare soil at all times. Shredded hardwood bark is the best for ornamental beds and alfalfa hay is the best for vegetable gardens. Partially completed compost is also excellent.

Do not apply pre-emergent herbicides. They only control a small number of annual weeds such as grass burs and crab grass, and those can be controlled with proper culture. A little air, water, and fertilizer is all that's needed. Post emergent herbicides have no place in proper horticulture either. We should encourage health and life in the soil and on the land. There's too much concentration on killing things. The most dramatic example of this abuse is along the highways in Texas. While we are looking for ways to cut the state budget, millions are being spent to spray herbicides and further disturb the natural balance. What's the alternative? That's easy. Omit the herbicides, mow twice a year and allow the native grasses to reestablish. It's being done successfully in some counties already.

Weeds	Organic Solutions	Application
Weeds (general)	• Vinegar	• Spot spray 10 percent solution full strength on sunny day. 20 percent food grade is even better.
	• Chop with a hoe or hand remove	• This is still legal!
	• Accept a few	• Many "weeds" are herbs, wildflowers, and beneficial grasses.
Bermudagrass	• Vinegar	• Spray 20 percent food grade on hot, sunny day.
St. Augustine	• Dig out	• Use a sod cutter or hoe to remove rhizomes and stolons.
Nutgrass	• Aerate regularly	• Use an extra amount of mechanical aerifying.
	• Mulch	• Cover weeds in beds with a thick blanket of mulch.
	• Hand remove	• Nut grass pulls out easily from healthy soil.
Johnsongrass	• Physically remove	• Can't stand to be mowed or regularly cut down.
	• Vinegar	• Spot spray at 20 percent concentration
Crabgrass	• Fertilizer	• Fertilize regularly with an organic fertilizer.
	• Mowing height	• Mow at a height of 3 inches or more.
Dallisgrass	• Vinegar	• Spot spray with 20 percent food grade on a hot, sunny day.
	• Hand remove	
Poison Ivy	• Physically remove plants but protect skin	• Do not do if you are highly allergic.
	• Tecnu	• Apply to skin to prevent or to relieve rash pain.

Controlling Animal Pests

When animals become a nuisance in your garden or flower beds, they can usually be controlled with all-natural products.

Animals	Organic Solutions	Application
Armadillos	• Live traps	• Pied Piper or Have a Heart.
Birds	• Cats	• I'd rather have the birds.
	• Onion/garlic spray	• Most birds are beneficial and a natural mix of life in the garden will usually control populations.
	• Birdscare Flash Tape	• Install per instructions.
	• Soapy water	• Last resort: spray roosting birds with a mild soap solution.
Cats	• Dogs	• Or keep the cats indoors.
	• Citrus extract or peelings	• Apply to problem areas.
	• Live traps	• Pied Piper or Have a Heart.
	• Dry cayenne or habenero pepper	• Spread around problem area.
Deer	• Hinder	• Apply per label.
	• Soap bar	• Hang in trees in problem areas.
	• Blood meal	• Spread around problem area.
	• Electric fence	• Install around protected area.
Dogs	• Live traps	• Pied Piper traps or Have a Heart.
	• Dog runs	• It is not cruel to house dogs in dog runs when not at home.

Animals	Organic Solutions	Application
Dogs	• Dog-B-Gone home brew	• 1 part cayenne pepper, 2 parts mustard powder, 2 parts flour, or use straight cayenne pepper.
Gophers	• Black Hole Gopher Trap	• Install in tunnel per instructions.
	• Gopher spurge	• Plant Gopher spurge, *Euphobia lathyrus* around the perimeter of problem area.
	• Garlic, castor beans	• Plant as a barrier to garden areas.
Mice	• Traps	• Still looking for a better one.
	• Baits	• Apply Havoc in bait station.
	• Cats	• The natural way.
	• Peppermint	• Use ground up pieces of mint or cardboard soaked in peppermint oil as repellent.
Moles	• Same as for gophers	• At least you have nice sandy soil.
Rabbits	• Low and recessed fences	• Electric fences are even better.
	• Cayenne pepper	• Dust onto problem area.
	• Blood meal	• Spread around problem area.
Raccoons	• Live traps	• Pied Piper traps or Have a Heart traps.
	• Electric fence	• Install around garden area.
Rats	• Death traps	• Still looking for a better one.
	• Live traps	• Pied Piper traps or Have a Heart traps.
	• Bait stations	• Havoc per label.
Skunks	• Live traps	• Pied Piper traps or Have a Heart traps.
		• Be careful of the spray and bites. Many skunks are rabid.
Snakes	• Introduce bull and king snakes	• These guys look fierce but are great friends.
	• Roadrunners, guineas, and other snake-eating birds	• They control the dangerous snakes like rattlers, copperheads, coral, and water moccasins.
	• Most garden snakes are beneficial.	• Protect nature's biodiversity.
Squirrels	• Live traps	• Pied Piper traps or Have a Heart traps.
	• Fox urine	• Apply liquid to problem areas. Works as a repellent.
	• Blood meal and/or cayenne pepper	• Spread around problem area.
Turtles	• Underwater traps for aquatic turtles	• Pied Piper traps.
	• Land turtles are mostly beneficial	• Fence off from the vegetable garden.

CHAPTER 7

Organic Solutions

Differences in Organic Fertilizers

In general, most of the 100% organic fertilizers are effective and recommended for certain uses. I'll try to give you some general guidelines and then review all the specific products I have used.

First of all, watch out for the term "organic based." There's nothing wrong with these products, unless you want to go organic. They aren't organic. They are synthetic fertilizers with organic matter added. Also watch out for the coverage trick. Some organic fertilizers give instructions to apply them to a larger area than they will effectively cover. If you are a beginning organic gardener, the rate to use is 20 lbs/1,000 sq ft for all products listed below unless otherwise noted. The 20-lb rate is necessary to start the reversal of the soil's chemical drug dependency and to begin rebuilding soil humus. After the soil's health has been increased, applications can be reduced to 10 lbs/1,000 sq ft. Recommended rates of less than this should be questioned.

In a bag of synthetic fertilizer, say a 15-5-10 analysis for example, 30% of the contents of the bag is fertilizer. The other 70% is usually filler and salt. The N-P-K analysis of an organic fertilizer will be lower, such as 4-2-0, 5-2-4, or 3-1-2, but 100% of the ingredients in the bag is food for the soil. Because organic fertilizers are primarily plant derivities, they contain at least some quantity of all the trace minerals the soil and plants need. There are often 60 trace minerals or more in organic fertilizers. Organic fertilizers also contain carbon, organic matter, humus (which is decomposed

organic matter), and most of these products also contain hormones, enzymes, and beneficial fungi and bacteria.

Organic fertilizers are naturally timed-released so they don't glut the plants with nutrients at the wrong time. Most synthetic fertilizers break down and are immediately available at application. Sulfur and plastic coated products are the exception. Organic products break down and release nutrients to the plants when the plants are growing the fastest and need the nutrition.

Here's a run down of the most available and useful organic fertilizers, soil amendments, and biostimulants.

Fertilizers and Biostimulants

Agri-Gro

A liquid biological, nutritional solution containing microorganisms beneficial to the soil and plant growth. For use on all agricultural and ornamental crops. Works best when mixed with molasses.

Agrispon

A liquid metabolic stimulator that encourages root and top growth and helps control pathogens of all sorts indirectly through biological activity. It's used for soil, foliage, and seed treatment to enhance plant growth and health. It reduces drought stress and salt stress and makes better use of all fertilizer elements, especially nitrogen. By increasing microbial activity, Agrispon increases nitrogen fixation by microorganisms.

Alfalfa Meal

Alfalfa provides many nutritional benefits not only for plant use, but for soil organisms as well. One very important ingredient is triacontanol, a powerful plant growth regulator. Orchid and rose growers make an alfalfa tea and spray it directly on as a foliar fertilizer. Alfalfa is very high in vitamins, plus N-P-K-Ca, Mg, and other valuable minerals. It also includes sugars, starches, proteins, fiber, and 16 amino acids. Sprinkle lightly over garden and water, or use about a handful (depending on the size) around each rose, tree, or shrub.

Alfalfa Tea

In a 5-gallon bucket, put 1 cup alfalfa meal. Fill bucket with water; let it set overnight. The result will be a thick tea. Apply generously to the root area of shrubs and flowers or use as a foliar spray after straining.

Bat Guano

A natural, all-purpose fertilizer containing nitrogen and lots of trace elements. The analysis will vary with the age of the guano. It has natural fungicidal qualities and almost no chance of being contaminated with pesticides or chemicals. It is an excellent supplemental fertilizer for flowers. It is best to apply once or twice during the growing season. It looks very mild but has as much as 10 percent nitrogen, so be careful not to overuse.

Bioform

Liquid fertilizer made from fish emulsion, seaweed, and molasses. Analysis is 4-2-4-3S. The sulfur in the molasses has virtually eliminated the fish smell. The product also contains a biostimulant/soil penetrant. This same company now makes a deodorized fish emulsion, analysis 3-1-1.

Blood Meal

Excellent organic source of nitrogen and phosphorus. Good to use as a mix with cottonseed meal. Expensive, but it's good to use occasionally. Analysis can range from 12-2-1 to 11-0-0.

Bone Meal

Excellent slow-release source of calcium and phosphorus recommended for bulbs, tomatoes, and other vegetables. Analysis will range from 2-12-0 to 4-12-0 with 2 to 5 percent calcium.

Cattle Manure

Manure is one of our greatest natural resources. It has to be handled properly and not over used in any one area. Using too much of anything can cause problems. Manure can be properly used in several ways.

Cow manure is a good ingredient for the manufacture of compost or for use directly on agricultural fields. Dairy cow manure is best because it has the least chance of chemical contamination. It should be composted prior to using in the home vegetable garden. Hog manure has similar properties and uses, but it has a higher analysis, usually around 2-5-1 compared to cattle manure's 2-1-1.

Cedar Flakes

Good for chiggers, fleas, and lowering the pH of the soil. An excellent material to use on the floor of greenhouses. Cedar flakes will help control harmful nematodes.

Chelators

Chelated iron and other chelated nutrients are used when a direct dose of a particular nutrient is needed to quickly solve a deficiency. Chelated products are organic compounds with attached inorganic metal molecules that are more available for plant use. Compost, humus, humic acid, and microorganisms have natural chelating properties.

Chicken Manure

Chicken litter is a good natural fertilizer high in nitrogen. Pelletized forms are better because they are not as dusty. Approximate analysis ranges from 5-3-1 to 6-4-2. Unfortunately commercial chickens are still fed lots of unnatural things. Best to compost before using.

Colloidal Phosphate

Soft rock phosphate is a mixture of fine particles of phosphate suspended in a clay base. It is an economical form of natural phosphorus and calcium. Unlike chemically made phosphates, rock phosphate is insoluble in water, will not leach away, and therefore, is long-lasting. Has 18 percent phosphorus and 15 percent calcium as well as trace elements. Florida is the primary source.

Compost

The best fertilizer and the key to any organic program. Nature's own product, high in nutrients, humus, humic acid, enzymes, vitamins, and microorganisms. Compost has magical healing and growing powers and can be used successfully on any and all plants. Analysis will vary due to ingredients.

Compost can be made at home or purchased commercially. The best composts are those made from a variety of organic materials such as hay, sawdust, paunch manure, leaves, twigs, bark, wood chips, dead plants, non-greasy food scraps, pecan hulls, grass clippings, and animal manure. The manure percentage in compost should not be more than 20 to 25 percent of the volume. The best manure to use is whatever is locally available: chicken, turkey, cattle, horse, or rabbit.

Cottonseed Meal

A good natural fertilizer with an acid pH. Analysis will vary and ranges from 6-2-1 to 7-2-2 with trace elements. Should be composted to detoxify the chemicals used in cotton farming. Does have odor. Good organic source of nitrogen. Best use is as a nitrogen source for the compost pile.

Earth-Rite Products

A line of humus-based products that also provide N-P-K and trace elements.

Earth Safe Products

A line of organic fertilizers manufactured by the Carl Pool Company. "Turf Toughener" is an all-natural turf fertilizer made from molasses, feather meal, meat and bone meal, blood meal, alfalfa meal, fish meal, cottonseed, and soybean meals. Analysis is 4-1-5; tomato and vegetable food is 4-6-5; premium lawn food is 9-3-6.

Earthworm Castings

An effective organic fertilizer that is high in bacteria, calcium, iron, magnesium, and sulphur, as well as N-P-K, and has over 60 trace minerals. Earthworm castings make an excellent ingredient in potting soil, in flats when germinating seed, and to toss into each hole when planting vegetables, herbs, bulbs, or other ornamentals.

Fertilaid

All-purpose fertilizer made of tankage (blood meal, bone meal, and natural urea), chicken and fish waste, 37 cultures of soil-borne bacteria, 28 trace elements, 20 percent humus, 20 percent humic acid. It is a good soil detoxifier and many users say that it has fungicidal properties. Its only drawbacks include availability, dustiness, and inconsistency.

Fish Emulsion

A concentrated liquid fish fertilizer for use directly in the soil or as a foliar feed. The analysis will range from 4-1-1 to 5-2-2. It is reported to be a very effective insect repellent. Great all-purpose spray when mixed with liquid kelp. Some fish emulsion products have an odor for about 24 hours—a pretty strong one in fact. However, some of the newer products on the market have been greatly deodorized.

Fish Meal

A natural fertilizer originally used in this country by Indians growing corn. Has a high analysis of approximately from 7-13-3 to 8-12-2. It is stinky, but very effective especially for problem areas during transition from chemical to organic.

Glauconite

See greensand.

Granite Sand

Sand-like residue from the granite quarry. Excellent way to add slow-release minerals to planting beds. Much better than sharp sand. Contains 5 percent potash.

Greensand

Often sold as Jersey greensand glauconite. It is a naturally deposited, undersea, iron potassium silicate. It's an excellent source of potash with a normal analysis of 0-1-5. It's best used with other fertilizers and a good potting soil ingredient.

GreenSense

A granulated organic fertilizer made from composted animal manure (cow, pig, or sheep), activated charcoal, alfalfa, molasses, and iron sulfate that offers a quick greening effect. It is very effective and economical. Pelletizing eliminated the dust problem, and the molasses and charcoal took care of the manure odor.

Gypsum

This natural material is calcium sulfate and is an excellent source of calcium and sulfur. Gypsum also neutralizes plant toxins, lowers soil pH, removes salts from the soil and opens the soil structure to promote aeration and drainage. Gypsum is approximately 23 percent calcium and 17 percent sulfate.

Horse Manure

Horse manure is higher in nitrogen than most other farm animal manures and is an excellent material to use for the manufacture of compost. Fresh manures should not be tilled directly into the soil unless they are applied a month before planting or composted first. Sheep manure has similar properties and uses.

Humates

Leonardite shale is basically low-grade lignite coal and is a good carbon source. Percentage of humic acid will vary. May be mixed into liquid form or used in the dry form. Excellent source of humic acid and trace minerals.

Hydrogen Peroxide

H_2O_2 is water with an extra oxygen molecule. It is a good product for oxygenating the soil. It's a fascinating compound in that at 3 percent it's used medicinally, at 20 percent it's lethal, and at 35 percent it's explosive.

Kelp Meal

A dry fertilizer made from seaweed. Analysis will range from 1-0-2 to 1-2-8, with lots of trace minerals. It is an excellent source of plant hormones that stimulate root growth and regulate plant growth. Seaweed also provides soil conditioning substances that improve the crumb structure or tilth. Good natural source of copper and boron.

Kricket Krap

One hundred percent all-natural cricket manure from Augusta, Georgia. The fish bait crickets are fed a high protein diet of fish meal, soybean, blood meal, chicken chowder, corn, and molasses. Analysis is 4-3-2 plus magnesium and calcium.

Lava Dust

The sand-sized and smaller waste material left from lava gravel is an excellent, high energy soil amendment material. It can be used in potting soils and bed preparation. It is a very high energy sand and loaded with trace minerals.

Leather Tankage

Leather tankage is a slaughter house byproduct high in nitrogen. Several organic fertilizers are derived from leather tankage. Some tankage contains chemicals used in the tanning process.

Lime

A major calcium fertilizer, dolomitic lime contains 30 to 35 percent magnesium. High calcium lime contains only 10 percent magnesium. High calcium is preferred because most low calcium soils usually contain too much magnesium.

Liquid Seaweed (Kelp)

A product made from seaweed that will green plants quickly. Loaded with trace elements and hormones, it acts as a root stimulator. Makes an excellent all-purpose spray when mixed with fish emulsion that fertilizes and helps control insects and fungi. Also acts as a chelating agent, making other fertilizers and nutrients more available to the plants.

Maestro-Gro

A line of organic fertilizers that has a bone meal base. Products include a wide variety of ingredients such as bone meal, fish meal, feather meal, rock phosphates, kelp meal, greensand, and microorganisms. Texas T is an excellent general purpose product within this line.

Manalfa

Cross between alfalfa and cow manure. Be careful using products pelletized with clay that might cause a buildup over time.

Medina

A dairy cow manure extract used for stimulation of microorganisms in the soil. Medina Plus contains trace elements and seaweed as an added benefit. Hastagro is a Medina product that is a low chemical fertilizer with an analysis of 6-12-6, also containing seaweed.

Milorganite

Sewer sludge fertilizer from Milwaukee. Has been widely used on golf courses. Had a scare for a while that the product caused Lou Gehrig's disease, but was proved to be false. It's best not to use any sewer sludge product on edible plants.

Molasses

Sweet syrup used as a soil amendment to feed and stimulate microorganisms. Contains sulfur, potash, and other trace minerals.

Old Farmer's Almanac

A granulated organic fertilizer made from composted animal manure (cow, pig, or sheep), activated charcoal, alfalfa, molasses, and iron sulfate that offers a quick greening effect. It is very effective and economical. Pelletizing eliminated the dust problem, and the molasses and charcoal took care of the manure odor. It is the same base product as GreenSense with a 3-1-2 analysis.

Orgro

Organic fertilizer made from composted chicken and turkey manure. It is manufactured in Arkansas by the Releaf Corp. The analysis is 4-2-4.

Rabbit Manure

The average analysis of rabbit manure is from 2-1-5 to 3-2-1. Mixed with leaves, sawdust, straw, grass, and other vegetative materials, it makes an excellent compost. Can be used directly as a fertilizer, but it's better to compost first.

Ringer

Ringer is the brand name of a group of natural products for landscaping, lawns, and vegetable gardens. The base for the products is chicken feathers, blood meal, soybean meal, and bone meal. The products contain soil microorganisms, enzymes, and organic matter.

Seaweed

Best used as a foliar spray. Excellent source of trace minerals. Should be used often. Contains hormones that stimulate root growth and branching. The 60-plus trace elements found in seaweed are present in the proportions found in plants.

Sewer Sludge Compost

Most cities should produce this product. It is an excellent lawn fertilizer, but probably should not be used on vegetables or other edible plants. Heavy metal contamination is a concern.

Soil-Sul

A Carl Pool product made from copperas and gypsum that is mixed at 2 cups per 5 gallons. Used to cure chlorosis and root rot.

Sul-Po-Mag

A mined source of sulfur, potassium, and magnesium. A naturally occurring mineral containing 22 percent sulfur, 22 percent potash, and 11.1 percent magnesium that is naturally granulated.

Superthrive

A liquid product made from vitamins and hormones. Excellent supplemental food for flowering plants. Use at 3 drops per gallon at each watering for best results. Can be mixed with other products. Works well as a root stimulator.

Sulfur

A basic mineral often lacking in alkaline soils. Applying granulated sulfur at 5 to 10 lbs/1,000 sq ft twice annually can bring base saturation of calcium down and raise magnesium. Be careful not to breath dust, over apply, or use when planting seed. It can act as a preemergent. Sulfur dust is also used as a pesticide in some situations.

Sustane

A granulated fertilizer made from composted turkey manure. It has some odor for 24 to 36 hours but has shown excellent soil improvement and reduction of diseases. One of the fastest working 100 percent organic fertilizers. Analysis is 5-2-4.

Tomas

A manufactured organic fertilizer containing a variety of ingredients such as feather meal, fish meal, and bone. Analysis will vary due to different formulations.

Turkey Manure

Turkey manure is a high nitrogen manure that is an excellent ingredient for compost. Best to compost before using.

Zinc

Important fertilizer element for pecans and other crops. Will defoliate fruit trees if misused. Not needed in acid soils or balanced soils. Zinc is a trace element found in most organic fertilizers. Do not apply on an annual basis without good soil test information. Many soils have plenty of zinc already and too much is toxic to plants.

Rate Chart

Product	Rate	Frequency/Comments
Agrispon	1 tsp/gal of water per 1,000 sq ft, 13 oz/acre	Once a month to help release nutrients in the soil. May be mixed with other liquid products.
Alfalfa meal	20 to 25 lbs per 1,000 sq ft	Once a year in conjunction with other organic fertilizers.
Bat guano	10 to 20 lbs per 1,000 sq ft	Once a year to flowering plants or at each flower rotation.
Bioform	2 to 3 Tbs per 1,000 sq ft	Spray with water all plantings at least three times per year. Can be mixed with other products.
Blood meal	10 lbs per 1,000 sq ft	May be combined with cottonseed meal (4 parts cottonseed meal to 1 part blood meal).
Bone meal	10 to 20 lbs per 1,000 sq ft	Once a year when planting bulbs or flowers. Watch for calcium buildup.
Chelated iron	1 qt/acre or 1 Tbs/gal	Spray as needed for a quick temporary fix of iron deficiency.
Cow manure	20 to 30 lbs per 1,000 sq ft up to 5 tons per acre.	Use composted manure to avoid weeds; raw material good to use on agricultural fields. Watch for build up of phosphates and nitrates.
Cottonseed meal	20 to 30 lbs per 1,000 sq ft	Use once or twice per year. May be combined with blood meal or other meals
Colloidal phosphate	25 to 50 lbs per 1,000 sq ft	Use once per year to give a long-lasting source of phosphorus and calcium. Put small handful into planting hole of new plants.
Compost	1/4-inch depth on lawns; 2-inch depth in beds	Once a year to lawns and planting beds is ideal. Not important if beds are mulched.
Compost on fields	900–1,200 lbs/acre	Important addition to use as needed to raise the health of unbalanced soil.
Dillo dirt	1/4-inch depth on lawns	Once or twice per year on lawn and planting beds.
Earth Safe	10 lbs per 1,000 sq ft	Use 20 pounds per 1,000 sq ft the first year. 10 lbs per 1,000 thereafter.

(continued on next page)

Rate Chart Continued

Product	Rate	Frequency/Comments
Earthworm castings	20 lbs per 1,000 sq ft	Use once per year or at each annual flower rotation on flowering plants as a supplemental food. Put a small handful in each planting hole.
Epsom salts	1 Tbs per gal	Spray monthly if needed. Can be mixed with other sprays. For soils deficient in sulfur and magnesium.
Fertilaid	20 lbs per 1,000 sq ft first year	Two or three times a year; twice thereafter at 10 lb/1,000 sq ft.
Fish emulsion	2 oz/gal of water per 1,000 sq ft	Spray all plants 2 to 3 times per year or any time extra greening or pest control is needed.
Fish meal	20 lbs per 1,000 sq ft	Once or twice a year to lawns or planting beds as a supplemental fertilizer. Use 10 pounds per 1,000 sq ft after the first year.
Granite sand	10 lbs per 1,000 sq ft up to 5 tons per acre	Once a year as a mineral supplement. Can also be used to top-dress new solid sod installations.
Greensand	10 to 20 lbs per 1,000 sq ft	Excellent mineral supplement.
GreenSense	10 lbs per 1,000 sq ft	20 lbs per 1,000 sq ft should be used the first year.
Humate (Dry)	1½ lbs per 1,000 sq ft	Use high quality humate (40 to 50 percent humic acid) @ 50 lbs/acre once per year.
Humate (Liquid)	½ oz/1,000 sq ft	Spray all foliage lightly three times per growing season. Can be mixed with other liquid products.
Hydrogen peroxide (H_2O_2)	½ oz of 35 percent material per gal/1,000 sq ft or 8 oz of 3 percent material per gal per 1,000 sq ft	Can be mixed with other materials but always add the H_2O_2 first.
Lava sand	10 lbs per 1,000 sq ft up to 5 tons per acre	Once a year as a mineral supplement. Can also be used to top-dress new solid sod installations.
Maestro-Gro (Texas T)	20 lbs/1,000 sq ft the first year; 10 pounds thereafter.	Other formulations may have different rates. Check label.
Manalfa	800 lb/acre or 20 lbs/1,000 sq ft	10 lbs/1,000 sq ft after 1st full year.

Rate Chart Continued

Product	Rate	Frequency/Comments
Manure on fields	500 - 1,000 lbs/acre	In the beginning, as much as 5 tons per acre can be used until fertility levels increase.
Medina	1 qt per 1,000 sq ft	Apply to salty or contaminated soil as needed.
Medina Plus	4 oz per gal of water to cover approximately 1,000 sq ft	Apply as a foliar spray to trees, shrubs, flowers, and vegetables two to three times a year.
Micro Life	20 lbs/1,000 sq ft	Apply 2 to 3 times per year to all planting areas.
Molasses	1 oz per gal of water or other liquids	Apply as a foliar and soil spray to fertilize and feed microbes.
Organic fertilizers in general	20 lbs/1,000 sq ft	½ tsp/4" pot, 1 tsp/gal, 1 Tbs/5 gal container. Water in after application.
Pene-Turf	4-8 oz/acre or .10 oz/1,000 sq ft (30 drops per gal)	Residential 1 tsp/1,000 sq ft.
Poultry manure	20 lbs per 1,000 sq ft the first year; 10 pounds thereafter.	Apply twice per year as a good natural source of nitrogen.
Ringer	10 lbs per 1,000 sq ft	20 pounds per 1,000 sq ft the first year.
Seaweed (Liquid kelp)	½ to 1 oz per 1,000 sq ft	Apply to lawns and planting beds once a month as a supplement between applications of dry fertilizers.
Seaweed (Kelp meal)	10 to 20 lbs/1,000 sq ft	Apply to lawns and planting beds once a month as a supplement between applications of dry fertilizers.
Seaweed and fish emulsion	Mix 1 oz of seaweed and 2 ozs of fish emulsion per gallon of water	Apply as a general foliar spray to aid insect and fungus control and as a foliar feed. Spray all plants and lawns.
Solubor	1 lb/acre or .4 oz/1,000 sq ft	Spray very carefully after determining a boron deficiency from a proper soil test.
Soybean meal	20 lbs per 1,000 sq ft	Apply twice per year.
Sul-Po-Mag	20 lbs per 1,000 sq ft	Use once per year on soil needing sulfur, magnesium, and potassium.
Sustane	20 lbs per 1,000 sq ft first year	Reduce to 10 lbs/1,000 sq ft twice per year after first year.
Tomas	10 lbs per 1,000 sq ft	20 pounds per 1,000 sq ft the first year.
Vinegar	½ oz per gal	Mix with other liquid products 1 to 2 gal of mix per 1,000 sq ft.

Organic programs use sprayers to apply liquid fertilizers rather than poisons.

Antidesiccants

Also called antitranspirants, these products are made from pine oil and are non-toxic and biodegradable. They are sometimes used for the prevention of powdery mildew on roses and crepe myrtles. They work by spreading a clear film over the leaves. Not highly recommended for use as fungicides. Best used to prevent dryout of plant foliage.

Bacillus thuringiensis (*Bt*)

A beneficial bacteria applied as a liquid spray or powder to kill caterpillars. Sold under a variety of names such as

Thuricide, Dipel, Bio-Worm. Use *Bacillus thuringiensis* 'Israelensis' (Bti) in water for mosquitoes. Use Bioform or molasses with *Bt* for extra effect. Sugar in the molasses provides protein and keeps insect-killing bacteria alive on the foliage longer, even during rain. Encapsulated *Bt* products such as Foray are now on the market. They have a longer residual on plant.

Baking Soda

Mixed at the rate of 4 teaspoons per gallon of water, baking soda makes an excellent fungicide for black spot, powdery mildew, brown patch, and other fungal problems. Add one teaspoon of liquid soap or vegetable oil to the mix. Be careful to keep the spray on the foliage and not on the soil, as it can alter soil chemistry. Baking soda is composed of sodium and bicarbonate. Both are necessary in the soil, but only in very small amounts.

Bordeaux Mix

A fungicide and insecticide usually made from copper sulfate and lime. Good for most foliar problems and an effective organic treatment for disease control on fruits, vegetables, shrubs, trees, and flowers such as anthracnose, botrytis blight, peach tree curl, and twig blight. Wet down decks and other hard surfaces before spraying. Some staining is possible.

Copper

Trace mineral that in liquid form is an effective fungicide for powdery mildew, black spot, peach leaf curl, and other diseases. Copper is also an ingredient in Bordeaux mix.

Demize

Demize is a citrus oil extract used for killing fleas indoors. It is not a true organic product but has low toxicity, has a fresh citrus fragrance, and works quite well.

Diacide
(Now called Perma-Guard)

A natural insecticide containing diatomaceous earth, pyrethrum, and PBO (Piperonly butoxide). Pyrethrum will kill beetles, leafhoppers, worms, caterpillars, ants and other crawling insects on contact. Relatively nontoxic to animals and people. Apply at the first sign of an insect problem, but do not use as a preventative.

Diatomaceous Earth (D-E)

Diatomaceous earth is approximately 5 percent aluminum, 5 percent sodium, and 86 percent silicon. It is the skeletal remains of microscopic organisms (one-celled aquatic plants) that lived in seawater or freshwater lakes millions of years ago in the western United States. The broken skeletons have razor sharp edges that scratch the exoskeleton of insects causing them to desiccate and die. Apply using a dusting machine (manual or electrostatic) covering plants or lawn areas entirely. Do sure to use a dust mask when applying! A better way to apply is to mix 2 tablespoons of diatomaceous earth together with 1 teaspoon of pyrethrum in 1 gallon of water and spray as a liquid. D-E is nonselective, so use sparingly. Breathing dusty material can cause lung problems. As a food supplement, use at 1 to 2 percent of the food volume for feeding pets or livestock.

Dormant Oil

Long-standing organic treatment for scale and other over-wintering insects. Petroleum-based and will kill beneficial insects, so use sparingly. It's recommended to spray dormant oil at temperatures between 40° and 80° when rain is not expected. It works by smothering the insects and their eggs. Effective against scale, aphids, spider mites, and others. Do not use sulfur as a fungicide without waiting 30 days after using dormant oil.

Floating Gro-Cover

Gardening fabrics are designed to cover plants in a moist greenhouse warmth while allowing water, light, and ventilation for proper plant respiration. These row cover materials protect foliage from chewing insects, prevent harmful insects from laying eggs, and reduce diseases carried by pests. Birds, rabbits, and other animals are discouraged from feeding on plants.

Garlic/Pepper Tea

An organic insect and disease control material made from the juice of garlic and hot peppers such as jalapeño, habeñero, or cayenne. This is one of the few preventative controls that I recommend. However, its use should be limited because it will kill small beneficial insects. It is effective for both ornamental and food crops.

Imidan

Imidan is reported to be the best control for plum curculio that damages apples, plums, peaches, and other stone fruits. Imidan is a chemical pesticide but seems to be the least-toxic choice. Apply at petal fall and 10 days later.

Lime Sulfur

An organic fungicide (calcium polysulfide) for fruits, berries, roses, nuts, and ornamental plants. Spray plants as buds swell, but before they open. It is effective for powdery mildew, anthracnose, peach leaf curl, and brown rot. It controls insects such as scale and mites.

Liquid Copper

A flowable formulation of copper salts for fungal control on roses, vegetables, fruits, and ornamentals. It is a good control of powdery mildew, bacterial blights, and anthracnose.

Nicotine Sulfate

An old-time organic pesticide used for the control of hard-to-kill insects. Although it is a quickly biodegradable product, it is dangerous to handle and should only be used as a last resort. Remember how dangerous nicotine is the next time you light up. It is one of the few effective controls for cutter ants.

Nosema Locustae

A biological control for crickets and grasshoppers. It works the same way *Bt* works on caterpillars. It's applied as a dry bait and the insects eat the material, then get sick and are cannibalized by their friends. Charming isn't it—but it works. Brand names include Nolo Bait, Grasshopper Attack, and Semispore.

Oils

There are now four types of spray oils: dormant, summer, horticultural, and vegetable.

Dormant oils are petroleum based, relatively free of impurities and have been used as far back as 1880. Dormant oils have lower volatility and more insect-killing power than the other oils, but they can be more toxic to plants. These oils should only be used during the winter months when plants are dormant. Summer oils, also petroleum based, are lighter, less poisonous to plants, more volatile, and less effective on insects. They can be used during the heat of summer on some hard-to-kill bugs. Horticultural oils are the lightest and most pure petroleum oils. They also can be used for spraying pecan trees and fruit trees, but they are also effective on shrubs and flowers that have scale or other insect infestations. Vegetable oils are plant extracts. They are environmentally safe, degrade quickly by evaporation, fit into organic or integrated pest management programs, are nonpoisonous to the applicator, are noncorrosive to the spray equipment, and kill a wide range of insects. The state of Texas is also pushing toward vegetable oils. Drilling lubricants can no longer be petroleum oils.

Organic Plus

A pure diatomaceous earth product labeled for the control of a wide range of garden and household pests.

Precor

An insect growth regulator that controls fleas by preventing the larvae from developing into adults. It is often used indoors with *Demize*. It's not a true organic, but fits into an organic program because of its low toxicity.

Pyrethrum

Available in liquid or dry forms. Will kill a wide range of insects including aphids, beetles, leafhoppers, worms, caterpillars, and ants. It is short-lived and relatively nontoxic to animals. Pyrethrum is made from ground painted daisy (*Chrysanthemum cimerariae-folium*). Artificial substitutes, called pyrethroids, should be avoided. Pyrethrin is the active natural ingredient in pyrethrum.

Rotenone

One percent solution can bc uscd to kill aphids, worms, beetles, borers, and thrips. Five percent solution is effective for use on fire ants, pill bugs, and hard-to-kill type beetles. Rotenone is dangerous if not handled carefully, but is still considered an acceptable organic product. There are products available containing a combination of rotenone and pyrethrum. Rotenone is particularly dangerous to fish.

Ryania

Root extract from the ryania shrub. Can be used as dust or spray to control moths, corn borers, and other problem insects. Ryania is a relatively strong organic pesticide.

Sabadilla Dust

Made from the crushed seeds of a tropical lily. Effective on some of the hard-to-kill garden pests such as thrips, cabbage worms, grasshoppers, loopers, leafhoppers, harlequin bugs, adult squash beetles, and cucumber beetles. Relatively nontoxic to man.

Soap

Nonphosphate liquid soaps and water mixed together into a spray make a good control for aphids and other small insects. Strong solutions can damage plant foliage, and even weak solutions can kill many of the microscopic beneficial insects. So use sparingly.

Sulfur

Finely ground sulfur is used by mixing with water or dusting on dry to control black spot, leaf spot, brown canker, rust, peach leaf curl, powdery mildew, and apple scab. Mix with liquid seaweed to enhance fungicidal properties. Sulfur will also control fleas, mites, thrips, and chiggers. To avoid leaf burn, do not use when temperature is 90° or above.

Tanglefoot

Spread on the bark of trees to control gypsy moths, canker worms, climbing cutworms, and ants. Made from natural gum resins, castor oil, and vegetable waxes. Can be used on tree trunks to discourage sap sucker damage.

Triple Action 20

Triple Action 20 is a synthetic fungicide but has extremely low toxicity and biodegrades very quickly. It is said to give excellent control of fireblight. Use at 1 teaspoon per gallon. It is also sold as Consan 20.

Vinegar

Vinegar can be an effective tool for controlling a few problem fire ant mounds. Pour it directly into the center of the mound. Use the strongest dilution available. Five percent and 10 percent vinegars are commonly available in the grocery store. Vinegar is an effective herbicide on a hot, sunny day, especially 20 percent food grade. It's a nonselective herbicide, so be careful to keep it off your good plants.

Weed Fabric

Controls weeds and conserves soil moisture. It is a synthetic fabric that allows maximum air and water movement, while at the same time blocking out weed growth. Not recommended. Use mulch in order to maintain the natural processes in the soil.

Yellow Sticky Traps

Nontoxic bright yellow cards that trap insects with their sticky coating. They are also used to monitor insect populations. Particularly effective in greenhouses against white flies.

Homemade Remedies

Roach Control

Eliminate the food and water sources. Fix dripping faucets and leaky pipes. Do not leave dirty dishes, food scraps, pet food, or any other tasty morsels out for the bugs to snack on. Eliminate cardboard boxes if possible. The small tunnels make good mating and hiding places.

Plug any holes or cracks where roaches can gain access to the house or hide to mate. Steel wool can be used to fill voids around pipes, etc. Use silicon caulking to fill cracks.

Apply a light dusting of boric acid to areas such as behind and between appliances where roaches like to party. For additional control, mix silica gel or diatomaceous earth together with the boric acid. Use light dustings. If the material can be seen after application, you probably put out too much.

For even more control, make a bait by mixing 4 parts flour, 2 parts sugar, 1 part boric acid, and enough water to create little cakes. Put the cakes behind appliances where roaches hide. Keep out of reach of pets and children.

Pharaoh Ant (Sugar Ants) Bait

Ingredients:

- 1 teaspoon creamy peanut butter
- 1 pat of butter or margarine
- 1 tablespoon any light syrup
- 1 teaspoon boric acid powder

Blend the above ingredients over low heat until smooth. Be careful not to burn the solution. Put the finished bait into lids or other small containers. The ants will find them. This amount will make several bait stations. Feed ants as long as they will take the bait. Do not use this recipe on your waffles or pancakes. Remember that boric acid is poison.

Another recipe is a mixture of boric acid, powdered sugar, and water to make a thin paste to put in shallow containers.

Flea Control

First of all convert over to organic fertilizers and avoid pesticides. If the natural populations of insects and soil microorganisms thrive, the competition for food will help to control fleas and other insect pests.

Bathe your pets every two weeks in a mild soap and water bath. Use a non-phosphate biodegradable soap at 1 teaspoon per gallon. Brush or use flea combs on the pets regularly and feed garlic and brewer's yeast supplements. Spray diatomaceous earth and pyrethrum mixed in water into all outdoor infested areas. Don't use this as a preventative because beneficial insects will be destroyed.

Clean and vacuum regularly and spray citrus peel extract products such as *Demize* inside the house to kill adult fleas. Spray insect growth regulators such as *Fleatrol* and *Precor* to prevent young fleas from developing into adults.

Fire Ants

First of all, go organic and encourage biodiversity. Then treat large-scale infestations with *Logic* at 1 lb/acre on a dry day. Make sure the ants are foraging by putting out a piece of chicken or some jelly. Knock out individual problem mounds by pouring one of the following into the center of the mound: strong vinegar with diatomaceous earth or a pyrethrum/rotenone product.

Garlic/Pepper Tea

Liquify two bulbs of garlic and two cayenne or habenero peppers in a blender 1/3 full of water. Strain the solids out and add enough water to the garlic/pepper juice to make one gallon of concentrate. Shake well before using and add 1/4 cup of the concentrate to each gallon of water in the sprayer. Two tablespoons of vegetable oil per gallon of concentrate will make the tea stronger but, I doubt it's needed.

Dog-B-Gone Home Brew

One part cayenne pepper, 2 parts mustard powder, 2 parts flour, or use straight cayenne pepper. Dust on the mulch, soil, and plants in areas where animals are a problem.

Oil Concentrate

Homemade vegetable oil concentrate can be made by mixing 1 cup vegetable oil and 1 tablespoon soap in a gallon of water to make concentrate. Then use 1 cup of concentrate per gallon of spray. Some gardeners use the simpler formula: 1 tablespoon of vegetable oil and 1 teaspoon soap in one gallon of spray. Acceptable oils for this use include soybean oil, corn oil, sunflower oil, cottonseed oil, and olive oil. This organic pesticide is used to spot control outbreaks of aphids, red spider mites, lace bugs, flea beetles, and other problem critters.

Bug Juice Spray

Slugs and pill bugs can be effectively controlled by using a spray made from the bodies of the pest species. To control pill bugs, mix 1 ounce of ground pill bugs with 2 ounces of water to make a paste and then dilute 1 ounce of the bug concentrate in 1 gallon of water. Spray a heavy amount of the bug juice on problem areas. This same technique works for slugs and other hard-to-kill insect pests such as Mexican bean beetles, armyworms, stink bugs, and cutworms.

Note: Keep insecticides away from children and pets and don't breathe the dust of any dusty product. Remember, anything can injure or kill if mishandled.

Appendix

Soil Test Procedures

I recommend soil tests that use the cation exchange capacity (CEC) test. Some labs call it Total Exchange Capacity (TEC).

1. *Prepare a map of the areas to be tested.* A good map makes your sampling repeatable from year to year and is useful at the time of fertilization.

   Divide the landscape, field, or pasture into areas where the soil has the same color, slope, surface, texture, internal drainage, and past history of erosion. Each area should have the same plant type (i.e., beds, turf). As a general rule, any area that is different in slope, texture, color, etc., and large enough to be fertilized separately should also be sampled separately.

2. *Collect the sample.* Using a soil probe, or stainless steel trowel, push the probe down to a depth of 6½ to 7 inches (4 inches for no-till, pastures and lawns). Remove any grass or thatch on top and put the rest of the probing into a soil sample bag or plastic container. Ziploc bags are fine, as long as they have *never* been used. To avoid possible contamination, do not use paper sacks from the grocery store, bread wrappers, etc. Avoid using previously used buckets. Probe the soil every 50 to 100 paces, always taking a probe for every one or two acres on larger areas. Only a small amount of soil is necessary for analysis.

3. *Label the bags.* Indicate name and area number on the sample bag. Make sure the labeling on the bag matches the number of the area on the map it is to represent. It is helpful to label the bags to match the areas before taking the sample. Soils may be sent in dry or wet.

4. *Mail the samples.* Send the samples to soil testing services that include an exchange capacity test (CEC). Extension services usually do not do this. Tests based on the pH only do not give information about which nutrients are available to the plants. The cost of basic tests will vary but generally are in the range of $20 to $30. Texas labs include A&L Plains Agricultural Laboratories, Lubbock, Texas, and Western Agricultural Labs, Lubbock, Texas.

Soil samples can be taken with stainless steel probes or garden trowels.

Soil samples should never be put in previously used bags.

Soil Test Results

Ideal Chemical Balances Based on Five Different Soil Types

Service Representative				Date		
Field		1	2	3	4	5
Sample		IDEAL	IDEAL	IDEAL	IDEAL	IDEAL
Lab No.		sandy	sandy loam	light clay	medium clay	heavy clay
Total Exchange Capacity		5.00	12.00	20.00	30.00	40.00
pH of Soil Sample		6.50	6.30	6.30	6.30	6.30
Organic Matter, Percent		3.50	5.10	5.10	5.10	5.10
ANIONS NITROGEN:	lbs/acre	85	100	100	100	100
SULFATE:	p.p.m.	25	25	25	25	25
PHOSPHATES: as (P_2O_5) lbs/acre	Desired Value Value Found Deficit	234 500	240 500	250 500	275 500	320 500
EXCHANGEABLE CATIONS CALCIUM: lbs/acre	Desired Value Value Found Deficit	1200 1200	3264 3264	5440 5440	8160 8160	10880 10880
MAGNESIUM: lbs/acre	Desired Value Value Found Deficit	240 240	346 346	576 576	864 864	1152 1152
POTASSIUM: lbs/acre	Desired Value Value Found Deficit	293 293	468 468	780 780	1170 1170	1560 1560
SODIUM:	lbs/acre	23	41	69	104	138

BASE SATURATION PERCENT

	1	2	3	4	5
Calcium (60 to 70%) } 80%	60.00	68.00	68.00	68.00	68.00
Magnesium (10 to 20%)	20.00	12.00	12.00	12.00	12.00
Potassium (2 to 5%)	7.50	5.00	5.00	5.00	5.00
Sodium (.5 to 3%)	1.00	0.75	0.75	0.75	0.75
Other Bases (Variable)	4.00	3.75	3.75	3.75	3.75

	1	2	3	4	5
EXCHANGEABLE HYDROGEN (10 to 15%)	7.50	10.50	10.50	10.50	10.50
Chlorides (p.p.m.)	60.00	80.00	80.00	80.00	80.00
Boron (p.p.m.)	1.00	1.20	1.50	1.50	1.50
Iron (p.p.m.)	200.00	300.00	300.00	300.00	300.00
Manganese (p.p.m.)	135.00	200.00	200.00	200.00	200.00
Copper (p.p.m.)	5.00	5.00	5.00	5.00	5.00
Zinc (p.p.m.)	15.00	15.00	15.00	15.00	15.00

Common Measurements and Equivalents

One pinch or dash	= $^1/_{16}$ teaspoon	1 gill	= $^1/_2$ cup (4 ounces liquid)
1 teaspoon	= 60 drops	1 cup	= 16 tablespoons (8 ounces liquid)
1 tablespoon	= 180 drops	1 pint	= 2 cups (16 ounces liquid)
1 ounce	= 360 drops	1 quart	= 2 pints (32 ounces liquid)
1 teaspoon	= $^1/_6$ ounce	4 quarts	= 1 gallon
1 tablespoon	= 3 teaspoons ($^1/_2$ ounce liquid)	1 gallon	= 4 quarts
		1 gallon	= 16 pints
1 gallon	= 769 teaspoons	1 gallon	= 32 cups
4 tablespoons	= $^1/_4$ cup (2 ounces liquid)	1 peck	= 8 quarts
$^1/_3$ cup	= 5 tablespoons plus 1 teaspoon	1 bushel	= 4 pecks
		1 pound	= 16 ounces (dry measure)
$^1/_2$ cup	= 8 tablespoons (4 ounces liquid)	1 sq. yd.	= 9 sq. ft.
		1 cu. yd.	= 27 cu. ft.

Linear Measure

1 foot	= 12 inches
1 hand	= $^1/_3$ foot = 4 inches
1 span	= 9 inches
1 yard	= 3 feet
1 rod	= 16$^1/_2$ feet = 5$^1/_2$ yards
1 furlong	= 40 poles = 220 yards
1 mile	= 8 furlongs 1760 yards = 5280 feet = 320 rods
1 league	= 3 miles
1 degree	= 69 $^1/_8$ miles

Square or Area Measure

1 square foot	= 144 square inches
1 square yard	= 9 square feet
1 acre	= 160 square rods = 43,560 sq. ft.
1 section	= 640 acres = 1 square mile

Cubic or Volume Measure

A legal cord of wood is 4 feet high, 4 feet wide, and 8 feet long.

1 cubic foot	= 1728 cubic inches
1 cubic yard	= 27 cubic feet
1 cord of wood	= 128 cubic feet
1 board foot	= 144 cubic inches = $^1/_{12}$ cubic foot

Liquid or Fluid Measure

1 pint (pt)	= 2 cups
1 quart (qt.)	= 2 pints
1 gallon (gal.)	= 4 quarts
1 barrel (bbl.)	= 31$^1/_2$ gallons
1 acre foot	= 325,000 gallons

Dry Measure

1 quart	= 2 pints
1 peck	= 8 quarts
1 bushel (bu.)	= 4 pecks

Metric Equivalents (Linear)

1 millimeter (mm)	= .0394 in.
1 centimeter (cm)	= .3937 in.
1 decimeter (dm)	= 3.937 in.
1 meter (m)	= 39.37 in. = 1.1 yard
1 decameter	= 393.7 in. = 10 yd. 2.8 ft.
1 hectometer	= 328 ft. 1 in.
1 kilometer	= 3280 ft. 1 in.

Common Equivalents

1 bushel	= 2150 cubic inches or 1$^1/_4$ cubic feet
1 gallon	= 231 cubic inches
1 cubic foot	= 7$^1/_2$ gallons
1 cubic foot of water	= 62$^1/_2$ pounds (62.43 lb.)
1 gallon of water	= 8$^1/_3$ pounds (8.345 lb.)
1 cubic foot of ice	= 57$^1/_2$ pounds

Application Rates

Bulk Material

1 cu. ft. equals	1 cu. yd. equals 3 cu. ft. bag	Bagged material	2 cu. ft. bag
12 sq. ft. 1″ deep	1296 sq. ft. ¼″ deep	36 sq. ft. 1″ deep	96 sq. ft. ¼″ deep
6 sq. ft. 2″ deep	648 sq. ft. ½″ deep	18 sq. ft. 2″ deep	48 sq. ft. ½″ deep
4 sq. ft. 3″ deep	324 sq. ft. 1″ deep	12 sq. ft. 3″ deep	24 sq. ft. 1″ deep
3 sq. ft. 4″ deep	162 sq. ft. 2″ deep	9 sq. ft. 4″ deep	12 sq. ft. 2″ deep
	108 sq. ft. 3″ deep		8 sq. ft. 3″ deep
	81 sq. ft. 4″ deep		6 sq. ft. 4″ deep

Dilution Chart

Gallons of Water

Dilution	1 Qt.	1 Gal.	3 Gal.	5 Gal.	10 Gal.	15 Gal.
1-10	3 oz.	12 oz.	2¼ pts.	2 qts.	3¾ qts.	5½ qts.
1-50	4 t.	5 T.	7½ oz.	12½ oz.	25 oz.	37½ oz.
1-80	1 T.	2 oz.	6 oz.	10 oz.	20 oz.	30 oz.
1-100	2 t.	2½ T.	3½ oz.	6¼ oz.	12½ oz.	19 oz.
1-200	1 t.	4 t.	2 oz.	3½ oz.	6½ oz.	10 oz.
1-400	½ t.	2 t.	2 T.	1½ oz.	3 oz.	5 oz.
1-800	—	1 t.	1 T.	5 t.	1½ oz.	2½ oz.

Soil Nutrient Availability

	Low	Normal	High	Very High
Calcium	< 20%	20 – 60	60 – 80	> 80
Magnesium	< 10%	10 – 25	25 – 35	> 35
Potassium	< 5%	5 – 20	20 – 30	> 30
Phosphorus	< .1%	.1 – .4	.5 – .8	> .8
Nitrogen	< 1 ppm	1 – 10	10 – 20	> 20
Nitrate	< 5 ppm	5 – 50	50 – 100	> 100
Sulfate	< 30 ppm	30 – 90	90 – 180	> 180
Sulfur	< 10 ppm	10 – 30	30 – 60	> 60

Percent represents available percentages in the soil, ppm represents parts per million

Glossary

Acid cation. A cation that tends to increase soil acidity. In practice, aluminum and hydrogen are the only significant acid cations.

Acid soil. Soils with a pH less than 7. If the pH is near 6, a soil is considered slightly or moderately acid; if below 5.5, it is very acidic.

Actinomycetes. A white fungus-like soil microorganism important in the decay of organic matter.

Aeration. A mechanical process of punching holes used to relieve the effects of soil compaction.

Aerobic. An environment containing oxygen. In the soil, aerobic conditions favor organisms that oxidize organic residues and produce carbon dioxide as a major byproduct.

Agrispon. A mineral and plant extract product that stimulates microorganisms and basic soil and plant functions. Manufactured in Texas by Appropriate Technologies.

Alkaline soil. Soils with a pH greater than 7.

Amino acids. The building blocks of proteins. They are made up primarily from nitrogen and carbohydrates, but many also contain sulfur, phosphorus, and other minerals.

Ammonium nitrate 33-0-0 (N_4NO_3). A water soluble chemical compound containing approximately 33.5% nitrogen, one half of which is in the ammonia form and one half in the nitrate form.

Ammonium phosphate. A solid fertilizer material manufactured by reacting ammonia with phosphoric acid.

Ammonium sulfate 21-0-0 ((NH_4)$_2$$SO_4$). A solid material manufactured by reacting ammonia with sulfuric acid.

Anaerobic. Without oxygen. Anaerobic decomposition is less efficient than aerobic organisms. Nitrogen fixation by free-living organisms usually occurs under anaerobic conditions.

Anhydrous ammonia 82-0-0 (NH_3). A gas containing approximately 82% nitrogen. Under pressure, ammonia gas is changed to a liquid and usually is stored and transported in this form. Anhydrous ammonia is used to make most of the solid forms of nitrogenous fertilizers and also is used for direct application to the soil either as a gas or in the form of aqua ammonia. The most soil-destructive fertilizer in the world.

Anion. An ion with a negative electrical charge. Sulfur, phosphorus, boron, chlorine, and molybdenum exist in the soil as anions.

Anion exchange. A condition, analogous to cation exchange, where one anion can replace another at the surface of a clay mineral.

Antidesiccants. Liquid sprays used to coat the foliage of plants for the purpose of reducing transpiration in hot weather and increasing cold tolerance in winter.

Bacillus thuringiensis (Bt). Biological insecticides that specifically target caterpillars and other problem insects.

Banding fertilizer. The process of spreading fertilizer in bands rather than broadcasting it. The fertilizer may be spread along a line about two inches to the side of a planted seed and sometimes two inches below. It is considered one of the best methods for using commercial soluble fertilizers, especially phosphorus.

Base cations. A cation that tends to increase the soil pH. In practice the term is restricted to calcium, magnesium, and potassium.

Bat guano. Bat droppings.

Biodiversity. Biodiversity of life is not just important, it's critical. The outstanding characteristics of nature are variety and dynamic stability. A healthy situation exists when we create ranches, farms, gardens, and landscapes that have a complex mix of microorganisms, insects, animals, and plants. To understand nature is to grasp the concept that nature is a whole and can't be subdivided. Everything relates to everything else.

Biostimulant. Organic products, usually liquids, used to stimulate soil microbiotic activity. Examples include Medina, Agrispon, Agri-Gro.

Blood meal. A dry organic fertilizer made from the blood from slaughterhouses. Normal analysis will be approximately 12-0-0.

Bone meal. Cooked bones ground to a meal without any of the gelatin or glue removed. Steamed bone meal has been steamed under pressure to dissolve and remove part of the gelatin.

Borax ($Na_2B_4O_7 \cdot 10H_2O$). A salt (sodium borate) used in fertilizer as a source of the minor plant food element boron. Borax contains about 11% of the element boron. It is available in food stores and is a suitable fertilizer for supplying boron.

Bordeaux mix. A fungicide and insecticide made by mixing solutions of copper sulfate and lime or of copper arsenate and phenols. Use the first one.

Buffer capacity. The degree to which a substance can resist changes in its characteristics.

Burned lime. Limestone heated to drive out carbon dioxide. Same as quicklime.

Calcareous. Containing calcium or calcian carbonate.

Calcite. Limestone containing mostly calcium carbonate, $CaCO_3$. A more common name is ground agricultural limestone.

Calcium carbonate ($CaCO_3$). The principal component of calcitic limestone and one of the principal components of dolomitic limestone, of which magnesium carbonate, $MgCO_3$, is the other. Marl and oyster shells also are composed primarily of calcium carbonate.

Carbohydrates. Stabilized structures of sugars. Carbohydrates form the skeleton of the plant, and they are a means for storing energy for a long period of time.

Cation. An ion with a positive electrical charge. Calcium, magnesium, potassium, copper, iron, manganese, and zinc exist in the soil as cations. Nitrogen may be present either as a cation (ammonium) or as an anion (nitrate).

Cation exchange. A process in which the small number of cations dissolved in the soil water (soluble cations) change place with the much larger number of cations associated with the soil micelles (exchangeable cations).

Cation exchange capacity. A measure of the ability of the soil components to attract cations and hold them in exchangeable form. The exchange capacity depends upon the amount of clay, the type of clay, the organic content, and the degree of humification of the organic matter.

CEC. An abbreviation for Cation Exchange Capacity.

Chelation. The chemical process by which an organic substance binds a cation having more than one electrical charge. Chelation is similar to cation exchange. Cation exchange holds the majority of the major cation nutrients (calcium, magnesium, potassium), while chelation holds the cation trace elements (copper, iron, manganese, zinc).

Clippings. Leaves cut off by mowing.

C/N ratio. An abbreviation for Carbon/Nitrogen ratio.

Colloidal. A state of matter where finely divided particles of one substance are suspended in another.

Colloidal phosphate. Waste material from rock phosphate mining operation. An excellent slow-release source of phosphorus, calcium, and trace elements.

Compaction. The pressing together of soil particles by foot or vehicular traffic.

Companion planting. Using plants together that differ from each other but assist one another with insect and disease control.

Compost. Nature's fertilizer created by the rotting of vegetable and animal matter.

Composted manure. Animal manure that has been taken through the process of natural composting in order to kill pathogens and weed seed.

Cool-season turfgrass. Those turfgrasses primarily used in the northern United States, such as Kentucky bluegrass, tall fescue, and ryegrass.

Copperas ($FeSO_4 \cdot 7H_2O$). Ferrous (iron) sulfate used as a trace nutrient fertilizer, especially in alkaline soils.

Copper sulfate ($CuSO_4 \cdot 5H_2O$). Most common source of copper for fertilizer. Also used as an insecticide and fungicide. A common name is blue vitriol.

Cottonseed meal. Fertilizer meal made from ground cottonseed.

Cover crop. A crop that improves the soil on which it is grown. Many plants are sown primarily as cover crops to cover the ground, improve it, and protect it for a succeeding cash crop. Other plants, such as alfalfa, clover, and most grass-legume sods, can serve as both a cash crop and a cover crop.

Cross-pollinate. To apply pollen of a male flower to the stigma or female part of another flower.

Curculio, plum. Worm that attacks the fruit of plums and other orchard trees.

Cutting height. The distance between the ground and the blades of the mower.

Cyanobacteria. Blue-green algae, a form able to fix nitrogen from the air.

Cytokinin. A plant hormone that can modify plant development by stimulating or altering the cellular RNA.

D-E. Abbreviation for diatomaceous earth.

Damping off. A disease of seeds and young seedlings caused by fungi.

Denitrification. The conversion of nitrates in the soil to some form of gaseous nitrogen, which escapes into the atmosphere and is lost.

Diacide. Organic insecticide made primarily from diatomaceous earth and natural pyrethrum.

Diammonium phosphate (21-53-0). A solid fertilizer material made by reacting ammonia with phosphoric acid.

Diatomaceous earth (D-E). An off-white dust from skeletal remains of diatoms. Used as an insecticide and food supplement. Diatomaceous earth is very absorptive and abrasive.

Dicotyledon (dicot). A plant with two seed leaves.

Dioecious. Plants that have the male reproductive system on one plant and the female on another.

DNA. (Deoxyribonucleic acid). Nucleic acid found in all living cells.

Dolomite. A material used for liming soils in areas where magnesium as well as calcium are needed. Made by grinding dolomitic limestone that contains both magnesium carbonate, $MgCO_3$, and calcium carbonate, $CaCO_3$.

Dormant oil. Petroleum-based oil used for smothering overwinter insects such as scale.

Dormant turf. A brown-colored turf that has temporarily ceased growth due to unfavorable environmental conditions.

Earthworm castings. Earthworm droppings

Epiphytic. Referring to plants growing without soil and receiving their nutrients from the air.

Epsom salts. Magnesium sulfate. It is used as a fast acting source of magnesium and sulfur normally used as a foliar feed.

Exchangeable cations. Those cations that are electrostatically attracted to soil particles. The sum of the exchangeable cations and the soluble cations are considered to constitute the available cations for plant take up.

Exudates. Root system discharge materials.

Fertigation. The application of fertilizer through an irrigation system.

Fertilaid. An organic fertilizer made from slaughterhouse waste such as bone meal, blood meal. Product claims to contain living microorganisms. (4-2-0).

Fertilizer. Any material or mixture used to supply one or more soil or plant nutrients.

Fish emulsion. An oily liquid fertilizer made from fish waste or whole fish.

Flowers of sulfur. Finely granulated sulfur dust used to acidify an alkaline soil.

Foliar burn. An injury to the leaves of the plant caused by the application of a fertilizer or pesticide.

Foliar spray. Liquid plant nutrients applied by spraying on the foliage.

Footprinting. Discolored areas, or impressions, left in the lawn from foot traffic when the turf is in the first stage of wilt.

French drain. A drainage device in which a hole or trench is backfilled with sand or gravel.

Fungicide. A product used to control diseases caused by fungi.

Geotropism. The effect of gravity on plants.

Granite sand. Sand made from weathered or ground-up granite rock.

Green manure. A cover crop used to smother weeds, to protect the soil, and to hold nutrients that might otherwise be leached. Traditionally a green manure is planted after the harvest of a cash crop, but an alternative is a "living mulch," where a cover crop is sown before harvesting the cash crop.

Greensand. A material called glauconite that is a naturally deposited undersea, iron potassium silicate. It's an excellent source of potash with a normal analysis of 0-1-5. It's best used with other fertilizers.

Guano. Decomposed dried excrement of birds and bats and is used for fertilizer purposes. The most commonly known guano comes from islands off the coast of Peru and is derived from the excrement of sea fowl. It is high in nitrogen and phosphate, and at one time was a major fertilizer in this country.

Gumosis. Stress-related gumming of the vessels in fruit trees. Sometimes caused by the chloride in (KCl) potassium chloride. Potassium sulfate (KSO_4) will not cause the problem.

Gypsum. ($CaSO_4 \cdot 2H_2O$). The common name for calcium sulfate, a mineral used in the fertilizer industry as a source of calcium and sulfur. It is a good source of sulfur and is also used to improve alkaline soils having a high sodium content.

Hay. Grass, clover, or the like that is cut while still green and used as a fodder or mulch.

Herbicide. A product used for weed control.

Humus. The Latin word for *soil* or *earth*. It is the broken-down form or organic matter.

Hydrogen peroxide. (H_2O_2). An oxygenating compound used for soil conditioning and bacteria fighting.

Hydromulching. A method of seeding using a mixture of seed, fertilizer, and mulch sprayed in a solution on the soil surface.

Hydroseeding. Same as hydromulching but without the mulch.

Hydrosprigging. Same as hydromulching but uses sprigs instead of seed.

Ion. An electrostatically charged atom formed when a salt is dissolved in water. The dissolved salt breaks up into both positively and negatively charged ions.

Ionic charge. The electrical charge associated with ions. Cations have a positive electrical charge and anions a negative charge.

Insecticide. A product used to control insects.

Integrated pest management. Buzz word for using a little bit of organics and a varying bit of chemicals.

Irrigation, automatic. An irrigation system using preset timing devices.

Langbeinite. Sul-Po-Mag.

Layering, soil. An undesirable stratification of a soil.

Leaching. The movement (usually loss) of dissolved nutrients as water percolates through the soil.

Leather tankage. Waste from the leather tanning industry.

Lignin. Works with cellulose to form the woody cell walls of plants.

Lime. Technically, lime is calcium oxide. In agricultural usage, however, the term is used to denote any liming material.

Lime sulfur. Organic pesticide used for disease control.

Localized dry spot. An area of soil that resists wetting.

Magnesia. Magnesium oxide used as an emergency source of magnesium.

Magnesium sulfate. ($MgSO_4 \cdot H_2O$). A soluble salt used as a source of magnesium. Common forms are the mineral kieserite and Epsom salts.

Manalfa. Organic fertilizer made from a blend of livestock manure and alfalfa.

Manganese sulfate. ($MnSO_4 \cdot H_2O$). A solid chemical compound used as a source of manganese for plants.

Manure. Manure most commonly refers to animal dung, but the term is also used in association with green manuring.

Meq/100 g. The unit of measure of cation exchange capacity and exchangeable cations. It is shorthand for "milli-equivalents of exchangeable cations per 100 grams of soil." A milli-equivalent is $1/100$ of an equivalent, and an equivalent is the quantity of a cation that will exchange with one gram of hydrogen ions.

Micelle. Shorthand for micro-cell. It refers to a colloidal clay or humus particle with many negative electrical charges. It attracts positively charged cations.

Milorganite. Sewer sludge fertilizer from Milwaukee.

Mineral oil. Oil made from refined petroleum products.

Molybdenum. One of the essential micronutrients.

Monoammonium sulfate. Synthetic fertilizer containing phosphorus, sulfur, and ammonia. 11-48-0.

Monoecious. Plants that have male and female flowers on the same plant.

Monovalent. An ion, either an anion or cation, carrying a single electrical charge.

Multivalent. An ion carrying more than one electrical charge. Chelation can only bind multivalent cations.

Muriate of potash (KCl). The principal source of potassium for synthetic fertilizer. Potassium chloride, usually is sold on the basis of a material containing 95%–99% KCl, with a K_2O equivalent of 60%–62%.

Mycorrhizae. Fungi that penetrates roots of plants to extract carbohydrates. Its unique value is that in return it passes mineral nutrients to the plant. It can be a major source of available phosphorus. It is similar to the rhizobia bacteria that inhabit legume roots and fix nitrogen.

Nectar. A sweet liquid secreted by plants. The main raw material of honey.

Nematodes. Small hair-like organisms that attack root systems and other soil-borne organisms.

Nitrate inhibitors. Substances that retard the ability of soil organisms to transform ammonium to nitrates. Their purpose is to avoid the denitrification that occurs with heavy fertilizer applications of urea, ammonium salts, or liquid ammonia.

Nitrate of soda. Sodium nitrate ($NaNO_3$). A fertilizer material containing approximately 16% nitrogen. The principal source of sodium nitrate has been the natural deposits of the salt in Chile. It is also produced synthetically.

Nitrification. A process that takes place in the soil whereby soil microorganisms form nitrates from organic matter and the ammonia forms of nitrogen.

NPK. A shorthand notation for "Nitrogen-Phosphate-Potash."

Open pollinated. Unlike hybrids, plants that will return true from seed.

Organic matter. Organic substances in differing stages of decay, varying from litter to very stable humus.

Osmosis. Diffusion of fluid through a membrane.

Overseeding. Seeding a dormant turf with a cool-season grass in order to provide color during the winter.

Parthenocarpic. Organisms that don't need to be pollinated to reproduce.

Peat. A low-quality humus in which the nitrogen is completely lost through anaerobic fermentation.

Pesticide. A chemical used to control any turfgrass pest such as weeds, insects, and diseases.

pH. An abbreviation for potential hydrogen. It is used chemically to express the hydrogen ion concentration of a solution. More simply, pH is a scale from 1 to 14, used to denote the relative intensity of acidity or alkalinity. A neutral solution or soil has a pH of 7.0. Values below 7.0 denote more acid conditions and those above 7.0 more alkaline conditions.

Phosphate. The fertilizer oxide form of phosphorus (P_2O_5).

Phosphoric acid. 0-52-0 to 0-55-0 (H_3PO_4). An inorganic acid used in the manufacture of concentrated calcium phosphates, ammonium phosphates, and sometimes for direct application through irrigation water.

Phytophthora. Latin name for a genus of fungi that causes plant dis- ease, generally a root and crown rot pathogen.

Photosynthesis. Nature's process of manufacturing carbohydrates from carbon dioxide (CO_2) and water (H_2O) with the use of light energy and green plant pigment called chlorophyll.

Plant metabolism. Those functions of a plant that use energy stored in sugars and carbohydrates to enable the plant to grow and reproduce.

Plugging. Establishing a turfgrass using plugs of sod.

Pollen. A mass of microspores in a seed plant. Looks like a fine dust.

Polysaccharides. Carbohydrates (complex sugars) of high molecular weight including starch and cellulose.

Potash. A term used to denote the potassium oxide (K_2O) equivalent of materials containing potassium.

Potassium chloride. 0-60-0 (KCl). Muriate of potash.

Potassium magnesium sulfate. ($2MgSO_4K_2SO_4$). Also called Sul-Po-Mag and langbeinite. From natural salt deposits primarily in New Mexico and some European countries. Organic source of K, Mg, and S.

Potassium sulfate. (K_2SO_4). A solid material with a K_2O equivalent of 45%–52%. Also called sulfate of potash.

Proteins. The active, amino acid components of a growing plant. Proteins carry out the bodily activities of the plant using the energy from sugars and carbohydrates.

Protozoa. One-celled microscopic animals.

Pyrethrum. Natural insecticide made from the powder of the crushed painted daisy. *Chrysanthemum cinerariaefolium.*

Quicklime. Burned lime, roasted to drive out carbon dioxide and increase the solubility.

Reel mower. A mower that cuts grass by means of a reel guiding the leaves against the cutting edge of the bedknife.

Renovation. Improving the vigor of a low-quality soil.

Rhizobia. A group of bacteria that penetrates the roots of legumes, extracting carbohydrates from the plant, and capable of fixing atmospheric nitrogen.

Rhizome. A below-ground stem capable of producing a new plant.

Rhizoshere. The soil area immediately adjacent to the root hairs of plants.

Rock powders. Naturally occurring materials with fertilizing value. The most common rock powders are limestone, rock phosphate, granite dust, greensand, langbeinite (sulfate of potash magnesia), and basalt.

Root nodules. Nodules attached to the roots of legumes and certain non-legumes. These nodules contain nitrogen-fixing bacteria or nematodes.

Rotary mower. A mower that cuts grass with a high-speed blade that runs parallel to the soil surface.

Rotenone. Natural insecticide made from the extract of a certain plant root.

Sabadilla. Natural insecticide made from the extract of a tropical lily.

Salt index. The relation of solubilities of chemical compounds. Most nitrogen and potash compounds have a high index, and phosphate compounds have a low index. When applied too close to seed or on foliage, the ones with high indexes can cause plants to wilt or die.

Scald. Grass that dies under "standing water."

Scalping. The excessive removal of leaves during mowing, leaving mostly stems.

Seaweed. Saltwater plants used for fertilizer.

Secondary elements. The secondary plant food elements as traditionally defined are calcium, magnesium, and sulfur.

Silicon. A nonmetallic element that is the most abundant element next to oxygen in the earth's crust.

Slag. A byproduct of steel, containing lime, phosphate, and small amounts of other plant food elements such as sulfur, manganese, and iron.

Soap. A cleansing and emulsifying agent made by action of alkali on fat or fatty acids.

Sod. Plugs, squares, or strips of turf still connected to soil.

Soft rock phosphate. Colloidal rock phosphate. A byproduct of rock phosphate mining.

Soil. An ecological system consisting of inorganic minerals, organic matter, and living organisms.

Soil pH. The pH of the water in soil. It controls the availability of phosphorus and trace elements and the diversity of soil organisms. The soil pH for most soils is in the range 5.0 to 9.0, with 7.0 being neutral.

Soil structure. The distribution and size of aggregates in the soil. A good soil structure contains aggregates of widely varying size.

Sprigging. Establishing a lawn using sprigs or stolons.

Stolon. An above-ground stem capable of growing a new plant.

Straw. The aboveground vegetative growth of a plant, usually a small grain or annual legume.

Sugar. The direct product of photosynthesis. Sugars store the energy absorbed from the sun in the plant leaves.

Sulfate of potash-magnesia. ($2MgSO_4 \cdot K_2SO_4$). A naturally occurring solid material, also called langbeinite, found in salt deposits primarily in New Mexico and in several European countries. The commercial product usually has a K_2O equivalent of about 21%, and contains 53% magnesium sulfate and not more than $2^1/_2$% chlorine. It is used in fertilizer as a source of both potash and magnesium.

Sulfur. Normally referred to as a secondary element. It is actually a primary nutrient and is critical in the synthesis of proteins.

Sul-Po-Mag. Mined material consisting of sulfur, potassium, and magnesium. (See sulfate of potash-magnesia).

Superphosphate. The first manufactured phosphorus fertilizer, prepared originally by dissolving bones in sulfuric acid. 0-18-0 to 0-20-0.

Superphosphoric acid. 0-67-0 to 0-76-0.

Tankage. Process tankage is made from leather scrap, wool, and other inert nitrogenous materials by steaming under pressure with or without addition of acid. This treatment increases the availability of the nitrogen to plants.

Thatch. A layer or organic matter that develops between the soil and the base of the plant.

Top-dressing. Spreading a thin layer of soil on the lawn to smooth the surface.

Transition zone. An east-west zone through the middle of the U.S. between the northern area, growing cold-season turfgrasses, and the southern area, growing warm-season turfgrasses.

Triple superphosphate. Rock phosphate dissolved in phosphoric acid.

Urea. 45-0-0 - $CO(NH_2)_2$. A solid synthetic organic material containing approximately 45% nitrogen.

Urea-form. Synthetic fertilizer (38-0-0).

Vertical mowing. The use of a mechanical device that has vertically rotating blades for thatch control.

Vitamin. Organic substances that are essential in tiny quantities to the nutrition of most plants and animals.

Volatilization. The process of liquid becoming a gas.

Warm-season turfgrass. Those turfgrasses used primarily in the southern United States, such as bermudagrass, St. Augustinegrass, zoysiagrass, centipedegrass, and buffalograss.

Wilt. The discoloration and folding of leaves caused by either excessively dry or excessively wet conditions.

Zinc sulfate. ($ZnSO_4 \cdot 7H_2O$). White vitriol, a solid material used as a source of zinc.

Resources

A Field Guide To Texas Snakes by Alan Tennant is the best basic guide for snakes found in Texas. Gulf Publishing Company.

A Field Guide To Texas Trees by Benny Simpson is a very complete book and an excellent tool for Texas tree identification. Gulf Publishing Company.

Acres USA Primer - by Charles Walters is one of the best overall guides on organics. Acres USA.

Agriculture Testament and **Soil and Health** by Sir Alfred Howard. These state-of-the-art guides to organics and using compost to bring soil back to health were written in the 1940s, but are still two of the best publications on the market. Oxford and Rodale Press.

Birder's Guide to Texas by Edward A. Kutac is the best basic guide for birds in Texas. Gulf Publishing Company.

Bread from Stones by Julius Hensel is a classic explaining the role of earth minerals in the production of wholesome food crops. Acres USA.

Common Sense Pest Control by William Olkowski, Shiela Daar, Helga Olkowski is an excellent reference for low toxicity pest control. The Taunton Press.

Growing Fruits, Berries & Nuts Southwest-Southeast by Dr. George Ray McEachern is an excellent book on selecting and growing pecans, fruit trees, and berry plants. Gulf Publishing Company.

Herb Gardening in Texas, Second Edition by Sol Meltzer is the best introduction to growing herbs in Texas. Gulf Publishing Company.

How To Grow Native Plants of Texas and the Southwest by Jill Nokes is the best book available on propagation of native Texas plants. Gulf Publishing Company.

How to Have a Green Thumb Without an Aching Back, Exposition Press, **Gardening Without Work,** Devin-Adair, and **The No Work Gardening Book,** Rodale Press, by Ruth Stout are great. She is a humorous writer, a philosopher, and an advocate of mulching. They are hard to find as are Sir Alfred Howard's books, but the Tracery in Dallas can usually track them down for you.

Introduction To Soil Microbiology -Second Edition by Martin Alexander. John Wiley & Sons.

Know It and Grow It II by Dr. Carl Whitcomb is an excellent general reference for plant materials of the south. Lacebark Press.

Landscape Design . . . Texas Style by Howard Garrett. This book is a well-kept secret about my design and landscape philosophy as well as a rather decent reference book on landscape construction and regional plant material selection. Taylor Publishing.

Let It Rot by Stu Campbell explains the art of composting in clear and easy to read instructions. This is the best book on composting I have found. Garden Way Publishing.

Native Texas Plants: Landscaping Region by Region by Sally and Andy Wasowski is an excellent tool for use in selecting and using native Texas plant materials. Gulf Publishing Company.

Natural Insect Repellents for Pets and People by Connie Moore and Janette Grainger is a clear and simple guide to using herbs and other organic techniques for pet care. Published by The Herb Bar.

Nature's Silent Music by Dr. Phil Callahan explains how to preserve the health of the land by avoiding toxic chemicals and working within nature's laws and systems. Acres USA.

Odena's Texas Herb Book, Lavender Hill Cook Book, Little Sprout (for children), **Saffron: Spice of Kings** by Odena G. Brannam. Lavender Hill Herb Farm.

Organic Gardening Magazine is the oldest reference on organic gardening. Joe and Robert Rodale are both now dead but their book and inspiration live on.

Perennial Garden Color by Dr. William C. Welch is the best basic guide for the selection and use of perennials in Texas. Taylor Publishing.

Plants of the Metroplex III by J. Howard Garrett covers organic planting techniques and the recommended trees, shrubs, groundcovers, vines, herbs, and flowers of Texas. Lantana Publishing.

Rodale's Color Handbook of Garden Insects by Anna Carr is a field guide of practical information for gardeners, farmers, and homeowners. Rodale Press, Inc.

Rodale's Garden Problem Solver by Jim Ball addresses more than 700 specific gardening problems and answers thousands of general gardening questions on insect and animal pests, weeds, propagation and diseases. Rodale Press, Inc.

Roses Love Garlic and **Carrots Love Tomatoes** both by Louise Riotte. **Carrots Love Tomatoes** shows you how to arrange your garden for the most complementary relationships. Topics included are flower and vegetable interplanting, plants that deter insects and diseases, and planting to keep weeds down. **Roses Love Garlic** explains companion planting with flowers. It tells you how to combine flower and vegetable gardens, introduces you to many unique plants, and explains how to use them. Garden Way Publishing.

Seaweed and Plant Growth by Dr. T. L. Senn explains in detail the wonderful powers of seaweed as a fertilizer and root stimulator. It explains how seaweed can be used as a supplement to the fertilization program to improve plant resistance to stress of all kinds, including cold tolerance. Senn.

Shepherd's Purse Organic Pest Control Book is an excellent book on organic insect control. It is available through The Book Publishing Company in Summertown, TN.

Silent Spring, by Rachel Carson. If you don't convert to organics after reading this classic, you never will. The Riverside Press, Cambridge.

Soil Fertility by Robert Parnes, Ph.D., is a comprehensive technical reference manual that explains using a non-chemical fertilizer program to create and maintain healthy, balanced soil. AgAccess.

Southern Herb Growing by Madalene Hill and Gwen Barclay is an excellent book on general herb growing. It includes color photos, cultural needs and uses of over 130 herbs. It also contains recipes. Shearer Publishing.

The Albrecht Papers by William Albrecht, are a compilation of a series of papers by the late Dr. Albrecht and are the bible for managing soil health. Acres USA.

The Basic Book of Organic Gardening by Rodale includes the definition of an organic gardener, the

secrets of the best organic gardeners, alternatives to insecticides and
vegetable gardening information.
Rodale Press, Inc.

The Bug Book by John and Helen
Philbrick is an excellent little reference book on organic insect control
with emphasis on how to take
advantage of beneficial bugs. Garden Way Publishing.

The Chemical Free Lawn Care by
Warren Shultz is a book offering
detailed information on how to
establish and maintain lawns using
organic techniques. It's a well-writ-
ten and easy-to-follow book on nontoxic alternatives. Rodale Press, Inc.

**The Complete Guide to Texas Lawn
Care** by Dr. William E. Knoop is a
very thorough turf reference book
for the south. T G Press.

**The Encyclopedia of Natural Insect
& Disease Control** is a comprehensive reference on controlling insects
and diseases in the garden, orchard,
and yard without chemicals. Rodale
Press, Inc.

**The Encyclopedia of Organic Gar-
dening** is a comprehensive book
covering everything from bee keeping to vegetables, including information on nearly 700 fruits, flowers,
vegetables, and ornamentals. Rodale
Press, Inc.

**The Garden-Ville Method (Lessons
in Nature)** is written by my mentor
and the king of compost, Malcolm
Beck, one of the most knowledge-
able people on organics in the country. Beck.

The Herb Garden Cookbook by
Lucinda Hutson is not only a great
cookbook but also has excellent
basic information on the culture of
herbs. Gulf Publishing Company.

The One-Straw Revolution by
Masanoku Fukuoka is a wonderful
introductory book to natural farming. Rodale Press, Inc.

The Secret Garden by Frances Hodg-
son Burnett. For children of all ages,
this delightful book introduces the
reader to the magic of nature.
Alfred A. Knopf, Inc.

The Soil of the Ghost Moth, by Dr.
Phil Callahan explains why insects
are attracted to plants. Acres USA.

The Soul of the Soil by Grace Ger-
shuny and Joseph Smillie is a little
book that's a nice guide to ecological soil management. GAIA Services.

The Vegetable Book by Dr. Sam Cot-
ner is quite simply the best book
available on growing veggies in
Texas. T G Press.

Weeds Control Without Poisons by
Charles Walters. A thorough review
and explanation of how to control
weeds through soil management.
Acres U.S.A.

General Sources

Acres USA. A monthly newspaper
that covers organic agriculture, ecological farming, and bio-dynamics.
P.O. Box 9547, Kansas City, MO
64133, 816-737-0064.

All Natural. A mail order catalog for
organic products, 13600 Murphy
Rd., Stafford, Texas 77477, 713-499-
8461.

Bat Conservancy International. P.O.
Box 162063, Austin, Texas 78716,
Merlin Tuttle, Bert Grantges.

Bio-Integral Resource Center (B.I.R.C.).
Box 7414 Berkeley, CA 94707. This is
the source of legitimate Integrated
Pest Management information.

Other groups and institutions have often misused the term.

Gardens Alive. A quarterly magazine and mail order catalog for organic techniques and products. Natural Gardening Research Center, Hwy 48, P.O. Box 149, Sunman, IN 47041.

Holistic Resource Management is an international nonprofit organization helping people learn how to stop the desertification of the planet. Alan Savory is the founder and he and his staff teach regular courses on holistic management. P.O. Box 7128, Albuquerque, New Mexico 87194, 1-800-654-3619.

Lavender Hill Herb Farm, 8755 Quinn Dallas, TX 75227

National Wildflower Research Center. A nonprofit organization dedicated to the re-establishment of native vegetation in Texas. 2600 FM 973 North, Austin, Texas 78725, 512-929-3600.

Native Plant Society of Texas. Box 891, Georgetown, Texas 78626.

Natural Food Associates P.O. Box 210, Atlanta, Texas 75551, 1-800-594-2136

Rodale Press. Publishers and editors of many books on organics and related subjects including the monthly magazine *Organic Gardening*. 33 East Minor Street, Emmaus, Pennsylvania 18098.

Texas Department of Agriculture. Austin, Texas, 512-463-7536.

Texas Horticulturist. A monthly horticultural newspaper published by the Texas Pecan Growers Association, 4348 Carter Creek, Suite 101, Bryan, Texas 77802, 409-846-3285.

Texas Organic Grower's Association (TOGA) The state organization of organic producers.

Specialty Organic Growers and Suppliers

Biofac (Beneficial insects) 512-547-3259, P.O. Box 87, Mathis, Texas 78368.

Bio Insect Control (Beneficial insects) 806-293-5861, 710 S. Columbia, Plainview, Texas 79072.

Biome, P. O. Box 6706, Houston, TX, 77082, 1-800-998-1701.

Biosys (Organic products) 415-856-9500, 1057 E. Meadow Circle, Palo Alto, CA 94303.

Blue Cottage Herb Farm (Herbs) 903-498-4234, Rt. 1 Box 1075 Kaufman, Texas 75142.

Burpee Seed Company, 215-674-4900, 300 Park Avenue, Warminster, PA 18974.

Herbal Gems (Herbs) 214-876-2130, Box 775, Frankston, Texas 75763.

Integrated Pest Management, 818-287-1101, 305 Agostino Road, San Gabriel, CA 91776.

Johnston Seed Co. (Native Seed) P.O. Box 1392, 411 West Chestnut, Enid, Oklahoma 73702.

M&R Durango (Beneficial insects) 800-526-4075, P.O. Box 886, Bayfield, Colorado 81122.

Native American Seed Co. (Buffalograss and wildflower seed) 214-539-0534, 3400 Long Prairie, Flower Mound, Texas 75028.

Natural Gardening Research Ctr. (Organic products) 812-623-3800, P.O. Box 149, Sunman, IN 47041.

Nature's Control (Organic products) 503-899-8318, P.O. Box 35, Medford, OR 97501.

Necessary Trading Co. (Organic farming products) 703-864-5103, P.O. Box 603, New Castle, VA 24127.

The Orchard (Organic Orchard) 214-771-2097, Rt. 2 Box 22 A, Rockwall, Texas 75087.

OrCon, Inc. (Beneficial insects) 213-937-7444, 5132 Venice Blvd., Los Angeles, CA 90019.

Organic Cotton Pillows and Furniture 825 Northlake Dr., Richardson, Texas 75080, Dona Shrier, 214-235-0485.

Organic Pest Management (Beneficial insects) 206-367-0707, P.O. Box 55267, Seattle, WA 98155.

Peaceable Valley School, Old River Rd., Washington, TX 77880, 409-878-2353.

Pied Piper Traps (Live animal traps) 445 Garner-Adell Rd., Weatherford, Texas 76086, Joe Piper, 817-682-4663.

Professional Pest Management, Rt. 12 Box 346-31, Lubbock, TX 79424, 806-794-6761.

Rincon-Vitova Insectaries (Beneficial insects) 800-248-BUGS, P.O. Box 95, Oak View, CA 93022.

Seeds of Change (Catalog for open pollinated seed) 505-535-2255, P.O. Box 280, Gila, New Mexico 88038.

Seed Saver Exchange (Seeds) 319-382-5990, Kent Wheely, Rt. 3 Box 239, Decorah, Iowa 52101.

Spray and Grow, 1-800-288-6505, P.O. Box 722038, Houston, Texas 77272.

Turner Seed Company (Native Seed) Route 1, Box 292, Breckenridge, Texas 76024, 1-800-722-8616.

Many retail and wholesale nurseries now offer "organic" products. Always be sure to ask. The list shown includes companies that strictly specialize in these products.

Month-by-month Garden Maintenance

Plant

- Fruit and pecan trees, grapes, berries, asparagus, onions, English peas, garlic, anemones, and ranunculus.
- Balled-and-burlapped or containerized—trees, shrubs, and vines.
- Transplant plants during dormant period.
- Spring flowers and vegetable seeds indoors.
- Cold-hardy color: dianthus, pansies, flowering kale, and cabbage (if the weather is mild).
- Complete tulip, daffodil plantings in early January. "Force" bulbs in pots indoors.

Fertilize

- Root stimulator to new shrubs and trees monthly until established.
- Asparagus beds in late January.

Prune

- Shade trees and summer flowering trees. Remove dead and damaged limbs.
- Summer-flowering trees including crepe myrtles (remove no twigs larger than a pencil in diameter), abelias, altheas.
- Evergreen shrubs.

- Fruit trees. (Best time is just before bud break.)

Water

- Spot water any dry areas to avoid plant desiccation.

Pest Control

- Dormant oil if needed to scale-prone plants such as oaks, hollies, camellias, euonymus, pecan, and fruit trees. Vegetable oil spray is more environmentally friendly than petroleum dormant oils.
- Houseplants: spray with garlic/pepper tea or soap mixture for mealy bugs, spider mites, and scale.

Odd Jobs

- Have soil tests run.
- Turn compost pile monthly or more often and keep moist.
- Plan spring landscape improvement projects and begin construction activities.
- Prepare garden soil by adding missing minerals and mulching bare soil.
- Take mower, tiller, trimmers into shop for repairs before spring.
- Feed the birds!

February

Plant

- Broccoli, brussels sprouts, cabbage, cauliflower, onions, English peas, asparagus, potatoes, other cold-tolerant vegetables.
- Petunias, pansies, pinks, snapdragons, alyssum, calendulas, glads, cannas, and daylilies.
- Fruit trees and berries.
- Transplant existing landscape plants.
- Transplant crowded perennials.

Fertilize

- All planting areas with a 100 percent organic fertilizer @ approximately 20 lbs/1,000 sq ft. If the soil is already healthy, the rate can be reduced to 10 lbs/1,000 sq ft.
- Cool-season flowers with earthworm castings and bat guano at 10 lbs/1,000 sq ft.

Prune

- Shade and ornamental trees lightly to remove dead, diseased, and crossing limbs.
- Peaches and plums to encourage 45° angle growth. Grapes, by 80 to 90 percent. Best time to prune all fruit and nut trees.
- Evergreens and summer-flowering plants.

- Bush-form roses (not climbers).
- Prune or mow winter-damaged foliage from liriope, ophiopogon, honeysuckle, and Asian jasmine. English ivy and other ground covers should be hand pruned if needed.

Water

- Winter annuals and dry soil areas as needed.

Pest Control

- Giant bark aphids: no treatment needed in most cases.
- Dormant oil (vegetable oil is best) for serious infestations of scale insects. Be sure to keep mixture shaken while using.

Odd Jobs

- Adjust and repair sprinkler system.
- Have soil tested. Watch for accumulations of phosphorus.
- Have maintenance equipment repaired for spring use. Sharpen hoes, pruning tools, and mower blades.
- Add compost and top-dressing mulch to all unhealthy soil areas.
- Turn the compost pile regularly.
- Food the birds!

March

Plant

- Trees and shrubs.
- Finish cool-season vegetable plantings. Begin warm-season crops after last killing freeze date.
- Best tomatoes for Texas: Celebrity, Carnival, Spring Giant, Jackpot, Better Boy, Porter, Sweet 100. Plant a mixture of varieties and include some open-pollinated choices.
- Continue to plant cool-season annuals such as petunias and snapdragons. Begin planting warm-season types after last killing freeze.

Fertilize

- All planting areas with a 100 percent organic fertilizer at approximately 20 lbs/1,000 sq ft (if not done in February).

Prune

- Spring-flowering shrubs and vines only after they finish blooming: flowering quince, spirea, forsythia, weigela, azaleas, camellias, Caroline jessamine, wisteria, climbing roses, etc.
- Fruit trees before bud break.

Water

- Annuals and other dry soil areas as needed.
- Wildflower areas in dry years.

Pest Control

- Loopers and caterpillars: *Bacillus thuringiensis* (*Bt*) biological worm spray.
- Pillbugs, snails, slugs: diatomaceous earth/garlic tea, beer traps, rotenone/pyrethrum products.
- Aphids: soap and water or garlic tea. A blast of water and a release of ladybugs is even better.
- Black spot, powdery mildew, bacterial leaf spot: baking soda at 4 teaspoons per gallon.
- Sycamore anthracnose: Bordeaux mixture as leaves emerge.
- Fruit tree sprays; garlic/pepper tea and baking soda. Spray the baking soda only as diseases appear.
- Fertilizer sprays are all that's needed once healthy soil is established.

Odd Jobs

- Turn the compost pile.
- Use completed compost for bed preparation. Use partially completed compost as a top-dressing mulch.
- Mulch all bare soil.
- Feed the birds!

April

Plant

- Turfgrass from plugs, sod, sprigs, or seed.
- Roses from containers.
- Container-grown fruit and pecan trees.
- Warm-season flowers including (sun) periwinkles, cosmos, portulaca, copper leaf, marigolds, zinnias, lantana; (shade) caladiums, coleus, begonia, impatiens, and nicotiana.
- Warm-season vegetables including melons, okra, southern peas, corn, squash, beans, cucumbers, eggplant, peppers, and tomatoes.
- Container flowers, in pots and baskets. Use a potting soil mix containing compost.
- Summer and fall-flowering perennials.
- Herb garden plants in beds, pots, and hanging baskets.
- Repot houseplants if needed.

Fertilize

- Summer-flowering shrubs and roses with 100 percent organic fertilizers.
- Spray rose foliage with Epsom salts and garlic tea.
- Apply an organic root stimulator monthly to newly planted trees and shrubs.
- Liquid spray: organic foliar fertilizers on all foliage.

Prune

- Spring-blooming vines and shrubs immediately after bloom.

- Pick-prune hedges to be wider at the bottom for better light and thicker growth.

Water

- All planting areas deeply but infrequently during dry periods.
- Potted plants as needed.

Pest Control

- Release green lacewings for thrips in roses, glads, as well as for general insect control.
- Snails, slugs, pillbugs: diatomaceous earth and garlic/pepper tea, beer traps or pyrethrum/rotenone.
- Release trichogramma wasps for pecan casebearers.
- Ticks, fleas, and chiggers: diatomaceous earth/pyrethrum products.
- Bacterial leaf spot of peaches and plums: bordeaux mixture, baking soda and water, or garlic/pepper tea.
- Aphids: water blast followed by release of ladybugs.
- Black spot on roses: baking soda spray.
- Fruit sprays: garlic/pepper tea.
- Fire ants: broadcast baits for large areas. Pour vinegar with diatomaceous earth into individual mounds or use pyrethrum/rotenone products.

Odd Jobs

- Mow weekly and leave clippings on the lawn.
- Turn compost pile.
- Continue to add new vegetative matter and manure to existing and additional compost piles.
- Mulch all bare soil.
- Feed the birds!

May

Plant

- Lawn grasses from plugs, sod, seed, sprigs, or by hydromulching. Plant buffalograss in sun.
- Tropical color in beds or pots: bougainvillea, mandevilla, allamanda, penta, hibiscus, and others.
- Trees and shrubs.
- Warm-season annual color plants.
- Cannas, glads, caladiums, and other summer bulbs. Mums and other fall perennials.
- Groundcovers from $2^1/_4$-inch or 4-inch pots.
- Hot-weather vegetables, including southern peas, okra, and melons.

Fertilize

- All annual flowers and potted plants with bat guano, earthworm castings, cottonseed meal, or other 100 percent organic fertilizers.

Prune

- Climbing roses after their bloom.
- Spring-flowering shrubs, vines, shrubs, and trees after their bloom.
- "Pinch" away the growing tips of mums weekly.

Water

- All planting areas deeply but infrequently during dry periods.
- Potted plants regularly.

Pest Control

- Release trichogramma wasps for pecan casebearers and moth larvae.
- Fleas, ticks, and chiggers: diatomaceous earth/pyrethrum products.
- Cabbage loopers and other caterpillars: *Bacillus thuringiensis* (*Bt*).
- Aphids on tender new growth: strong water blast, soap and water or garlic/pepper tea.
- Release green lacewings and ladybugs for general insect control.
- Lace bugs on azaleas, sycamores: soap and water or garlic/pepper tea.
- Weeds: hand remove or use mechanical devices.
- Fire ants: use baits for large areas. Pour vinegar with diatomaceous earth into individual mounds or use pyrethrum/rotenone products.

Odd Jobs

- Mow weekly and leave clippings on the lawn.
- Turn compost pile and continue to add new ingredients.
- Mulch all bare soil.
- Feed the birds!

Plant

- All warm-season grasses; bermuda, zoysia, St. Augustine, and buffalo.
- Summer annual color, such as portulaca, marigold, zinnia, periwinkle, lantana, copperleaf, amaranthus, cosmos, and verbena.
- Tropical color: bougainvilleas, hibiscus, pentas, allamandas, mandevillas, etc.
- Crepe myrtle, while in bloom to be sure of color.
- Shrubs and trees.
- Fall tomatoes.

Fertilize

- All planting areas with a 100 percent organic fertilizer. This should be the second major fertilization.
- Foliar feed all plantings and lawns with fish emulsion and seaweed.
- Iron deficiency results in yellowed leaves with dark green veins on the newest growth first. Apply iron and sulfur products. Epsom salts spray will also help in alkaline soil areas.

Prune

- Blackberries to remove fruiting canes after harvest. Prune new canes to encourage side branching.
- Remove spent flowers from daisies, daylilies, cannas, and other summer flowers.
- Dead and damaged wood from trees, shrubs, as needed.

Water

- All planting areas deeply but infrequently during dry periods.
- Potted plants regularly. Daily waterings are needed for some plants.

Pest Control

- Spider mites: garlic/pepper tea or soap and water. Spray every 3 days for 9 days.
- Fleas, ticks, chiggers: diatomaceous earth/pyrethrum products.
- Bagworms: *(Bt) Bacillus thuringiensis*.
- Webworms in pecans, persimmons: *Bt* and include one teaspoon of liquid soap to improve penetration.
- Scale insects, including mealy bugs: summer-weight horticultural oil.
- Black spot on roses, mildew, and other fungi: baking soda and water.
- Weeds: hand remove and work on improving soil health.
- Lacebugs, elm leaf beetles: pyrethrum, garlic/pepper tea, summer-weight horticultural oil.

Odd Jobs

- Mow weekly and leave clippings on the lawn.
- Turn compost pile.
- Mulch all bare soil.
- Feed the birds!

July

Plant

- Color for fall: marigolds, zinnias, celosia, Joseph's coat.
- Container-grown nursery stock.
- Warm-season lawn grasses.
- Tomatoes, peppers, melons, other warm-season vegetables for fall garden.

Fertilize

- All planting areas with 100 percent organic fertilizer if not done in June.
- As needed to correct iron deficiency. Use iron/sulfur products.
- Spray all plantings with fish emulsion/seaweed products, and biostimulants.

Prune

- Roses to encourage fall bloom.
- Dead or damaged limbs.
- Flowering plants to remove spent flower heads.

Water

- All planting areas deeply but infrequently during dry periods.
- Outdoor container plants daily, others as needed.

Pest Control

- Chinch bugs: diatomaceous earth/pyrethrum products.
- Elm leaf beetles, lace bugs: pyrethrum, summer-weight horticultural oil or appropriate *Bt*.
- Spider mites: soap and water or garlic/pepper tea. Spray every 3 days for 9 days.
- Fleas, ticks, chiggers, bermuda mites: diatomaceous earth/pyrethrum products.
- Webworms in pecans, persimmons, bagworms: *Bacillus thuringiensis* (*Bt*) with 1 teaspoon soap per gallon.
- Leaf rollers: *Bacillus thuringiensis* (*Bt*).
- Scale insects on euonymus, hollies, camellias. Use summer-weight oil. Apply dormant oil during winter.
- Weeds: hand remove or use mechanical devices.

Odd Jobs

- Mow weekly and leave clippings on the lawn.
- Turn compost pile, add new ingredients, and start new piles.
- Mulch all bare soil with partially completed compost or other coarse textured material.
- Feed the birds!

August

Plant

- Fall color such as mums, asters, marigolds, zinnias, and celosia.
- Fall-flowering bulbs such as spider lilies, fall crocus, and fall amaryllis.
- Finish warm-season vegetable plantings of beans, corn, cucumbers, melons, and squash.
- Cool-season vegetables, including broccoli, cauliflower, brussels sprouts, cabbage, spinach, potatoes, lettuce, carrots, beets, radishes, and English peas.
- Finish planting warm-season lawn grasses: buffalo, bermuda, St. Augustine, and zoysia.
- Wildflower seed.

Fertilize

- Foliar feed all planting and lawns with liquid organic fertilizer.

Prune

- Trim spent flower stalks and blossoms of annuals and perennials to stimulate regrowth of stems and blooms.
- Remove dead and damaged wood from shrubs and trees.

Water

- Water deeply and as infrequently as possible. Your garden and land-scape will usually need more water this month than any other.
- Potted plants and hanging baskets daily.

Pest Control

- Grubs worms: good soil culture is the best control. Beneficial nematodes and milky spore.
- Chinch bugs: diatomaceous earth.
- Aphids: soap and water, garlic tea. Water blast and release of ladybugs.
- Fire ants: Use baits for large areas. Rotenone/pyrethrum for individual mounds.
- Chewing insects: diatomaceous earth/pyrethrum products.
- Cabbage loopers: *Bacillus thuringiensis* (*Bt*).
- Borers in peaches, plums and other trees: Rotenone/pyrethrum, mulch root system.
- Release beneficial insects if needed: praying mantids, ladybugs, green lacewings.

Odd Jobs

- Mow weekly and leave clippings on the lawn.
- Turn compost pile.
- Feed the birds!

September

Plant

- Cool-season, leafy, root crops such as carrots, beets, turnips, etc.
- Wildflower seeds.
- Finish warm-season lawn grass plantings by early September.
- Transplant established spring-flowering bulbs, iris, daylilies, daisies, and peonies.
- Perennials.
- Cool-season grasses.

Fertilize

- All planting areas with a 100 percent organic fertilizer at approximately 10 lbs/1,000 sq. ft.
- Foliar feed all planting and lawns.

Prune

- Root-prune wisterias that failed to bloom.
- Remove spent blooms of summer-flowering perennials.
- Remove surface tree roots if needed, but no more than 20 percent of root system per year.

Water

- Water deeply during dry spells.
- Potted plants and hanging baskets regularly.

Pest Control

- Brown patch in St. Augustine: baking soda and water.
- Webworms, tent caterpillars: *Bacillus thuringiensis* (*Bt*).
- Grub worms: milky spore and beneficial nematodes.
- Cabbage loopers on broccoli, cauliflower, cabbage, brussels sprouts: *Bacillus thuringiensis* (*Bt*).
- Aphids on tender new fall growth: garlic tea or water blast followed by release of ladybugs.
- Spray compacted soil with Li'l Perk or Pene-Turf.
- Fire ants: use baits for large areas. Vinegar plus diatomaceous earth for individual mounds.
- Roses for black spot and powdery mildew: baking soda, seaweed, garlic/pepper tea.
- Iron chlorosis (yellowed leaves, dark green veins, newest growth first): chelated iron. In calcareous soils apply sulfur at 5 lbs/1,000 sq ft twice per year.

Odd Jobs

- Mow weekly and leave clippings on the lawn.
- Turn the compost pile.
- Feed the birds!

Plant

- Pansies, violas, pinks, snapdragons, flowering cabbage and kale, English daisies, Iceland poppies, wallflowers, and other cool-season flowers.
- Complete wildflower plantings.
- Trees, shrubs, vines, and spring- and summer-flowering perennials.
- Strawberries.
- Cool-season grasses.

Fertilize

- Foliar feed all plantings and lawns with fish emulsion/seaweed products. Test soil annually to monitor accumulations of phosphorus and balance of all minerals.

Water

- Newly planted wildflower area if no rain.
- Newly planted annuals.

Prune

- Pick-prune shrubs as needed, but save major pruning for winter.
- Remove dead and damaged wood from trees.

Pests

- Brown patch in St. Augustine: baking soda and water.
- Peach leaf curl: Bordeaux mixture and garlic/pepper tea.
- Cabbage loopers in garden: *Bacillus thuringiensis* (*Bt*).

Odd Jobs

- To reflower a poinsettia, give it uninterrupted darkness 14 hours each day and light for 10 hours until December, then move to a well-lighted location.
- Mow weekly and leave the clippings on the lawn.
- Build new compost piles and turn old ones.
- Use completed compost to prepare new planting beds.
- Use partially completed compost as a top-dressing mulch for ornamentals and vegetables.
- Feed the birds!

November

Plant

- Trees and shrubs.
- Spring bulbs, including daffodils and grape hyacinths. Pre-cool tulips and hyacinths for 45 days at 40° prior to planting.
- Spring- and summer-flowering perennials, including daisies, iris, daylilies, lilies, thrift, lythrum, etc.
- Spring-flowering annuals, including pansies, pinks, snapdragons, flowering cabbage and kale, English daises, California and Iceland poppies.
- Winter-hardy nursery stock.
- Cool-season grasses.

Fertilize

- Bulbs, annuals, and perennials with earthworm castings and other gentle organic fertilizers.
- Indoor plants with earthworm castings and other low-odor organic fertilizers.

Water

- All planting areas at least once if no rain.

Prune

- Begin major tree pruning. Remove dead limbs before leaves fall. Too early for fruit trees
- Pick-prune shrubs to remove longest shoots if needed.

- Remove spent blooms and seed heads from flowering plants.
- Cut off tops of brown perennials; leave roots in the soil.

Pests

- Watch roots of removed annuals for nematodes (knots on the roots). Treat infected soil with biostimulants and compost.
- Watch houseplants for spider mites, scale, aphids. Spray as needed with Agrispon, Neo-Life soap, and a mild vegetable oil solution.
- Watch lawn for signs of grubworm damage. Grass will be loose on top of ground. Treat with milky spore and beneficial nematodes.

Odd Jobs

- Have landscape and garden soils tested now to determine soil balancing needs.
- Pick tomatoes the night before the first freeze; let them ripen indoors.
- Put all fallen leaves, spent annuals, and other vegetative matter into the compost piles.
- Add mulch to your garden—do not cultivate.
- Mulch all bare ornamental beds for winter protection
- Turn compost piles.
- Feed the birds!

December

Plant

- Trees and shrubs.
- Living Christmas trees (after use) that are adapted to the area's climate and soils.
- Spring bulbs, including tulips and hyacinths.

Fertilize

- Greenhouse plants with bat guano or earthworm castings and other organic fertilizers.
- Houseplants, once or twice during winter, with earthworm castings or other odorless organic fertilizers.

Water

- Any areas that have become dry to help protect against winter cold injury.

Prune

- Peaches, plums, and other fruit trees, just prior to bud break is ideal.
- Apples to remove vertical shoots.
- Evergreens to adjust the appearance.
- Shade trees to remove dead and damaged wood.

- Cut off tops of spent perennials; leave roots in the ground.

Pests

- Bark aphids on trees: no treatment needed.
- Scale insects on shade and fruit trees: dormant oil.
- Cut mistletoe out of trees. Remove infested limbs if possible.
- Spray houseplants to control scale, mealy bugs, spider mites, and other insects.
- Remember that henbit, clover, and other wildflowers are beautiful, so don't worry about spraying them.

Odd Jobs

- Pick tomatoes the night before first freeze.
- Clean and oil tools before storing for winter.
- Run mower, trimmer engines dry of gasoline, drain and change oil. Take to repair shop now to avoid the spring rush.
- Mulch all bare soil.
- Turn compost piles.
- Feed the birds!

Index

Boldface numbers indicate major discussion.

B

Bacillus thuringiensis, 112, 121, **178**, 192
Bacteria, 68, 77, **78**, 80
Bacterial blight, **158**, 160
Bacterial leaf scorch, 159
Bactimos, 142
Bagworms, **137**, 153
Baking soda, 112, 117, 159, **178**
Balanced soil, 68, 123
Bald cypress, 17
Basic maintenance program, 131
Basil, **47**, 152
Bat guano, 100, 117, **169**, 175, 193
Bats, 8
Bay, **46**, 120
Beans, 124
Bed preparation, 101
Bees, 137
Beetles, 80, 81, **137**, 146, 153
Beets, **57**, 124, 126
Begonia sp., 33
Beneficial insect release schedule, 151
Beneficial insects, 8, 112, 121, 128, **146**, 150
Berberis trifoliolata, 19
Bermudagrass, **64**, 130, 163
Berries, **59**, 127, 128
Big bluestem, 66
Bignonia capreolata, 27
Bio insect control, 152
Biodiversity, **5**, 8, 193
Biofac, 152
Bioform, 100, **169**, 175
Biome, 152
Biostimulants, **168**, 193
Birds, 8, **164**
Black gum, 17
Black spot, 112, 117, 118, **159**, 160
Blackberries, **59**, 127, 128
Black-eyed peas, 66
Black-eyed Susan, 52, 55
Blood meal, 100, **169**, 175, 193
Blossom end rot, 159
Blue grama, 66
Blueberries, **60**, 127, 128

Bluebonnet, 54, 55
Bluestem, 66
Bolting, 112
Bone meal, 71, 100, **169**, 175, 193
Borage, **46**, 152
Borago officinalis, 46
Borax, **70**, 193
Bordeaux mix, 71, **178**, 193
Borers, 137, 153
Boron, **70**, 72, 187
Boston ivy, 28
Bothriochioa saccharoides, 66
Bougainvillea, 26
Bouteloua sp., 66
Branch bark ridge, 111
Branch collar, 110, 111
Brassica oleracea acephala, 34
Broadfork, 88
Broccoli, **57**, 124, 126
Brown patch, 158, **159**, 160
Brussels sprouts, **57**, 126
Bt, 3, 112, 178
Buckwheat, 66
Buffalograss, 64, **65**, 130
Bug juice spray, 183
Bulb planting dates, 119
Bulbs, **116**, 119
Bur oak, 16
Burford holly, 22
Burned lime, 193
Burning bush, 20
Bush beans, **57**, 126
Bushy bluestem, 66
Butterflies, 11
Butterfly weed, **38**, 55

C

Cabbage, **57**, 124, 126
Cabbage loopers, 138
Cabbage worms, 151, 153
Cabling, 112
Calcite, 193
Calcium, **70**, 72, 187
Calcium carbonate, 193
Calcium sulfate, 171
Callicarpa americana, 20

Superphosphate, 200
Superphosphoric acid, 200
Superthrive, 174
Sustainable, 3
Sustane, 100, **174**, 177
Sweet William, 34
Sweetgum, 17
Switchgrass, 66
Sycamore, 18
Symphoricarpos orbiculatus, 25
Symphytum officinale, 50
Synthetic fertilizers, 168

T

Tagetes sp., 37, 50
Tahoka daisy, 55
Tanacetum vulgare, 50
Tanglefoot, 181
Tankage, 100, 200
Tansy, **50**, 120, 140, 152
Tarragon, 46
Taxodium sp., 17
TEC, 102
Termites, 80, 81, **145**, 157
Tex Turf 10, 64
Texas ash, 14
Texas bluegrass, **65**, 66
Texas buttercup, 54
Texas cover crops, 66
Texas Department of Agriculture, 139
Texas redbud, 13
Texas sage, 23
Texas smoke tree, 20
Texas T, 176
Texas trees, 109
Texas wildflowers, 55
Thatch, **83**, 200
Thatch buildup, 99
Tomas, 100, **174**
Thrift, 42
Thrips, **145**, 157
Thyme, 31, **51**, 120, 152
Ticks, **145**, 157
Tif, 64
Tim-Bor, 145
Toads, 8, 11

Tobacco horn worms, **145**, 151, 157
Tomato cages, 125
Tomatoes, **58**, 124, 126
Top-dressing, 200
Topsoil, 101
Total exchange capacity, 102
Trace minerals, 70
Trachelospermum asiaticum, 31
Transition zone, 200
Transplanting, 107, **133**
Tree borers, 153
Tree chips, 95
Treehoppers, 157
Trees, **12**, 106, 108, 110
Triacontanol, 95, 169
Trichogramma wasps, 137, 138, **149**, 151
Trifolium incarnatum, 55
Trifolium repens, 31, 55
Trimming, 131
Triple Action 20, 159, **181**
Triple superphosphate, 200
Tripsacum dactyloides, 66
Trumpet vine, 27
Tulips, 119
Turk's cap, 41
Turkey manure, 174
Turnip greens, 126
Turnips, **58**, 124
Turtles, 11, 165

U

U. S. Forest Service, 112
Ulmus parvifolia, 17
Uniola paniculata, 66
Urea, 200
Urea-form, 200

V

Vegetable oils, 180
Vegetable planting, 126
Vegetable planting structures, 125
Vegetable varieties, 57
Vegetables, 123, 124
Verbascum thapsus, 51

Verbena, **37**, 55
Vertical mowing, 200
Viburnum, 25
Vinegar, 109, 115, 117, 177, **181**
Vines, **26**, 113
Viola hybrids, 37
Virus, 161
Vitamins, 93, 200
Volatilization, 200

W

Walnuts, 97, 128
Warm-season turfgrass, 200
Wasps, 11, **149**, 150, 157
Water, 70
Water oak, 17
Watercress, 51
Watering, 115, 117, 121, 129
Watermelons, 58
Wax myrtle, 17
Webworms, 112, 157
Weed control, 161
Weed fabric, 182
Weeds, 101, 115, 117, 129, 131, **161**, 163
Western Agricultural Labs, 186
Western soapberry, 17
White ash, 17
White clover, **31**, 66

White Dutch clover, 55
White yarrow, 55
Whiteflies, **145**, 150, 157
Whitefly parasites, 150
Wild petunia, 43
Wildflowers, **52**, 121, 122, 130
Willow leaf holly, 22
Willow oak, 17
Wisteria, 28
Wood fern, 29
Woodchucks, 80
Woodlice, 81
Wormwood, 48
Wound dressings, 109, 111

Y

Yarrow, **39**, 44, 45, 53
Yaupon holly, 14
Yeast, 68, 77, **79**, 80
Yellow Sticky Traps, 182

Z

Zinc, 70, 72, **76**, 174, 187
Zinc sulfate, 200
Zingiben sp., 51
Zinnia, 37
Zoysia, 64, **65**

━ MORE GARDENING BOOK GREATS ━

A Garden Book for Houston and the Texas Gulf Coast
4th Edition
Edited by the River Oaks Garden Club of Houston
Now in its seventeenth printing, here's everything a gardener needs to know—design, soil improvement, drainage, watering, lawns, trees, shrubs, vines, groundcovers, bulbs, flowers, and gardens for color, shade, fragrance, or vegetables.
396 pages, color photos throughout, index, appendixes, 7" x 10" hardcover.
ISBN 0-88415-350-9   #5350   **$27.50**

Native Texas Plants
Landscaping
Region by Region
Sally Wasowski with Andy Wasowski
Stunning photos and witty informative text that Lone Star gardeners love.
406 pages, color throughout, region plans, specialty plans, bibliography, index, 8" x 11" paperback.
ISBN 0-87719-201-4   #9201   **$27.95**

Native Texas Gardens
Maximum Beauty Minimum Upkeep
Sally Wasowski and Andy Wasowski
"The Wasowskis have loaded *Native Texas Gardens* chock-full of excellent design ideas and reference information, plus a big dose of common sense.... a must read for every Texan who dreams of a beautiful landscape free from high maintenance costs, big water bills, and a sore back."
—Chris S. Corby, Editor and Publisher, *Texas Gardener*
This colorful new book shows you how to install a native garden and convert to a natural landscape. When you go native, you:
➤ conserve water
➤ eliminate the need for toxic chemicals
➤ provide wildlife habitat
➤ cut your upkeep from hours per week to only hours per year.
February 1997. 208 pages, color photos, index, 8½" x 11" jacketed hardcover.
ISBN 0-88415-513-7   #5513   **$39.95**

❖ Visit Your Favorite Bookstore, Garden Center, and Nursery ❖